PITT SERIES IN
POLICY AND INSTITUTIONAL STUDIES

Pitt Series in Policy and Institutional Studies
Bert A. Rockman, Editor

PRESSURE, POWER AND POLICY

State Autonomy and Policy Networks
in Britain and the United States

Martin J. Smith

University of Pittsburgh Press

Published in the USA by the University of Pittsburgh Press, Pittsburgh, Pa., 15260

Published in Great Britain by Harvester Wheatsheaf,
a division of Simon & Schuster International Group

Copyright © Martin J. Smith 1993

Printed and bound in Great Britain

ISBN 0–8229–3778–6 (cl)
ISBN 0–8229–5522–9 (pb)
LC 93–60585

For my parents

CONTENTS

TABLES

ACKNOWLEDGEMENTS

In recent years the concepts of state autonomy and policy networks have provided significant additions to the understanding of state/interest group relations. Much of the discussion of these concepts has been restricted to journals and specialist literature. The intention of this book is to make policy networks and state autonomy accessible to students and to use these theories to enlighten the understanding of the empirical analysis of state/group interaction.

In developing my ideas on policy networks I have been greatly assisted by the work of David Marsh and Rod Rhodes. Their work has been an important influence, and they have both provided much support and encouragement throughout my academic career. A number of people have also assisted in the writing of this book. I would like to thank Neil Carter, Keith Dowding, Andrew Gamble, Wyn Grant, Jens Peter Folund Thompson, Deborah Haythorne, Jo Spear and Len Tivey for their comments on various drafts and related conference papers.

As with all my work, the greatest debt is owed to Fiona Devine. She uncomplainingly read many drafts and frequently provided insightful comments. I am sure that the book could have been much better if I had taken more notice of her. Finally, I would like to thank Christine Whittaker for photocopying my final copy and for letting me use her printer.

Martin J. Smith
Sheffield, November 1992

Chapter 1

PRESSURE GROUPS AND POLICY-MAKING

Pressure groups have long been central to the understanding of the policy process. Indeed, many studies of policy-making define groups as one of the key determinants of policy outcomes. The underlying argument of this book is that too much attention has been paid to the role of groups in the analysis of the policy process. It suggests that more consideration needs to be paid to the broad context within which groups operate. The important variables in understanding decisions are the nature of the relationships that exist between groups and the state – the types of policy networks – and the interests and activities of state actors – the degree of state autonomy. This book has two aims. The first is to introduce students to the concepts of policy networks and state autonomy and the second is to use these concepts to analyse a number of policy areas in Britain and the United States.

The key focus of analysis is not, therefore, groups but the nature of the relationships between state actors and groups, and the impact that these relationships have on policy outcomes. In the past, pressure group studies have been dominated by three theoretical traditions (which are discussed in detail in Chapter 2): pluralism, corporatism and marxism. Marxism, in a sense, sees pressure groups as having little importance and focuses on two groups in particular – the representatives of labour and the representatives of capital. It is concerned with the question of how the capitalist state is able to ensure the long-term interests of capital despite the presence of conflicts between capitalist interests and the existence of organised labour. Corporatism is likewise concerned with economic groups. For corporatism, the increased complexity of industrial society, combined with the concentration of power within particular groups, forces the state to incorporate groups into the policy process in order to ensure economic growth and to avoid class conflict. For pluralists, groups are central to the political process. They are a means of articulating the interests of various sectors of society and representing those interests to government. Policy is the outcome of various group pressures. The existence of a range of groups ensures that power is distributed widely through society. No single group or the state has the ability to dominate the policy process.

Pluralism and marxism are seen as society-centred approaches. In other words, they see policy as being determined by pressures within society. The state is responding either to the interest of classes or groups. Recently, theorists have claimed that the state has distinct interests and can determine policy outcomes. The state has the potential to take autonomous actions. It can act independently of groups in society. The argument of this book is that whilst pressure groups are important, their impact on policy depends on the interests of state actors and the types of relationships – the policy networks – that exist in specific policy areas.

Given this emphasis, it is important to define the state and pressure groups. The state is a distinct set of institutions which have the authority to make the rules that govern society and which, in the words of Weber, has a 'monopoly of legitimate violence' within a specific territory. Hence, the state includes such institutions as the government, the civil service, the judiciary, Parliament, local government. Consequently, the state is not unified (Hall and Ikenberry 1990; Jessop 1990). It is a set of institutions which provide the parameters for political conflicts between various interests over the use of resources and the direction of public policy. There are frequently conflicts between elected politicians and non-elected civil servants over policy. There is also conflict between politicians in different parts of the state over policy and resources. Therefore, it is very difficult to identify the state's interests because various parts of the state can have conflicting interests.

It is also difficult to identify the boundaries of the state. Some perspectives see the state as a clear set of defined institutions with official powers. Marxist theorists such as Gramsci and Althusser question the distinction between the state and the rest of society and argue that the state is integrated into many parts of civil society. For instance, Althusser (1971) saw organisations such as the church, schools and even trade unions as part of the Ideological State Apparatus.

It is indeed increasingly difficult to distinguish the boundaries of the state. Many parts of civil society are given institutional access to the state and play a role in the development of public policy. The state also funds a number of groups within society which, although in principle autonomous, are highly dependent on the state. In addition, the boundaries of the state are continually changing through privatisation, the hiving off of parts of the civil service and the creation of new regulatory bodies. Often the nature of these bodies is ambiguous. It is unclear whether they are part of the state or part of civil society.

Pressure groups are organisations which seek to represent the interests of particular sections of society in order to influence public policy (see Alderman 1984; Grant 1989a; Wilson 1990). Frequently, pressure groups have been classified according to whether they represent specific causes – for example anti-abortion, environment, or particular sections of society, such as trade unions, doctors, farmers, etc. Other writers have made a distinction between economic and non-economic groups. However, such classifications are unhelpful in actually explaining or analysing the influence of interest groups. A more useful distinction is made by Grant (1989a) who suggests that groups can be classified as 'insider' and 'outsider' groups.

Insider groups are regarded as legitimate by government and are consulted on a regular basis. Outsider groups either do not wish to become enmeshed in a consultative relationship with officials, or are unable to gain recognition (Grant 1989a: 14–15).

Policy network analysis develops the notion of insiders and outsiders by examining the mechanisms used for inclusion and exclusion and the impact that they have on policy.

Pressure groups and policy-making

Pressure groups have been central to political science in the post-war period. Some of the first empirical political scientists focused almost solely on the role of pressure groups. This has been particularly true in the United States where, according to Petracca (1992: 4), 'American political science has been dominated, indeed defined, by the study of groups.' The dominant tradition within the US has been pluralism, which placed a great deal of emphasis on groups. Within pluralism, power is dispersed throughout society rather than concentrated within the state. The state is seen as reflecting the various desires and interests of society. These interests are transmitted to the state by interest groups. People have various identities such as consumers, workers, residents and parents, and they join together in order to express their interests to government. Government, which has a duty to reflect the public interest, and not just sectional interests, takes account of the various pressures on it before determining the direction of policy. Society is made up of an array of groups that are often in conflict with each other and which are attempting to influence government. The large number of groups representing various interests ensures that no single interest can come to dominate the political system.

Groups are also important to pluralists because of their behaviouralist methodology. In explaining why certain policy outcomes occur, pluralists believe it is necessary to focus on observable behaviour. It is important to observe who is involved, how they act, and who makes the final decision. Pressure groups provide a visible and accessible policy actor. In examining the policy process, it is relatively easy to examine the resources and activities of pressure groups. Who did a pressure group lobby, what sort of tactics did they use, did they have meetings with officials and was the final policy outcome the one the interest group desired? Consequently, there are literally hundreds, if not thousands, of policy studies in Britain and the United States which concentrate on the activities of interest groups (see Alderman 1984; Ball and Millard 1986; Grant 1989a; Wilson 1990 for examples).

Pluralist pressure group studies suffer from a number of limitations. First, they concentrate on the resources of pressure groups, in terms of leadership, funding and membership density, and suggest that well-resourced pressure groups are often the most effective. However, there is no real reason why these resources should necessarily lead to high influence. For example, the British trade union movement was just as well-resourced on 2 May 1979 as it was on 3 May 1979 but with the election of the Conservative government a large part of its influence disappeared almost overnight. This suggests that what is important is not the resources but how they are perceived by other political actors. Resources are necessary for pressure groups to influence government but they are not sufficient for explaining that influence.

Second, by focusing on the observable behaviour of interest groups, pluralist studies tend to ignore large parts of the policy process. They are examining a snapshot of a political picture and in doing so ignore much of the context of the political process. The influence of pressure groups does not derive from how they use their resources but from the historical, ideological and structural context within which they operate. Pressure groups exist in a situation of past policy decisions. These past policy decisions frequently determine the pressure groups involved in decision-making, how they are involved, what policy options are feasible, and the final decision. For example, it is frequently argued that in Britain the City is an exceptionally privileged interest which has been successfully able to protect its financial interests (see Ingham 1984; Pollard 1981). The reasons for the success of the City are not because the City is well-resourced and an effective lobbyist. Rather, the British Empire made London the world's financial centre and the British economy internationally orientated. Consequently, British economic success has depended greatly on the success of the City (Gamble 1990). This has allowed the City to build a particularly close relationship to the government through the Bank of England over a long period of time (Moran 1984). As a result, when making economic policy, the government does not evaluate the demands of various interests in a detached way but is likely to pay close attention to the demands of the City.

Ideology also plays a major role in affecting how groups are perceived and what policy options are conceivable. Within each policy sector certain beliefs tend to dominate the policy process and provide the parameters for acceptable options. As a result interest groups which do not conform to these beliefs are ignored or excluded from the political process. With the dominance of new right ideology in Britain and the United States during the 1980s, groups which supported greater intervention in the economy, increased taxation or trade union interests, were almost completely excluded from the policy process.

The organisation of policy-making has a great impact on the influence of groups. Policy sectors have institutions which provide the means for making policy. These might include government departments, agencies, various advisory committees or other policy-making institutions. These organisations have their own standard operating procedures (SOPs) (Allison 1971). SOPs are rules for dealing with problems in a particular way. Consequently, when a problem recurs decisions do not have to be taken on the specific form of action that is necessary. These procedures frequently favour certain interests over others because they provide only a limited set of solutions. In addition, the organisation of policy-making creates certain institutions for including various interests and excluding others. Governments often set up advisory committees but only groups which abide by the 'rules of the game' have access to these committees. Hence, other interests do not have the same input into the policy process.

History, ideology and the organisation of the policy process thus structure the relations between groups and state actors. Pressure groups are not playing on a level field. Certain groups have structural advantages, i.e. advantages that cannot be changed by the decisions of individuals. Past policies, ideology and the way policy is made can advantage some groups over others. A decision to provide subsidies to farmers means that the policy process is geared to determining subsidies not abolishing them. A belief that farmers should be subsidised excludes the option of ending subsidies. A policy process that institutionalises the access of farmers to the policy process but does not provide consumers with representation ensures that farmers have considerable advantages over consumers. These advantages are not created by the deliberate observable acts of individuals or groups but develop over time as the result of a whole range of acts, intended and unintended consequences, and the repetition of routines (Giddens 1986).

Undoubtedly, the conscious, visible actions of pressure groups do have an influence on policy. There are numerous examples where this is the case. However, such an approach to the understanding of the policy process can only give a partial picture. Many of the factors affecting policy cannot be directly observed. Focusing on the resources and activities of pressure groups is unhelpful without an understanding of the ideological, historical and structural context within which these occur.

Third, the pluralists' concentration on the observable behaviour of groups leads to the error of concentrating on groups to the exclusion of state actors. As we will see in Chapter 3, state actors have interests that might conflict with the groups with which they deal. In addition, the state as an extremely large, well-financed and powerful organisation has the mechanisms to translate these interests into policy. Consequently, in many cases the main determinant of policy is not pressure groups but state actors. Pressure groups achieve access to government, and possibly influence, because of the decisions of state actors to adopt a particular policy or consult a particular group. On many occasions, although not always, the state has the ability to ignore or override groups. States can make groups illegal, create alternative groups, develop alternative administrative machinery or arrest group leaders. There are many occasions when governments simply ignore the demands of groups. The Conservative government in developing its trade union legislation during the 1980s, ignored the demands of the trade unions, in education it ignored the teachers' unions, and the most recent developments in health policy were made without consultation with the doctors. Moreover, on many occasions groups only develop influence once government chooses to devise a policy in an area. If the government does not intervene in health, agriculture or education, it is very difficult for doctors, farmers or teachers to influence policy.

This suggests that the relationship between the state and groups is extremely complex. The pluralist notion of power sees it as a zero-sum. In other words, if group A has power then group B loses it. Or if a group forces the state to adopt a particular policy, then the group gains and the state loses. However, the reality is that the power is the result of dependency (Rhodes 1981). If the state is to intervene in a policy area, it is easier if it has the cooperation of the relevant groups because this support increases the state's ability to implement policy. If groups are to influence policy they need to be recognised by the state as groups that can provide aid in the development of policy. Therefore group power depends on state recognition and state power depends on the support of groups. Again, this demonstrates that we need to examine policy sectors in order to understand the complexity of the relationships between groups and government and not focus solely on the way in which groups try to influence the state. This complexity is exacerbated because the state is not a unified body with a single set of interests. The state consists of a range of departments, sections within departments, agencies and actors who have different interests. Frequently, these interests conflict and therefore the understanding of policy requires not just an understanding of group/state relations but intra-state relations.

Policy networks and state autonomy

In order to explain why certain policy outcomes occur it is not enough to focus on the resources and activities of groups. It is necessary to analyse the relationships that exist between the state and groups and the interests and actions of state actors. Since the mid-1960s, US literature has accepted the notion that policy-making occurs in subsystems. In a policy subsystem a limited group of actors including members of Congress, administrators and pressure groups deals with a particular policy area or subarea autonomously from the wider political system (Freeman 1965). For Thurber (1991: 325):

> Policy subsystems can be characterized by networks of actors, their substantive policy domain, and various modes of decision-making. They are organised to make focused demands on the political system and to influence specific programs. . . .

Originally, subsystems were seen as iron triangles because the three participants – administrative agency, congressional subcommittee and pressure group developed a very closed relationship (see Salisbury *et al.* 1992; Thurber 1991). More recently, Heclo (1978) has suggested that the political system is becoming more open with issue networks replacing iron triangles. In an issue network the policy sector contains a large number of changing actors and there is little agreement on the policy goals.

In Britain, Richardson and Jordan (1979) introduced the notion of a policy community to refer to closed subsystems and more recently Rhodes (1988) and

Marsh and Rhodes (1992a) have attempted to systematise and clarify these terms in order to develop a more thorough account of policy networks (which is discussed in detail in Chapter 3). Policy networks are a means of categorising the relationship between groups and the state. Networks exist where there is some exchange of resources between state and groups. This can range from a limited exchange of information to the institutionalisation of a group in the policy process. Policy networks also range in their degree of integration from closed and close policy communities, with limited and stable participants, to open issue networks.

The notion of the policy network has a number of advantages over the traditional approaches to pressure groups. Pluralism, corporatism and marxism offer general theories concerning political systems. The notion of policy networks is much more flexible. It is a meso-level concept which is concerned with explaining behaviour within particular sections of the state or particular policy areas. Therefore, it can account for variations in group/government relations that exist in a range of policy arenas. With the concept of policy networks, the nature of state/group relations within a specific policy area is not assumed in the theory. This suggests that the state is fragmented rather than unified. Most theorists, whether marxist (Jessop 1990) or pluralist (Rhodes 1988), accept that the state is not unified but is an ensemble of many different institutions and agencies which are often in conflict. Policy networks provide a mechanism for assessing the various conflicting institutions. With policy networks, power is a relationship based on dependence and not a zero-sum. Power is something that develops within relationships between groups and state actors, and a policy network is frequently a mechanism for enhancing mutual power rather than taking power from one or the other.

Finally, policy networks allow analysis of the interest of state actors. In recent years an increasing number of writers (see for example Mann 1984; Nordlinger 1981; Skocpol 1985) accept that state actors have their own interests and the mechanisms for translating these interests into policy. Policy networks place the focus of analysis on the whole policy arena and not just groups. It thereby facilitates an examination of state actors in the policy process. Moreover, as is argued in Chapter 3, policy networks can also be a means for extending state autonomy by providing state actors with the capability of achieving their policy goals.

The concepts of state autonomy and policy networks suggest a number of propositions.

1. The type of relationships that exist between groups and governments varies greatly across, time, policy sector and states.
2. State actors have interests which are important in both the development of policy networks and policy. Moreover, state actors are very important in terms of pressure group power. Frequently it is not pressure groups that determine state policy but state policy affects the activities of groups. To that

extent our concern is more the impact of policy on groups than the impact of groups on policy.

3. The type of policy networks that exist affect the degree of state autonomy by affecting the ability of the state to make and implement policy.

4. The type of policy network affects policy outcomes.

5. Policy networks provide a context for understanding pressure groups. They are the enstructuration of past policies, of ideologies and of policy processes. Policy networks have to be examined historically because they are the result of developing relationships between groups and state actors.

6. The types of policy networks are very important in affecting how policy changes. As we will see in Chapter 4, the pressure for policy change can be economic, social, ideological and political but the type of change and the degree of change that occurs, is greatly affected by the nature of the policy network (see Marsh and Rhodes 1992b). Consequently, grand theories of political change are inappropriate, and pressure for change will produce a range of outcomes in different areas.

In order to examine the truth or otherwise of these propositions, this book takes a number of case studies in Britain and the United States. The case studies are agricultural policy, trade policy, industrial policy, health policy and consumer policy. Agriculture provides an interesting case study because it is frequently argued that farmers are powerful around the world. By comparing agricultural policy in Britain and the United States, it is apparent that policy has been made very differently in each country, distinct networks have developed and, despite the supposed power of the farmers, the impact of state actors on the development of policy is crucial. Industrial policy and trade policy are central areas because they involve business, which all approaches to pressure groups see as an important interest. Yet, by comparing business in Britain and the United States it is clear that the influence of business is highly variable and that it is simplistic to see the state acting in the interest of capital in either the short or long term. Health policy is a significant policy sector because it involves a professional group which has highly specialised knowledge. Again it enables an assessment of whether professional groups develop particular types of networks. The final case study is consumer policy. Here we are able to examine a policy network that involves a group lacking either economic power or professional knowledge and this will enable an assessment of whether the lack of crucial resources develops an alternative type of network. By examining a range of groups in different states we are able to isolate the variables that produce particular types of networks. By comparing a number of policy areas we can show that relationships change within networks and by comparing different states we can show that it is not just the state system that produces particular networks.

Britain and the United States provide useful comparisons in terms of examining pressure groups because they are such contrasting states and political systems. Britain has an executive-dominated, unitary political system. The parliamentary system with strict party discipline results in the government dominating the political process. The majority of policy decisions are made by central government only to be formally approved, in some cases, by the legislature. In addition, the British state is highly secretive, with access to central government controlled by civil servants. As a result the British state has a tendency towards elitism. Decisions are made by a small number of Ministers and civil servants.

Nevertheless, interest groups do have an important role in the policy process. As Jordan and Richardson (1982, 1987) point out, Britain does have a political culture or style that is highly consultative. It is seen as important to consult in order to simplify the policy process and to ensure the legitimacy of political decisions. However, consultation status is not a right but attributed to groups which abide by the 'rules of the game' (Rhodes 1988). These rules frequently mean not upsetting the closed nature of policy-making and abiding by the demands for secrecy. Thus, interest groups in Britain are provided with access to elite policy circles in return for accepting rules determined by government.

In the United States the political system is highly facilitative of pressure group involvement in the policy process. For Petracca (1992: 3), 'American politics is the politics of interests.' This is the case for a number of reasons. First, the separation of power means that policy-making in the United States is highly fragmented. Congress, the executive and the judiciary all have independent power and can affect policy outcomes. Consequently, there are many decision-making centres in the US – Congress, congressional committees and subcommittees, the presidency, administrative agencies and the Supreme Court. Each provides interest groups with many different access points. Further fragmentation occurs because of the federal nature of the US state. Many important decisions are made at state level which also has numerous decision-making centres. As the policy process is so fragmented, and there may be many decision-makers involved in making decisions on a single issue, they have an interest in attracting interest groups in order to increase their legitimacy and political support in intra-agency conflicts. For instance, Ronald Reagan used the business lobby in order to persuade Congress to support his tax-cutting measures. In addition, fragmentation makes policy-making and implementation extremely difficult, and interest groups are a mechanism for overcoming the separation of powers. They can be used to build a coalition between a Congressional committee and a particular administrative agency.

Second, the weakness of political parties and party discipline increases pressure group politics. As political parties are weak they rely heavily on pressure groups for funding and assistance in electioneering. Political Action Committees have been established whereby interest groups provide funds for election campaigns. As a result members of Congress are very dependent on interest groups and this increases their influence. Moreover, the lack of party discipline means that members of Congress do not have to follow a party line and, therefore, have a degree of freedom to vote according to the wishes of their interests. The need for funding, the frequency of elections and the weaknesses of parties mean that members of Congress are much more likely to take note of interest groups than British MPs. This is reinforced by the lack of party ideology which makes it less likely for the legislature, or Presidents, to stick to a particular set of policy proposals. Accordingly, they can be more open to pressure groups.

Third, the absence of class politics in the United States makes the American people much more willing to join an array of interest groups. In addition, with the size of the United States, group activity is much more important for achieving goals, particularly when the weak and diverse parties are poor at both aggregating and representing interests. Consequently, many commentators on US interest groups have suggested that the nature of the system, plus recent changes in US politics and society like greater education, reform of Congress and new government programmes, has led to an explosion of interest groups in the US (Berry 1989; Heclo 1978; Salisbury 1990). Even between 1981 and 1987 the number of lobbyists in Washington increased from 5,662 to 23,011 (Petracca 1992).

The difference in the British and American pressure group systems means that it provides an interesting comparison for the investigation of networks. With the consideration of different policy areas we can develop a number of propositions about the types of networks that we would expect to find in Britain and the United States:

1. Policy communities are more likely to develop where the state is dependent on groups for implementation.
2. Policy communities are more likely to develop where interest groups have important resources that they can exchange.
3. Issue networks will develop in areas of lesser importance to government, of high political controversy, or in new issue areas where interests have not had the time to establish institutionalised relationships.
4. Policy communities are more likely to develop in Britain than the United States.

The most likely policy sector for a policy community is British health policy because policy-making is generally elitist and closed, and in developing health policy the state would be highly dependent on professional knowledge both for the development and implementation of policy. Policy communities should also exist in industrial and trade policy where business was involved because of the high level of economic resources available to business. The greatest chance of an issue network should be US consumer policy. However, as we will see in the course of this book, these expectations are not necessarily fulfilled.

This book will show that policy networks and state autonomy can make an important contribution to the understanding of group/state relations. It suggests, however, that the notion of state autonomy is highly problematic and that it needs modification in the light of the policy network literature. The notion of state autonomy suggests a stark dichotomy between the state and the groups in civil society. In reality, the interests of state actors develop within the context of policy networks which are used to further state interests. Therefore, in analysing policy networks we need to be aware of the importance of state actors as well as interest groups and how state actors' interests develop in the context of group/state interactions. In analysing groups and policy-making it is inadequate to focus solely on groups. It is necessary to take an historical approach which examines the nature of the relationships that have developed in particular policy sectors. It is important to examine the mechanisms for inclusion and exclusion, the beliefs that are dominant in a policy area and the structures of the policy process.

Chapter 2 will outline the traditional theoretical approaches to group/ government relations and demonstrate their weaknesses by examining how they deal with business power. Chapter 3 develops the notion of policy networks and state autonomy and demonstrates that they provide a more sophisticated notion of policy-making. Chapter 4 deals with the issue of how policy networks change. It suggests that the general theories of change are inadequate for explaining political change and provides an alternative approach. The following chapters deal with the case studies of policy networks and each looks at the types of networks that developed in Britain and the United States, how they operated, how they affected policy and whether they have changed. The final chapter provides a comparison of the various policy areas and assesses the extent to which the propositions outlined above have been verified.

Part I
Theory

Chapter 2

PLURALISM, CORPORATISM AND MARXISM:
Traditional Approaches to State/Group Relations

Analysis of government/group relations has been conducted within the confines of three paradigms: pluralism, corporatism and marxism. Consequently, each of these theoretical schools provides a wide range of literature concerned with examining the interactions between groups and government. Undoubtedly these perspectives have offered many useful insights into understanding the impact of groups on policy outcomes. However, the chapter will demonstrate that each of these theories has important limitations and, therefore, does not provide a comprehensive account of state/group relationships. This chapter will outline the theoretical position of each of these perspectives. As all the theories pay particular attention to the role of business, the chapter will examine the empirical applicability of these theories by reviewing their analysis of business/government interaction. The chapter will demonstrate the problems with the theories and highlight the need for an alternative approach.

Pluralism

Pluralist theory has dominated much of the analysis of group/government behaviour. For many pluralists (Smith 1976; Latham 1953; Bentley 1967) groups are the key focus of analysis in understanding political behaviour. Moreover, pluralist theory was developed mainly in the United States where the role of groups is much more important in the policy process than in Britain. Pluralism has been subject to frequent criticism by corporatist and marxist theorists for offering a benign view of power (Jessop 1983a, b; Schmitter 1974). They accuse pluralists of suggesting that power is distributed equally, that the state is neutral and that access to the state is relatively open. However, in reality the pluralist view of group/government interactions is much more sophisticated than many of its critics allow (Jordan 1990c; Smith 1990d). There is no single theory of pluralism but there are strands which are common to most pluralists. First, pluralists accept that groups wield 'significant amounts of power' and therefore are important in determining policy outcomes (Easton 1967; Smith 1976).

Yet pluralists do not see all groups as having equal power. One of the key pluralist writers, David Truman (1951: 10), accepted that 'institutionalised relationships between an agency and its attendant interest groups' could develop.

Once established, these relationships prevent outside groups having access to the policy process. Therefore, pluralists claim that they can account for the sorts of relationships which other writers call corporatist. Jordan (1981) talks of the institutionalisation of pluralism and Kelso (1978) suggests the term 'corporate pluralism' where interest groups capture the government, the size of the policy arena is narrowed, and there is a tacit agreement for interest groups not to compete with each other. What distinguishes pluralists is not the rejection of institutionalised relationships but a rejection of the notion of a 'corporate state'. Cox (1988a: 301) claims that:

> to show that there are special interests shaping housing, welfare, defence and agriculture is not a refutation of the pluralist framework. To refute the pluralist framework one would have to demonstrate that the vast majority of policy made by the state were shaped by the same interest all or most of the time.

Pluralists, in analysing the impact of groups, focus on their resources. For pluralists, a group's impact on policy depends on the resources that it has available, and variations in resources lead to one group having greater influence than another. Truman (1951: 267–9) suggests that the access groups have to government depends on: the social position of the group; the extent to which it is organised; and the skills and organisation of the leadership. Pluralists also stress the importance of the size of the organisation and the degree of mobilisation, and the level of the group's legitimacy (Eckstein 1960).

Consequently, pluralists do not discount the importance of economic resources nor the advantages of business groups. Truman (1951) accepted that business has a 'favored position in the conventional myth pattern' and like Lindblom (1977) he believed that, 'The favored position of groups is furthered by the existence of an economic system under which businessmen's confidence and expectations of profit are of crucial importance to the health of the economy.' Likewise pluralists do not believe that the state is neutral. Truman recognised that the President has a degree of independence from groups but also realised that groups which provide the President with support, and of which he is a member, will have advantages (Truman 1951: 399–400). He further claimed that structural arrangements are rarely neutral, 'they handicap some efforts and favor others' (Truman 1951: 322).

So pluralists accept that certain groups, particularly business, have advantages in the policy process; that there are problems of access and that the state is not neutral. Truman also outlines the rules of the game that prevent certain groups from having access to government (Truman 1951). However, what distinguishes pluralism is the existence of certain checks which ensure that power is not concentrated in the hands of a few groups.

Pluralists highlight a range of internal and external constraints that prevent a single or limited number of groups from achieving too much influence. External constraints exist in the form of countervailing powers. Pluralists argue that the existence of one group is usually matched by an alternative countergroup (Galbraith 1953; Smith 1976). So, for example, in the case of the abortion issue, the development of the pro-abortion lobby led to the creation of the anti-abortion lobby (Marsh and Chambers 1981). Even if countervailing groups do not emerge, powerful groups are also externally checked by the existence of potential groups. Truman suggested that there are groups with shared interests that do not actually become organised. Nevertheless, these groups could become organised if a dominant group threatens their interests sufficiently. This threat ensures that political leaders take note of their interests without the potential groups taking political action (Truman 1951: 397 and 519). In addition, people have multiple membership of unorganised groups which balance the political system and these groups will be 'dominant with sufficient frequency ... so that ... both the activity and methods of organised interests are kept within broad limits' (Truman 1951: 448). If the government does not attend to the grievances of unorganised interests there is a danger that political consensus will break down as various deprived interests see that their interests are not being served by the political system (Finer 1966).

The internal checks are the important counterweights that exist inside government. Although a department may develop a close relationship with a pressure group it still has wider acquaintanceships and 'has to open its ears to all interested organisations' (Finer 1966: 102). The need to win elections forces the government to listen to many groups. Even if an individual department does not pay much attention to a range of interests, the views of other groups are represented 'by the fact that other departments also have checks and have different departmental views correspondingly'. This has led Wilson (1977) to talk of 'Whitehall pluralism'. He claims that even in the case of agricultural policy where the relationship between the Ministry of Agriculture and the farmers has been extremely close, pluralism was maintained. He argues that the interests of other groups was represented through Cabinet and Cabinet committees which allowed a wider discussion of agricultural policy and enabled the interests of non-farm groups to be considered (see Chapter 5). Therefore, the very system of government provides for the representation of a plurality of interests.

Although business is well endowed with resources, these checks prevent business from dominating the political process. Truman also believed that business was faced with problems of internal cohesion and this resulted in 'significant differences in economic and political power' (Truman 1951: 256). Dahl discovered, in his study of New Haven, a number of constraints on the power of economic notables: they were few in number; they often disagreed among themselves; the authority of business was mainly confined to business issues; and they participated only marginally in other policies (Dahl 1961: 71–6). Consequently, economic notables were no more consistent in influencing the political outcomes than any other group. Hence, Finer (1966: 118) denies that wealth provides groups with any extra resources over poor groups because 'there are such effective ways for poor associations to influence policy'.

These constraints are the major distinguishing feature of the pluralist analysis of pressure groups because they ensure the dispersal of power in modern industrial society. The complexity and interdependence of society, combined with a political system open to many interests leads to pluralism (Luhmann 1982). Although resources are not shared equally, those who lack one resource, like money, often have an alternative resource such as votes. For pluralists there is a wide dispersal of power between various leaders; constraints on leadership from non-elites and competing elites; and uncertainty over who benefits. So Hewitt (1974: 61) could conclude in his study of policy-making:

> From the evidence presented, it is clear that policy-making does not appear to be elitist in the sense that any single elite or interest is dominant. Instead the picture of national power that is revealed suggests a 'pluralist' interpretation since a diversity of conflicting interests are involved in many issues, without any one interest being consistently successful in realising its goals.

In his study, Hewitt selected a number of issues across four policy areas: foreign affairs; economic policy; welfare policy and social policy. He then analysed which groups were involved in each issue and he discovered that, 'Very few organisations were involved "significantly" in more than one issue' (Hewitt 1974: 54), thus demonstrating that no single class dominated the political process.

This position demonstrates the distinctiveness of the pluralist view of power and methodology. For Dahl (1957: 202–3) power is defined when, 'A has power over B to the extent that he can get B to do something he would otherwise not do'. In the decision-making process, power exists when A gets B to choose policy X when B would have chosen policy Y (Polsby 1980: 4). This view of power determines the pluralist methodology: 'actual behaviour is observed or reconstructed from documents, witnesses and so on, it is possible to determine empirically whether or not the same group realises two or more issue areas' (Polsby 1960: 477). Pluralists analyse who has power by looking at the process of decision-making and determining who was involved and who prevailed.

The pluralist view of state/government relations is much more sophisticated than critics allow. It acknowledges inequality of power, access and resources but also sees that certain constraints exist to ensure that a single group does not become too powerful. We will now examine how pluralism deals empirically with the problem of business and then we will examine the limitations of the pluralists' approach.

Pluralism and the power of business

Pluralists, who have been accused of developing a benign view of the role of business, recognise that business does have exceptional resources. They accept that business is likely to have a substantial impact on the political system. As

Vogel (1987: 405) admits: 'Clearly businessmen exercise considerable power over their employees, the political system and the economy as a whole.' His empirical work highlights the degree to which business interests have often been successful in influencing government policy (Vogel 1989). For most of the

> history of capitalism, the large business corporation in the United States effectively enjoyed a monopoly of the political and institutional power without parallel in the capitalist world in the twentieth century (Vogel 1978: 63).

The US government wanted to secure economic growth and therefore business did not need overt political activity in order for the government to adopt policies which favoured business interests (Vogel 1989). Despite setbacks in the 1970s, business again enjoyed considerable success in the 1980s by persuading the government to deregulate parts of the economy and to reduce corporate and individual taxation (Vogel 1989; McQuaid 1981). Business strongly supported the 1981 Recovery Tax Act and the result was tax cuts worth $169 billion to business and $500 billion to individuals over six years (Levitan and Cooper 1984: 55).

In Britain, pluralist research has also highlighted a number of business successes. The CBI influenced the government's 1975 Industrial Relations Act (Grant and Marsh 1977) and it was successful in persuading the Labour government against implementing the Bullock report on industrial democracy (Grant 1987). Nevertheless, for pluralists the influence of business does not depend on the nature of the state, the domination of a particular class or unobservable forms of power. Rather it is dependent on the resources available to business groups in a particular situation and the strength of opposition. Despite the ability of business to influence policy under particular circumstances, the power of business is limited by a number of factors.

Within the pluralist paradigm, business is able to influence government because it has a high level of the resources that are, in principle, available to all interest groups. Grant and Marsh point out that the CBI has over eleven thousand members from all sectors of British industry and this includes 75 per cent of companies listed in *The Times* top 200 companies. This secures the CBI a substantial income which it uses to maintain a professional leadership and an efficient organisation. The CBI has the ability to supply the government with important information and to develop policy documents which can be used as the basis of their demands.

The resources of high membership, professionalism, finance and specialist knowledge provide the CBI with a high level of legitimacy. As the CBI appears to be able to represent business and is clearly a serious organisation, government will be prepared to consult it on particular issues and accept its views as representing business (see Jordan and Richardson 1987). Consequently, the CBI has been able to develop insider status (Grant 1985). Grant and Marsh (1977: 109) discovered:

the CBI has extensive formal and informal contacts with both ministers and civil servants in a large number of government departments, although, of course, the majority of its contacts are with the Department of Trade and the Department of Industry and to a lesser extent with the Department of Employment.

The CBI is not the only business group that attempts to influence government. Increasingly important is the Institute of Directors and individual trade associations. The Institute of Directors is a much smaller organisation than the CBI and it also tends to be more political. Consequently, its links are through the Conservative Party rather than Whitehall. However, the fact that it established good relations with the former Prime Minister, Mrs Thatcher, meant that it became an increasingly influential organisation (Wilson 1985). Individual trade associations and even individual firms have been able to use their resources to establish important links with civil servants, Ministers and even the Prime Minister. For example, at GEC Lord Weinstock cultivated government support and effectively 'became his own government relations division' (Grant 1987: 94).

In the United States, the resources of business groups take a different form and the various business groups are less organised and comprehensive than in Britain. Before the 1970s business was almost completely unorganised politically. Although there were business organisations like the National Association of Manufactures (NAM), they were often divided, undertook little political activity and had limited contacts with government (McQuaid 1981; Vogel 1989; Wilson 1985). During the 1970s, business was feeling increasingly threatened by the demands of public interest groups. As a result of the success of environmental and consumer groups, business started to reorganise in an attempt to copy some of their tactics and forms of organisation (Vogel 1983). Throughout the 1970s business took action to increase its organisational resources. The number of businesses with government relations departments and Washington offices increased substantially (Vogel 1983). The Chamber of Commerce became a revitalised organisation. Between 1974 and 1980 its annual budget tripled and the membership doubled. It has established an important network which links local businesses to national politics by organising campaigns at the local level and giving them a national impact. The National Association of Manufactures has increased its political activities. In 1974 it established a Washington office and in 1975 registered itself as a lobbying organisation for the first time. NAM consciously became less ideological in order to improve relations with Congress and the administration (Levitan and Cooper 1984: 13).

In 1972 the Business Roundtable was formed due to the increasing perception amongst top companies of economic crisis and political threat. This organisation has a number of important resources. It is comprised of the Chief Executive Officers (CEO) of the largest US corporations. By 1980 it included the ten largest corporations in the *Fortune* 500 and forty of the top fifty companies. Consequently, it is financially very strong with the gross revenues of members being equal to about half the USA's GNP. The size and status of the

Roundtable's members enabled it quickly to establish good contacts with government and Congress (McQuaid, 1981).

The financial resources of business made it increasingly influential in US elections. Following the 1974 Federal Elections Finance Act, business can only donate money to election campaigns through Political Action Committees (PACs). However a whole range of PACs have now emerged which receive money from companies, trade associations and individuals (Wilson 1985). 'The number of business-related PACs increased from 248 in 1974 to 1,100 in 1976' (Vogel 1983). In the 1980 election campaign corporate PACs contributed $19.2 million and used much of this money to challenge incumbent Democrats in Congress (Vogel 1989).

The resources of finance, organisation and access enable business, according to pluralists, to employ a number of tactics. First, they have the finance to launch campaigns to try to influence public opinion. Second, they can develop contacts with legislatures in order to influence laws and, indirectly, the executive. In Britain this is less important but as Grant and Marsh (1977) point out, particularly over certain issues, the CBI maintains contact with MPs in the hope that they will put the CBI's argument in Parliament.

In the United States, influencing the legislature can take two forms. Business tries to obtain the support of members of Congress by supporting their election through PACs. Shipper and Jennings (1984) suggest that this support can be used as a means to threaten members of Congress. They describe how the Realtors' Political Action Committee published a series of report cards on members of Congress and financial support depended on answers to a seven-page questionnaire. Wright (1989: 713) claims that:

> Traditionally, groups have established and maintain access to elected officials through visible organisational connections to their geographic districts. Now it increasingly appears that groups achieve access through campaign contributions from their political action committees.

Business also increases its influence through Congress by establishing contact with members of Congress and particularly the chairmen of relevant congressional committees and subcommittees. Many companies now have Washington offices and the role of these offices is to highlight policies that will affect companies and to establish contacts that might be useful (Weidenbaum 1990: 374–9). With the reforms that have decentralised power within Congress, business has found a whole range of members of Congress with whom it needs to develop contacts.

Of crucial importance in terms of business tactics is the use of insider links to influence decisions by the executive. In Britain, the CBI is seen as the legitimate representative of manufacturing industry and this ensures access to the administration. When the government was developing its incomes policy it placed great importance on consultation with the CBI (Grant and Marsh 1977:

112–13). Pluralists have acknowledged that insider links are crucial for explaining the influence of the City. The City has established close links with government because of personal connections, contacts within the Conservative Party and the role of the Bank of England representing the interests of the City directly to government (Moran 1984; Wilson 1985).

In the United States insider links with the administration are often less important than in Britain because of a general distrust of the state and the adversarial nature of pressure group politics (Vogel 1987). Vogel (1988: 109) suggests that:

> Unlike in other capitalist nations, where there exist a wide array of official and quasi-official channels through which business can regularly communicate its views to public officials, in America corporate political participation tends to be much more *ad hoc* in nature.

However, there are still important insider connections. Members of business organisations and representatives of individual firms do establish contacts with members of the administration. McQuaid (1982) points out that between 1945 and 1960, forty-five to sixty chief executives were members of the business council which had an important role in advising the government on economic policy. Business has a wide range of resources which allow for a number of tactics to influence government and pluralists do not deny that business has significant success. What distinguishes pluralism is the recognition that the power of business is limited and that business does not completely dominate the political system. Unlike marxists and elitists, they do not see the state or policy being controlled by a single group or class. Pluralists maintain that there are a range of constraints on business power.

Pluralists reject the view of Bachrach and Baratz (1962), and of Lukes (1974), that the political agenda is skewed in favour of business. Vogel (1989) avers that the organisation of business in the 1970s was largely a response to new issues placed on the agenda by the consumer movement and the environmental movement. With increased consumer and environmental regulation, business was forced to organise politically in order to protect its interests.

For pluralists, business's lack of control of the agenda demonstrates the degree to which business has faced influential countervailing groups. In the United States, the 1970s saw the development of increasingly well organised and influential public interest groups which were able to place demands on government that did not favour the interests of business (Vogel 1989: 93). In Britain, the trade union movement had a high density, good organisation and perhaps a greater degree of unity than business groups. Unions, particularly in the 1970s also had close relations with government and often met the government on equal terms with business. According to a former leader of the CBI, Campbell Adamson, the Conservative Prime Minister, Edward Heath:

> loved the trade unionists more than he loved the industrialists. And not only did he

consider them the more important partner but actually he even seemed at times to be more able to agree with them than with his own kind as it were, the industrialists . . . (Whiteheadits87).

In the 1980s, the CBI faced new countervailing powers in the form of different sections of business. Particularly in the early 1980s the CBI believed that the government was more concerned with the interests of the City and of organisations like the Institute of Directors (Grant 1987; Leys 1985). Consequently, for pluralists, business is just one group amongst many. Vogel believes that business in the United States 'enjoys few privileges not enjoyed by other groups . . .'. It operates in the pressure groups' universe like any other group.

Business is also limited by its self-denying ordinance. There are many areas where business does not want to influence policy. The main concern of chief executives is to make a profit (McQuaid 1981: 114). The costs of participating in politics in terms of time, money and risk are high and therefore business will only participate if its interests are directly affected. Business's distrust of the state means that it does not want to participate in activity which might encourage intervention in its industry (Vogel 1978).

The impact of business on policy is also constrained by the absence of a united view. It is seldom the case that all of business is united in preference for, or opposition to, a particular policy. Businesses operate within a competitive market and often what is good for one business is bad for another. In Britain, the clearest division exists between the City and manufacturing industry, with the City preferring high interest rates and a high pound whilst manufacturing prefers low interest rates and a lower valued pound. However, further divisions exist between different sectors of industry – for example between electricity and gas, between manufacturing and services and between producers and retailers. Conflicts can even exist between firms in the same sector as in the case of BP receiving a tax concession which was not available for ICI (Grant *et al.* 1988). In both Britain and the United States, peak organisation either failed to develop, or failed adequately to represent, the interests of business as a whole. Vogel (1978: 67) suggests the lack of business organisation early on in the United States has resulted in the American bourgeoisie being 'the most fragmented in the capitalist world. The business community is largely a community in name only; its internal structures of authority remain remarkably decentralised.'

Finally, new right theorists and pluralists would argue that the concerns of politicians for winning elections override the concern for economic growth and, therefore, politicians are more likely to be influenced by the demands of voters than of business (Brittan 1975). Finer maintains that despite the close links between business and the Conservative Party, 'The Conservative Party exists to win elections.' Therefore the party has to 'temper the demands of its aligned interest groups' in order to win the votes which are not committed to either party. Hence, the vote is an important resource which enables unorganised people to take on the power of big business (Beer 1982). Finer makes the point that 'the Conservative Party must democratise the necessarily crude and sectional views of what are purely economic associations into something electorally viable.' This is remarkably similar to Poulantzas' view of the role of the relative autonomy of the state where the capitalist state must be relatively autonomous from the capitalist class in order to ensure that sectional interests do not destroy the capitalist system.

The result of these constraints on the influence of business is that business power is confined to certain policy areas and even in these it is often likely to be defeated on issues. Thus Vogel (1989) highlights a number of issues which demonstrate the declining influence of business in the United States. In particular, business faced a whole range of new regulation from the mid-1960s starting with the 1966 Traffic and Motor Vehicle Safety Act and the 1966 Fair Packaging Act which placed the interests of consumers above those of business. The 1960s and 1970s also saw increased regulation from the Consumer Product Safety Commission, the Federal Trade Commission and the Environmental Protection Agency. By the end of the 1970s there were many regulations which industry did not see as being in its interest (Weidenbaum 1977). Even in the 1980s with Reagan as President, business did not achieve as much as it might have hoped. By 1983 the level of the budget deficit was forcing Congress to consider new taxes and the government's deregulatory programme was making little progress (Vogel 1989).

Finer outlined how ineffective British business has been in preventing the government implementing its policies. Industry, despite strong opposition, had no choice but to accept the nationalisation of steel. Grant and Marsh (1977: 207) concluded:

> the CBI has had relatively limited impact on the major issues which have dominated British politics since its formation. As in other policy areas, it has been able to extract detailed concessions which are of benefit to its members. However, the CBI faces the fundamental difficulty that it is operating in a political environment that is increasingly unsympathetic to its aims and aspirations.

For pluralists, business is important but it is not all-dominating. They examine how pressure groups are organised, the resources they have and the tactics they use, and then determine how much influence a group has in a particular situation. The influence of business has to be ascertained through looking at policy decisions. Business influences government by working through the channels that exist for other interest groups. There is no unobservable structural power and there is not a capitalist state which is the 'ideal collective capitalist' or operating structural selectivity. Business groups have to lobby, develop contacts with departments, write letters and hope that they can influence outcomes. The reason why business is more successful than other groups is because it has more of the resources which are necessary for influence.

This theoretical and methodological position highlights some important aspects of the political process. It demonstrates the difficulty that business has faced in organising politically. It focuses on the actual political activity which business has taken in order to influence government policy. The pluralist approach to business shows how pressure groups organise and how they can establish contact with government. It also emphasises the important point that business does not always win and that it is necessary to account for how an economically strong sector is often politically ineffective. Nevertheless, there are problems with this approach.

Critique of pluralism

The problems of pluralism can be divided into general problems and those that relate particularly to its analysis of business. Although pluralism does not see all groups as equal, pluralists do believe that power in democratic societies is widely dispersed and that various resources are available to different groups and this allows them to influence policy. Hence Finer's view that even poor associations have access to resources. There are two problems with this view. First, it sees the dispersal of power as an ontological certainty. In other words, for pluralists, the distribution of power is part of modern society; it is a theoretical assumption. Like marxists, pluralists have their conclusions built into their theory and with a pluralist theory they reach pluralist conclusions. Second, pluralists exaggerate the ease of access. Jordan and Richardson (1987), whilst admitting that government consultation is often cosmetic, make continual reference to the ease of being consulted, the desire of departments to consult and their long lists of consultees. Finer (1966: 58) maintains that a good case will mean that an interest group will eventually get a hearing. This appears to deny that in many areas of policy, particular groups are denied access for long periods, as in the case of consumers and agricultural policy (Smith 1988).

This view of the ease of access to the political process is related to problems with pluralist methodology. Because pluralists are concerned with observable behaviour, they see evidence of consultation as an indicator of access and therefore influence. If A supports a policy Z, and the government consults A and chooses policy Z, A is seen to be influential. However, all that is demonstrated is a correlation between consultation with A and outcome Z. The relationship might not be causal. The government might have chosen Z for a number of reasons. By focusing on the observable, pluralists may frequently miss the real causes of a particular policy. As was highlighted in Chapter 1, pluralists fail to examine the structural and ideological context within which policy is made.

Pluralists frequently overemphasize the role of groups in the policy process without taking account of other determining factors. By focusing on the resources and behaviour of groups, pluralists pay insufficient attention to the structural and ideological context and the interests and activities of the bureaucracy and the government. They fail to recognise the ability of state actors to make policy independently of groups. The influence of groups does not derive solely from their resources but from the organisation of government. Often groups of equivalent resources fare very differently. These variations in influence are accounted for by the different organisations and institutions within government. Hall (1986: 19) points to the need for an institutional analysis of policy-making which 'emphasizes institutional relationships, both informal and conventional, that bind the components of the state together and structure its relations with society'.

Whilst rejecting structural power and pursuing a positivist methodology, pluralists do actually uncover unobservable phenomena. Truman acknowledges the power that potential groups have without having to take action. He claims that the willingness of legislators to react to pressure groups may 'not involve any overt act on the part of the group [or] any pressure on the legislator' (Truman 1951: 338). It would seem that Congress can act by anticipated reaction. Dahl (1961: 76) also found in New Haven that:

> the goals of businessmen are legitimized by a system of beliefs widely held throughout the community. Among other things, this system of belief gives legitimacy to business itself as an essential institution in American society.

He identifies anticipated reaction when he notes that these beliefs made politicians very wary about the influence of economic and political notables and so they avoided:

> issues that might unite the Notables in bitter opposition. Fortunately for the politicians, it is easy to avoid the implacable hostility of the Notables, for living conditions and the belief system have not – at least so far – generated demands for local policies markedly antagonistic to the goals of businessmen and Notables (Dahl 1961: 84).

Despite Dahl's claim that notables were not a ruling elite, and frequently lost in the policy process, it seems that no issues that fundamentally threatened the interests of the business elite were raised because of 'living conditions and the belief system'. This is the point that critics of pluralism have made; the system of beliefs prevents certain issues from reaching the political agenda (Lukes 1974; Gaventa 1980).

The existence of 'Whitehall pluralism' is also questionable. On many (the majority of) occasions other departments will not have the opportunity to represent alternative interests. In most instances, policy is made within departments without reference to Cabinet or Cabinet committees (see Crossman 1972). Even when policy is referred to interdepartmental committees the extent to which other departments will represent alternative interests is limited. Often Ministers are too busy to read the papers of other departments in order to offer constructive alternatives. They are also wary of criticising colleagues when they may want his/her support for their own department's policy (Headey 1974: 48

and 77–8). Perhaps most importantly, Ministers are likely to accept the broad thrust of policy and so will not suggest any real alternatives.

It is also doubtful that potential groups do exercise much influence over decision-makers. Departments do not represent their interests, not least because it must be difficult to recognise these interests. Moreover, it seems unlikely that potential groups pose much of an electoral threat. It is rare for a single issue to sway large numbers of votes (Butler and Stokes 1974) and the members of potential groups are likely to have many conflicting interests. Therefore, if a politician appeals to one potential group, or part of the group, he or she could lose the vote of another group. It seems likely that potential groups are those that have great difficulty organising, such as consumers or the elderly, who do not meet collectively, lack resources, often have conflicting interests and lack economic power. However much their interests are threatened, they are unlikely to become actual groups. Indeed the concept of a potential group is questionable. How can a potential group exist when the concept group involves some form of collective identity? A group can only exist once it is formed. Otherwise it requires the introduction of a marxian notion of 'objective' groups or interests which can exist without individuals having consciousness of their own groups.

The key problems of pluralism are methodological. It might be the case that a policy area is pluralistic. Yet if we are to understand the role of pressure group/government relations in the development of policy, they have to be placed within the context of state interests, ideology and structure. Yet the focus of pluralists is on groups and their observable behaviour, and hence, pluralists are unable to analyse the structural and the ideological. Nevertheless, they contradictorily discover evidence of unobservable activity with their notions of potential groups, belief systems and anticipated reaction. This methodology leads pluralists to see all groups as basically the same, if not equal, but with varying resources. This results in a denial that differences in resources can be built into the structure of society and the state. The dependence of Britain on invisible earnings means that the City has resources which are unavailable to any other group. This omission leads to a number of weaknesses in the pluralist analysis of business.

The most substantial problem with the pluralist approach is the tendency to treat business as just another interest group. Clearly, business has advantages that do not exist for other groups. First, businesses have ready-made organisations in the form of firms and consequently, they do not have to overcome the collective action problem faced by other interest groups (Olson 1965). Where businesses do have to join together, the benefits of their actions are often enjoyed by a small number of firms and so the incentives to organise are high (Olson 1965; Wilson 1980).

Second, because of its key role in the economy, business has resources unavailable to other groups (Lindblom 1977). The actions of business affect the lives of many people and the success of economies as a whole. This, as Lindblom points out, gives business a privileged position. Governments usually need successful economies for their own survival and so they are automatically receptive to the interests of business. Although trade unions have economic resources, their ability to organise and the problems they face in taking action are greater than those of business (Offe and Wiesenthal 1980). Consequently, business has advantages over other groups in establishing links with government. Business groups more immediately operate within the existing rules of the game. They are 'respectable', have resources they can exchange with government and are unlikely to be demanding radical change or threatening extreme political action. This enables business to establish institutionalised relations with government which are more intense, of greater duration and of higher quality than those of most other groups. The existence of these resources is not the result of chance or individual volition but due to the structure of capitalist society and of government – the resources are structural.

Third, business has access to financial resources far greater than those of other interest groups. Large multinationals have the resources to spend vast sums on lobbying, campaigns and publicity whilst other groups might depend on voluntary contributions or membership fees. Fourth, business through ownership of media has access to much greater sources of information than other groups and although television is less likely to be biased towards particular business causes, it is equally unlikely to question the existence of capitalism. Fifth, business does, especially in the United States, exist within an ideological framework which is generally favourable to business.

The existence of this ideology, the degree of institutionalisation and the importance of business for the economy means that business power does not always operate through the traditional lobbying techniques of pressure groups but through structural power. This is power that is exercised not through individual actions but by the organisation of policy-making and the beliefs of policy actors so that decisions are made in a certain way without business (or any group with structural power) having to act. By focusing on lobbying and the observable activity of business groups, pluralists are ignoring the context within which business operates and the other forms of power available. Moreover, the routinisation of these advantages (Giddens 1986) leads to business being systematically integrated into government and having structural power which is unavailable to most other groups. That pluralism to some extent failed to deal with the exceptional position of business, the increasing concentration and complexity of power and the changing role of the state led to a resurgence of corporatist theory in the 1970s.

Corporatism

Unlike pluralism, corporatist theories presuppose that power in modern societies and states is concentrated and that changes in the organisation of society have resulted in business having exceptional power. Consequently, certain corporatist theories propose that there is a dual state, with social and welfare issues being conducted in a pluralist arena whilst economic policy is conducted within a corporatist arena (Cawson and Saunders 1983). However, within corporatist theory – as with the others – there is no single definition of corporatism. Cawson (1986) identifies three main strands of corporatist theory: those which see it as an alternative economic system; those which see it as a mechanism of interest intermediation and those which see it as a distinctive form of state. We now outline these approaches to corporatism.

Corporatism as an alternative economic form

According to Winkler (1976: 103), 'Corporatism is an economic system in which the state directs and controls predominantly privately-owned business according to four principles: unity, order, nationalism and success.' Corporatism is an economic form that combines elements of capitalism and socialism. The four principles which Winkler identifies are intended to enable the state to cope with economic crisis as a result of economic restructuring. Corporatism is a mechanism for allowing the state to overcome the conflicts within society in order to achieve success in the national interest. The market economy is divisive and inefficient and therefore the state ensures unity through establishing an economic policy based on cooperation rather than competition. This unity enables the establishment of order which is the overcoming of the anarchic market. Nationalism is thus used as a means of establishing unity and order because it eliminates class conflict. Economic success can then be defined as national success rather than class success.

Winkler's notion of corporatism fitted into a developmental view of society. Corporatism was an inevitable stage which would be reached when the economy and business developed various characteristics. The problem for Winkler's theory was that very few societies reached this situation. Pahl and Winkler's prediction (1974) that Britain would become corporatist by the 1990s was undermined by the advent of Thatcherism and the attempt to return to the market.

Corporatism as a state form

For Jessop, corporatism is a particular form of representation which develops as a result of the 'changing requirements of capital accumulation' (Jessop 1990: 122). Jessop distinguishes between parliamentarianism and corporatism as different types of state forms which develop according to the varying requirements of capital accumulation. Under parliamentarianism:

> representation is secured through the participation of 'citizens' in policy-making of an elected government though voting and political rights. And intervention occurs

in the form of legislation or general policies enforced by a permanent rational–legal administration in accordance with the rule of law (Jessop 1990: 119).

Parliamentarianism is only adequate in certain situations and 'in others will prove incompatible with capital accumulation' (p. 122). Under corporatism:

> representation is mediated through a system of public 'corporations' which are constituted on the basis of their members' functions within the division of labour. And state intervention occurs through these same corporations and/or administrative agencies formally accountable to them. Thus, whereas representation and intervention are typically institutionally separated in parliamentary-bureaucratic systems, in corporatism they tend to be institutionally fused (Jessop 1990: 120).

Jessop maintains that parliamentarianism can only work in certain situations. It is appropriate during the stage of liberal capitalism when the state only has to provide the legal framework for the operation of capitalism but it is subject to crises of representation, and adversarial politics 'may encourage the abuse of executive power to secure electoral advantage at the expense of accumulation' (p. 124). Thus new forms of representation occur with new forms of intervention. Representation and intervention are merged into the same institutions and representation is based on functional criteria so that capital and labour can work together in the development and implementation of policy. In doing so, capitalism is protected because each partner accepts the 'legitimacy of the capitalist order' (p. 128). This leads Jessop to conclude that with the integration of capital and labour through the granting of concessions and legitimation of capital, liberal corporatism is 'the highest stage of social democracy' (p. 132). In some senses Jessop nearly goes as far as Winkler when he suggests that corporatism is 'a recurring element in modern societies. It is always tendential and in many cases more permanent; and it corresponds well in some respects to the nature and dynamic of capitalist relation.' So like Winkler, Jessop suggests that corporatism is a macro concept that appears at a particular stage of capitalist development.

This view creates a number of problems. In seeing the state develop from parliamentarianism to corporatism, Jessop established a very idealised definition of parliamentarianism. Jessop appears to endorse a Bagehot-like constitutional definition of a parliamentary system without question. In one section Jessop uncritically accepts the pluralist notion of adversarial politics which has been rejected by a number of authors (Gamble and Walkland 1984; Cox 1988c). Any empirical examination of parliamentary government will demonstrate that many of the characteristics that Jessop identifies never existed. This simplistic definition leads Jessop to create a notion of corporatism as a state form. However, he fails to recognise the implications of such an approach. What does it mean to say that corporatism is a state form? Does it mean that specific forms of representation and intervention occur throughout the state, purely in economic sectors, or just in certain aspects of economic policy? Can the different parts of the state take on different forms? Jessop (1980) suggests that the state is not unified. If this is the case, is a corporatist state form a possibility?

Corporatism as interest group intermediation

The most common use of corporatism is to see it as a means of understanding the relationship between interest groups and government where corporatism indicates that this relationship takes a very particular form. In Schmitter's (1974: 85–6) classic definition, corporatism refers to:

> a system of interest representation in which the constituent elements are organised into a limited number of singular compulsory, non-competitive, hierarchically ordered and licensed (if not created) by the state and granted deliberate representational monopoly within their respective categories in exchange for observing certain controls on their selection of leaders and articulation of demands and supports.

In this definition of corporatism, groups are seen as hierarchical organisations which face limited competition and are at least legitimised by the state (Williamson 1989). The strength of these organisations enables them to bargain with the state. The groups can offer the state legitimacy, information and assistance in implementation and, in return, they are offered a role in policy-making. Thus Cawson (1986: 38) suggests:

> Corporatism is a specific socio-political process in which organisations representing monopolistic functional interests engage with state agencies over public policy outputs which involve those organisations in a role which combines interest representation and policy implementation through delegated self enforcement.

Monopolistic and hierarchical groups have the resources to negotiate with government because they have the ability to implement any decisions which are agreed. Under corporatism, the role of groups is regulatory as well as representative. They are responsible for ensuring that their members accept agreed policy decisions. Hence, corporatism has advantages for both groups and government. The groups can influence policy and the government does not have to develop the capabilities to control social actors. This is also a much more limited notion of corporatism than that provided by the two previous definitions. Corporatism is seen as a particular form of representation and policy-making which can occur within certain parts of the state at specific times (see Cawson 1985). It is not a general theory of the state or the economy.

This definition of corporatism is much more limited than the other models. It tends to refer to economic policy and the meso level, although it can, in some countries, occur at the macro-level. Moreover, corporatism is likely to occur for a number of reasons and not because of general developments in capitalism. This leads Crouch and Dore (1990) to refine the definition even further and to talk of 'corporatist arrangements' rather than corporatism. This involves looking for specific relationships between groups and parts of government where, 'groups receive certain institutionalized or *ad hoc* benefits in return for guarantees by the groups' representatives that their members will behave in certain ways' (Crouch and Dore 1990: 3). The density of corporatist arrangements indicates the overall level of corporatism.

These three models of corporatism are all concerned with the interaction between the public and private. In Winkler's model this is largely in terms of the economy. For Jessop, it encompasses the state taking on specific forms of representation and intervention, and for the last model it refers to a specific form of interest group intermediation in particular sectors. The development of this last model is a result of the criticism that neither the corporatist economic mode nor the corporatist state form appears to exist anywhere, and hence, the corporatist model was refined so that it became more limited in its application (see Cox 1988a). We will now examine how corporatism has been used to examine business/government relations in order to evaluate the usefulness of corporatist theory.

Corporatism and business

For corporatists, business is central to an understanding of state/group relations. Usually, although there are exceptions (Cawson 1982), corporatist relations only develop between economic groups and the state. Often this includes both capital and labour but for most corporatists (especially for marxist corporatists) labour is included as a means of cooption in response to its increasing strength. Corporatism is a means of ensuring that trade unions accept an economic policy which is in the 'national interest' (Jessop 1990; Panitch 1977; Schmitter 1979; Vogler 1985). To quote Jessop (1990):

> since corporatism is constituted on the basis of economic–corporate interests, it provides no direct mechanism for defining the universal interest outside the capitalist framework. Class interests are defined and represented in and through the functionally heterogeneous but formally equal corporations, whose ability to cooperate and compromise depends on shared commitments to work within the fundamental limits of the capital relation.

Within corporatism, business is influential because it has the essential resources for the running of the economy. Business has control over particular areas of industrial policy and is important in terms of the control of labour, investment and the distribution of wealth. As capital becomes increasingly powerful and concentrated (Harris 1972; Middlemas 1979), business is institutionalised into state machinery and therefore has substantial potential influence on policy outcomes. In return for this influence, business assists government in the implementation of the government's economic policy. For corporatists, business influence occurs not through lobbying activity but through the integration of business organisations into the state.

Corporatists disagree over why corporatism occurs. Some see corporatism as a result of a certain stage of the development of capitalism which necessitates state intervention in order to ensure long-term accumulation (Harris 1972; Jessop 1982; Bonnett 1985). Others see it resulting from a need to limit the conflict between capital and a powerful labour movement in order to pursue the national interest (Crouch 1977; Middlemas 1979; Panitch 1977). As we have seen, corporatists also disagree on the level at which corporatism occurs. At the macro-level business can be involved in the development of economic policy, industrial policy and incomes policy. This usually involves the peak organisations of business in discussion with the peak organisations of labour and the government. Corporatism can also occur at the meso-level whereby industrial policy for a particular sector is developed in negotiation between a particular industry through trade associations (Cawson 1986). Finally, at the micro-level, particular firms can develop institutionalised relationships with government and use these to influence policy (Cawson *et al.* 1990; Grant *et al.* 1988). The following section will examine some empirical examples of corporatism.

Macro-level corporatism

For Middlemas (1979) the coming of the Second World War, and the increasing strength and legitimacy of the labour movement, resulted in economic actors becoming increasingly incorporated into the state. Middlemas claims that the post-war British state has seen the emergence of 'corporate bias', which is 'the tendency for industry, trade unions and financial institutions to make reciprocal arrangements with each other and with government while avoiding overt conflict . . .' (Middlemas 1986: 1). With corporate bias trade unions and business became governing institutions and were incorporated into government at many levels. Business was integrated into government through positions on advisory committees to government, quangos and royal commissions. By 1966 the CBI was represented on fifty-seven advisory bodies including such organisations as ACAS, NEDC and the Price Commission (Newman 1981). More importantly, in the post-war period, 'the centre of activity returned to the informal network of contacts between TUC, BEC and government' (Middlemas 1979).

Newman (1981: 91) maintains that, 'Tripartite consultation at the very highest level of national decision-taking soon found itself institutionalised as the regular order of the day.' The degree of corporatism was particularly apparent, according to corporatists, in two areas. From the late 1950s, Britain's economic crisis became increasingly evident and the government saw the need to intervene in the economy. This intervention necessitated the cooperation of business, and to a lesser extent the unions, and so the government incorporated business into the economic policy process. In 1962 the Conservative government created the National Economic Development Council (NEDC) as a forum for tripartite discussions for improving the productivity of British industry and the reports from the NEDC, and the sectoral 'little neddys', were a means of agreeing economic goals and policy. The Heath government after the 1972 Industry Act established an Industrial Development Unit to coordinate industrial policy (Jessop 1980). The Labour government of 1974 established sector working parties as a way of involving industry in developing policies to improve the performance of particular industries (Grant 1982).

The second area of macro-level corporatism is incomes policy. As incomes, inflation and strikes increased in Britain throughout the 1960s, the government became increasingly involved in controlling incomes. It was only able to do so through gaining the support of business and the unions. Consequently, incomes policy involved elaborate tripartite arrangements for negotiation. Throughout the 1960s and 1970s, there were a whole range of incomes policies agreed after discussion between industry, the unions and government (Riley 1988: 137). Crouch (1977) highlights how the 1964 Labour government attempted to achieve an incomes policy 'in the spirit of agreement and collaboration' by 'securing a tripartite declaration of intent to pursue a voluntary incomes policy'. A National Board for Prices and Incomes was established and the TUC and CBI were involved in monitoring wage claims and price increases.

It is highly questionable that macro-corporatism provides a useful description of state/business relations in either Britain or the United States. Critics of corporatism have suggested that it has never actually existed (Cox 1988c; Jordan 1984; Martin 1983). Although business did become more integrated into government, it is questionable how much influence this provided and to what degree business helped government implement policies. For example, the NEDC has never been a very effective body. Government accepted its reports when they reinforced government policy and ignored them when they did not. More importantly, government, business, and unions failed to develop the degree of consensus that is said to be necessary for corporatist arrangements to work. Indeed, much of British industry was not very happy with increased intervention in the economy (Marsh and Grant 1977).

Moreover, business peak organisations, as we have seen, are internally weak. The CBI is limited in its degree of representativeness and it has no sanctions that it can use on its members (Marsh and Grant 1977). Therefore, in bargaining with government, it is limited in what it can offer. As a result the majority of 'corporatist' agreements have been very unstable with agreements on incomes policies only lasting for a short period (Riley 1988: 137) and economic intervention being remarkably ineffective. Finally, macro-level corporatism does not seem a very good explanation of business/government relations in the 1980s and 1990s when the government has abandoned interventionist economic policy and incomes policy, and abolished, or reduced, the significance of many tripartite bodies.

Examples of macro-level corporatism are very difficult to find. Most corporatists have labelled Britain as an example of 'weak corporatism' (Williamson 1989: 150) and Middlemas (1979) believed that corporate bias was under stress from 1964 onwards. Macro-corporatism seems only applicable to a few, particular countries like Sweden and Austria. Even in these examples, questions have been raised concerning the applicability of the corporatist label. Moreover, the concept of macro-corporatism provides almost no insight into business government relations in the United States where business has failed, particularly at the peak level, to form integrated relationships with government (Salisbury 1979; Wilson 1982).

Meso- and micro-corporatism

Corporatists have recognised the failings of corporatist models and whilst accepting that corporatism might be rare at the macro-level, believe that it could be an appropriate description of business/government relations at the meso- (or sectoral) level and the micro- (or firm) level (Cawson 1985). Corporatists cite numerous cases of sectoral and micro-corporatism (see for example Birkinshaw *et al.* 1990; Cawson 1985; Crouch and Dore 1990; Williamson 1989). Boddy and Lambert (1990) outline how, as a result of shortages of mortgages, increasing house prices and rising interest rates, negotiations between the Department of the Environment and the Building Societies Association (BSA) led to the creation of a Joint Advisory Committee (JAC). The corporatist nature of this committee became apparent when in 1975 the JAC was used to establish borrowing guidelines for building societies. These guidelines were the result of 'straight bargaining between the societies and the government'. The BSA then assisted in the implementation of these guidelines by securing the agreement of the twenty largest building societies (Boddy and Lambert 1990: 151–2).

Bonnett (1985) found that despite the Thatcher government's opposition to state intervention and corporatist arrangements, the reality is that the linkages between government and industry remain very important in a number of areas. At the micro-level he describes how the government was closely involved in the development of the microelectronics industry providing subsidies, research and development and a number of bilateral deals such as the agreement for Acorn and the BBC to provide computers for schools. During the 1980s, the Industrial Development Advisory Board continued to advise Ministers on regional investment; in the development of North Sea oil there was much government industry bargaining and, 'Considerable public expenditure has been incurred in a huge public effort to stimulate development of the technological capacities of a specific industrial sector in Britain' (Birkinshaw *et al.* 1990: 81). At the micro-level the government has become involved with individual firms. In the case of ICL the government was closely involved in its development and accordingly, 'Enterprises on the scale of ICL are hardly likely to be refused access to make direct representations to ministers and officials' (Bonnett 1985: 96). So Birkinshaw *et al.* (1990: 82) can claim that even after ten years of Thatcherism:

'Notwithstanding the twin desires to reduce public expenditure and to rely on market forces to make economic decisions, the government continues to use corporatist mechanisms in support of markets and to organise markets.'

It has even been suggested that forms of meso-corporatism exist in the United States in particular sectors, at certain times, and in some regions. The Department of Defense has played a major interventionist role in the computer and semiconductor industries through providing substantial research funds (Vogel 1988). Brand (1984) points to the National Recovery Acts of the New Deal as being a 'corporatist experiment' with corporatist relationships developing in sectors such as oil. More specifically, examples of meso-corporatism are said to exist at the state level (Milward and Francisco 1983). State governors have been playing an increasing role in economic development with thirty-seven states having agencies for economic development (Hansen 1990). Often, as in Indiana, these bodies have representatives from industry and involve public and private officials discussing the state's economic strategy (Hansen 1990: 179).

Meso- and micro-corporatism certainly provide some important insights when discussing state/government relations. They highlight how relationships can vary on a sectoral basis; they concentrate on the forms of intermediation that exist between government and groups rather than simply analysing lobbying, and they recognise the role of the state in understanding the impact of groups on government. Yet, as Jordan (1981) has pointed out, we need to ask what is corporatist about these arrangements. Meso-corporatism seems to be using the notion of corporatism in a very loose way. In this model, corporatism refers to any relationship between government and industry and any state intervention in the economy. Birkinshaw *et al.* (1990) and Middlemas (1983) are applying corporatism almost as a blanket term for all government/industry relations, whether they are interventionist, bilateral or purely consultative. The label corporatism is used because the state provides a subsidy to an industry, because a state governor has a committee on economic affairs, or to describe professional self-regulation. The definition is so wide as to lose any meaning and to make it almost impossible to distinguish corporate from non-corporate relationships. '(N)eo-corporatism is said to exist whenever the state is involved in bargaining with any special interest and uses this interest to discipline its own members' (Cox 1988b: 38).

In addition this model says very little about influence and relationships between economic actors. Meso- and micro-corporatism almost completely ignore the third part of the corporatist equation – the role of labour. By concentrating on bilateral relations it ignores the question of how much impact these relationships have on policy outcomes. Corporatism is a mechanism for integrating conflicting economic interests into the state, but most meso-corporatist arrangements are bilateral. The limited role of trade unions in most of these relationships seems to suggest that they are not corporatist. It is a truism to say that if government is to provide assistance to an industry, there will be a relationship. However, corporatism is more than a government/industry relationship. It needs to be concerned with integrating conflicting economic actors into the policy process.

Finally, meso-corporatism seems to have difficulty in explaining the relationships that existed in Britain post-1979. After 1979 many of the relationships that existed at the macro-level disappeared or became insignificant. Although bodies like the NEDC and MSC continued with union and business representation, their influence and role have declined. Indeed the MSC was replaced with a new organisation that greatly reduced union representation and the NEDC was abolished in June 1992. Even at the meso-level government industry relations have changed. Boddy and Lambert point out that the building societies' JAC has become redundant since 1979. The Thatcher governments became increasingly disengaged from industry as privatisation increased. To use corporatism to describe the types of relationships that exist between business and government in Sweden, pre-1979 Britain and the Thatcher governments suggest that it is not a very precise or useful label.

As O'Sullivan (1988) has indicated, neo-corporatism is functionalist. It assumes that capitalist societies follow a certain developmental trajectory. Corporatism develops either, as in the models of Harris, Jessop and Winkler, because it is functional for capital, or because of the functional requirements of the state to deal with class conflict. Thus Panitch and Middlemas see corporatism developing as a way of coopting increasingly strong labour movements. This, as O'Sullivan indicates, creates a simplified view of recent history and the state. It undermines the nuances and complexities which differentiate modern twentieth-century states. What these explanations therefore ignore is that the British state, despite the level of capitalist development and class conflict, failed in ' "incorporating" either business or unions into the state' (O'Sullivan 1988: 19). Cox (1988c) characterises the post-war British state as being Keynesian with a pluralist bias. Most of the key economic actors were opposed to detailed state intervention in the economy.

Therefore, whilst corporatism has always been difficult to apply in the United States, it is now increasingly irrelevant to Britain. This suggests that corporatism is a specific and rare relationship and it is not a useful theory of government/industry relations. Rather than corporatism being something that occurs with specific economic developments, it is a description of a very particular relationship and therefore has little general use in explaining the way groups and government interact. An alternative approach to government/industry relations comes from the marxist school.

Marxism

There are numerous marxist theories of the state which attempt to account for the relationship between society and the state including structuralism, instrumentalism, class theoretical approaches, capital theoretical approaches, regulation theory and post-marxist theories (for a review see Jessop 1982, 1990). In this section we will briefly review the instrumental and structuralist approaches and Jessop's attempt to create a synthesis of a non-essentialist marxism, and then examine some empirical accounts of marxist approaches to business/government relations.

Instrumental approaches derive from Marx and Engels' position in *The Communist Manifesto* that the state is nothing but an Executive Committee for the bourgeoisie (for Marx and Engels' view of the state see Jessop 1982 and Dunleavy and O'Leary 1987). This view has been most eloquently expressed in modern times, in a more sophisticated form, by Miliband (1969: 23):

> In the Marxist scheme, the 'ruling class' of capitalist society is that class which owns and controls the means of production and which is able, by virtue of its economic power thus conferred upon it, to use the state as its instrument for the domination of society.

Miliband accepts that 'it is obviously true that the capitalist class, as a class does not actually "govern"' (p. 51). However he maintains (p. 61),

> that in terms of social origin, education and class situation, the men who have manned all the command positions in the state system have largely, and in many cases overwhelmingly, been drawn from the world of business and property or from the professional middle class.

He acknowledges (p. 55) that:

> Notwithstanding the substantial participation of businessmen in the business of the state, it is however true that they have never constituted, and do not constitute now, more than a small minority of the state elite as a whole. It is in this sense that the economic elites of advanced capitalist countries are not, properly speaking, a 'governing class'.

Even for instrumentalist marxists, business does not directly control the state. Rather the capitalist class dominates the state through a number of more indirect means. The state elite maintains an upper-class character with British civil servants mainly coming from Oxbridge and American decision-makers largely being the sons of professionals and proprietors (Hood and Harvey 1958). This elite, Miliband maintains in a more structuralist vein, 'accept the notion that economic rationality of the capitalist system is synonymous with rationality itself'. Hence, leaders adopt policies that favour the interests of capital. Business is also able to exert pressure directly through its control of financial and economic resources. Finally, business has control over sources of propaganda that enable it to win support for its interests and ensure the legitimation of the capitalist class. For Miliband, the state might not be directly controlled but senior civil servants and judges will ensure that policies which threaten the interests of capital do not slip into the public domain (Miliband 1982).

Poulantzas, in the famous Poulantzas–Miliband debate was highly critical of Miliband's approach, accusing him of adopting a pluralist methodology by concentrating on the individuals within government. For Poulantzas, it is not the character of individuals, but the nature of the capitalist state that determines policy outcomes. The class situation of bureaucrats is unimportant. They are servants of the ruling class not by their relations to the ruling class but because their 'internal unity derives from the actualisation of the objective role of the state' (Poulantzas 1969: 247).

For Poulantzas, the state is relatively autonomous from the capitalist class. This is necessary because the state's primary role 'is the maintenance of the unity of a social formation based in the last analysis on political class domination' (Poulantzas 1973: 54). The capitalist class is divided into fractions: for example national capital, multinational capital, finance capital, manufacturing capital. If one of these fractions directly controlled the state, they would rule only in their immediate self-interest. This would destroy the unity of the state and ultimately the capitalist economy. Therefore, the state has to be relatively autonomous in order to maintain unity through making concessions to various fractions and subordinate classes. The bourgeoisie cannot achieve internal unity and so it is necessary for a relatively autonomous state to do so (p. 284). In this way the state is able to ensure the long-term interests of the capitalist class.

This raises the question of how, if the state is relatively autonomous, the capitalist class is able to ensure that its interests are dominant? Poulantzas (1973: 115) points out that the state as a set of institutions does not have any power. It is 'the centre of the exercise of political power'. The state is an arena through which class conflict is pursued but this does not mean that these institutions are the instruments of social classes, 'They possess their autonomy and structural specificity' (p. 115). Thus in attempting to break with instrumentalism, Poulantzas seems to establish a contradiction. The capitalist state does not directly represent the economic interests of capitalists but their political interests. It is the dominant class's political power centre and organises their political struggle:

> In this sense, the capitalist state has inscribed in its very structures a flexibility which concedes a certain guarantee to the economic interests of certain dominated classes, within the limits of the system.

The state is relatively autonomous, it does not have power yet it ensures the political interests of the capitalist class through having their political interests 'inscribed in its very structures'. Although agency has no role in the activities of the state, the state is a very sophisticated institution which can be relatively autonomous yet at the same time makes careful decisions about what concessions should be made to the subordinated classes in order to ensure the capitalist interest. This autonomy enables the state to make concessions to the dominated classes, and so it reduces the economic power of the capitalist class in order to maintain political power (p. 193).

In his later work, *State, Power, Socialism*, Poulantzas attempts to provide a mechanism for explaining how capitalist interests achieve dominance. Poulantzas maintains that the state is not an 'intrinsic entity' but a 'relationship of forces' (1978: 128). He therefore sees the state as a 'specific material condensation of forces':

> The state and its policy, forms and structures therefore express the interests of the dominant class not in a mechanical fashion, but through a relationship of forces that makes of a state a condensed expression of the ongoing class struggles.

Poulantzas sees state outputs as a reflection of class struggle which are concentrated within the state. This however raises a number of problems. What is the mechanism within the state which enables it to reflect class structures? How can it reflect class struggle when it is apparently structured to ensure the long-term interests of the capitalist class and how is it able to maintain autonomy and unity if it is the condensation of forces? In addition, the notion of the state as a 'material condensation of class forces' is a metaphor that tells us little about the operations of the state and how the state reflects the behaviour of groups in society. Poulantzas' account is at such a high level of abstract theory that it says very little about the internal mechanism of the state and how various outcomes (whether in the capitalist interest or not) are produced.

Jessop has attempted to overcome the instrumentalism of Miliband and the determinism of Poulantzas by developing a non-essentialist theory of the state. In other words, a theory that is based on neither class nor economic reductionism. Jessop believes that the distinction between structuralism and instrumentalism is unhelpful. He points out that few studies exclusively adopt one or other of these approaches:

> Critics using this distinction often lack any sense of the dialectic between structure and agency, a dialectic which undermines the coherence of this dichotomy. They generally overlook the extent to which structural constraints can only be meaningfully defined in relation to specific agents pursuing particular strategies. . . . and they also ignore the extent to which the scope for agency (and thus power) is itself constituted in and through the operation of structures as well as strategic conduct (1990: 250).

Jessop attempts to avoid these crude distinctions and the determinism of either instrumental or structural approaches. He 'establishes relations between political and economic features of society without reducing one to the other or treating them as totally independent and autonomous' (Jessop 1982: 221). He rejects the view that the existence of a capitalist mode of production should necessarily imply 'the capitalist character of the state apparatus' (p. 222). For Jessop:

> the state is a set of institutions . . . that cannot exercise power . . . [S]tate power is a complex social relation that reflects the changing balance of power in a determinate conjuncture . . . [and it is] . . . capitalist to the extent that it creates, maintains or restores capitalism in a given situation. . . . (p. 221)

The state is a plurality of institutions whose unity is only constituted politically. Thus:

> the state system is the site of strategy. It can be analysed as a system of *strategic selectivity*, i.e. as a system whose structure and *modus operandi* are more open to some types of strategies than others. Thus a given type of state, a given state form, a given form of regime, will be more accessible to some forces than others according to the strategies they adopt to gain state power; and it will be suited more to some types of economic or political strategy than others because of the modes of intervention and resources which characterise the system (Jessop 1990: 260).

Jessop does, unlike some other marxists, consider the relationships that exist between the state and interest groups. He does this through outlining various mechanisms for representation and intervention. Jessop (1982: 228) believes that 'state forms and regime types can be distinguished in terms of differential articulation of political representation, internal organisation, and state intervention'. He then outlines five forms of representation/intervention: clientelism, corporatism, parliamentarianism, pluralism and *raison d'état*. However, as we saw above these forms of representation are presented as very crude ideal types which provide little insight into the nature of state/group relationships. Jessop offers no theory to help understand how parliamentarianism, or any other form of representation, actually works.

In offering a theory of the state that is anti-essentialist and rejecting the idea that any 'sub-system could be structurally "determinant in the last instance"' (Jessop 1990: 365), it has to be asked what is distinctive, or distinctively marxist, about Jessop's theory? He denies that the state is intrinsically capitalist, he denies that there is such a thing as state power and he accepts that the state is disunified – 'there are many different sub-systems and many more centres of power' (Jessop 1990: 365). There seems little here that a pluralist could disagree with (Cawson 1986). In particular, there seems to be a great deal of overlap with the neo-pluralist position which accepts the privileged position of business and the disunified view of the state (see McLennan 1989). However, Jessop does introduce the concept of strategic selectivity where the state has a bias towards particular strategies. But if there is no essentialism and the state has no power how can it (who can?) select particular strategies. In order to assess the

usefulness of marxist theories of group/government relations we will briefly
examine some empirical analyses of business/government relations.

Marxism and business power

In addition to Miliband's analysis, instrumentalist approaches have been used to
analyse business/government relations in the United States. In Domhoff's (1967:
84) view: 'Members of the American Upper Class and their employees control
the Executive branch of federal government.' He sees the large corporations
directly playing a role in the formation of public policy through access to the
'innermost private offices of the government in Washington' (Domhoff 1978:
62). The capitalist class is united by a series of interlocking directorates of large
corporations. For instance, commercial banks are tied on average to almost
twenty-six other firms (Mintz and Schwarz 1987: 37). These networks create the
potential for 'classwide principles of organisation' which creates a group of senior
managers who are propelled into 'a political leadership role on behalf of all large
business' (Useem 1987: 152).

These political leaders have a number of mechanisms available which allow
them to establish links with government. Businessmen become members of
government and so develop control over certain sections of the policy process
(McConnell 1966). For example, eight of the thirteen Secretaries of Defence
were businessmen (Anker, Seyboid and Schwarz 1987: 104). In addition, the
policy process begins within groups that are 'financed by major business
interests' (p. 105). Clawson and Clawson (1987) believe that it is business
domination of think-tanks which enabled the new right agenda to become
established in the United States. So instrumentalist approaches generally focus
on the background of individuals in positions of power and demonstrate how
these individuals are linked through social and economic networks and thus
ensure capitalist domination of the instruments of the state.

Structuralists concentrate not on the activities of business people and of state
elites, but on the nature of the state and the constraints that it faces. From this
perspective the British state is externally orientated due to its colonial past, the
level of overseas investment, the role of sterling in the international political
system and its overseas defence commitments (Jessop 1980: 24). This has
enabled a particular fraction of capital, namely the City, to have extraordinary
influence over public policy. The openness of the British economy and the
importance of the City to Britain's economic well-being meant that the City was
in an extremely strong position to prevent government adopting certain polices.
Every time the government attempted to concentrate on industrial policy money
would flow out of Britain and force the government to take measures to restore
confidence in sterling (Ingham 1984). The City did not have to undertake over-
lobbying activity. Its structural privilege was enough to give it influence over
policy.

David Coates (1980) demonstrated how the external constraints of the world capitalist economy were able to prevent the 1974–9 Labour government implementing its radical programme. The CBI and other peak organisations of industry were less effective in influencing the Labour government between 1974 and 1979 than they had been on the Labour governments of 1964 to 1970. It was not the main organisations of capital that were important. Rather Labour governments were forced:

> to seek forces of foreign credit: from Arab governments with massive petrodollar surpluses, from central banks and from the IMF. In seeking such credit, policy at home had to be tailored to meet foreign demands, initially indirectly, in that the Government felt itself obliged to follow internal policies which would persuade foreign creditors that an extension of credit was worthwhile and eventually directly, as the Labour Government found the IMF willing to lend an extra credit-tranche in December 1976 only in return for a written undertaking that domestic economic policy would follow the lines agreed in negotiation between Treasury officials and IMF investigators (Coates 1980: 158).

In addition, the Labour government was also constrained by the nature of the world economy. If Britain was to remain competitive in the world, labour costs had to be reduced. Therefore, rather than improving the living standards of the working class and ensuring 'a radical redistribution of wealth', the Labour government was forced to adopt an incomes policy which made the working class worse off and reduced the power of trade unions (Coates 1980).

Structural constraints do not only come from outside but are also part of the 'institutional ensemble' of the state. The state has 'structural selectivity' which means 'the very structures of the state system itself are realised in policy-making and implementation' (Jessop 1983b: 141). This selectivity would help to explain why a state imbued with the City's interests prevented the devaluation of the pound being discussed between 1964 and 1967 even though this destroyed Labour's industrial policy. Other examples include the way in which tripartite bodies such as the Pay and Incomes Board, despite apparent equality between capital and labour, actually biased outcomes to favour industry (see Crouch 1977). Marsh (1984) outlines how structural power prevented the acceptance of a radical economic policy by the 1974–9 Labour government. He demonstrates that the radical aspects of Labour's industrial policy were removed from the 1975 Industry Bill. The reason, he argues, is not because of the representations of the City and the CBI but:

> More significantly . . . the Prime Minister and the Chancellor consistently stressed the need to retain the confidence of both industry and the City. Indeed the preservation of confidence at a time when the pound was in trouble on the foreign exchanges was perhaps the major aim of the Government. This appears to be another example of structural power at work – the interests of capital shaped government policy not mainly because of the direct representations by its agents but because their interests were identified with the national interest (Marsh 1984: 25).

Marxism takes a distinct approach to business/government relations which is based on the presumption that eventually policy will favour the interests of capital. This creates particular problems. Marxists have difficulty in explaining why, if the state as an institution has no power, the state acts in the interest of capital. The answer they give is functionalist. The state acts in the interests of capital because it is a capitalist state (Crouch 1979; Frolund Thompson 1991). Despite attempts of latter-day marxists to move away from determinism, marxism allows no option other than business being the final victor in all policy areas. This creates great problems in explaining situations where capital does lose. Marxists have overcome this dilemma by seeing successes for subordinate classes as short-term concessions which are necessary for the long-term survival of capitalism or seeing the concessions as functional for the production of capital. This leads marxism into tautology. All state actions, whatever form they take, are in the interest of capital. Capital is bound to win because the state always acts in its interests. How do we know? Because the interests of capital are what determines the actions of the state and the actions of the state are in the interest of capital.

This leads to a further problem. How do state actors know what is in the interest of the state? Jessop (1990) suggests that there are no essential interests but that they are always related to state strategies. However, other marxists maintain that objective interests exist; yet it is unclear, apart from the maintenance of capitalism, what they are and even more unclear how state actors determine them. Are we to assume that the relative economic decline of Britain is in the interest of capital, or rather, state actors do not actually know how to increase the profitability of British industry?

Moreover, it also assumes that capital or individual capitalists have shared interests. Poulantzas tries to overcome this problem by suggesting that there are fractions of capital but even within a fraction, companies are in competition especially in the process of takeover. There is also great difficulty in determining the nature of these fractions. Capital could be divided between national capital and multinational capital, between service and manufacturing, between financial and manufacturing. Is a multinational manufacturing firm in the same fraction as a multinational financial firm or a national manufacturing firm? It is increasingly clear that links between financial and manufacturing sectors are becoming much greater, and so the divisions could be between different conglomerates rather than fractions (Marsh and Locksley 1983).

There are also difficulties within marxist theory of how capital actually influences the state. With structuralist approaches it is often unclear how structures actually work without introducing some notion of economism; i.e. the economy determines that the state acts in the interest of business. Poulantzas, in his later work, and Jessop have attempted to overcome this functionalism and economism by adopting a strategic relational approach (Frolund Thompson 1991). The state is then a site of particular class strategies; it is the condensation of class forces. However, what does this phrase mean? What is the mechanism whereby class struggle is reflected in the state and then in policy outcomes? As McEachern (1990: 20) maintains:

> If there are no guarantees, if there are no mechanisms internal to the state to provide that guarantee, then the whole argument about the analysis of the capitalist class needs to be recast so that it does not imply some automatic adjustment of state action to system and class-serving consequences.

Marxist theories have no meso-level theory for explaining how class interests become policy. Moreover, it is empirically inaccurate to claim that classes act. It is not classes that act but individuals and groups (Hindess 1989) and once they have acted how does the state respond to take account of new condensations? Marxists see the state reflecting the balance of class forces but are talking in metaphors rather than explaining how class interests become policy.

Similar problems arise with the notion of structural selectivity. Jessop accepts the notion of structural selectivity but maintains this does not mean 'that it always favours one class or set of interests' (1983b). If it does not, how selective is it and what is the mechanism of this selectivity? How structural is it if the mechanism of selection can favour different interests? Structuralist marxists also have difficulty in defining 'relative' autonomy. The mechanism to define and maintain this relative autonomy is uncertain. What is it that prevents the state either being dominated by capital or acting against its interests?

Instrumentalism is actually better at explaining how capital influences government. It looks at the connections between business and government through government organisation and the class structure. As McEachern (1990: 29) wrote of Miliband's account of the state:

> Although it lacked the analytical precision of Poulantzas's approach and lacked the elegance of later attempts to find the guarantees of the class effectivity of state action, it more than compensated for these deficiencies by its clear statement of what was involved in assessing the actors of the capitalist state and in exploring different arguments about why the state, constituted as it was in the political system, still generated solutions that were, on the whole, more favourable to capital than to labour. Poulantzas's alternative account, despite the great influence it had on the state debate, was less influential in generating detailed accounts of the actions of the capitalist state.

However, instrumentalists are using pluralist techniques and in doing so only concentrate on observable behaviour. Yet they do not really explain why coming from a particular class would make a state actor take a particular course of action. As Jessop (1983b: 140) reminds us, 'there is a wide variation in the background of politicians, officials, and economic spokesmen as well as a low correlation between social background and position on specific political issues of interest to capital.' In addition, they fail to demonstrate that business representation within government actually ensures that government acts in business's interest. Access to government does not equal influence. This approach leads instrumentalists to a reductionist position, seeing all policy outcomes as reduced to class domination.

Conclusion

This chapter has used the role of business to highlight the different approaches of pluralism, corporatism and marxism. When analysing the relationships between groups and government, pluralists concentrate largely on the role of groups; the resources they have and how they use them in political activity. Corporatists focus on a particular type of arrangement in group/government relations and marxists focus on the nature of the state and how it is organised to favour the interests of capital. Each of these approaches can bring something to the understanding of government/group interaction. Pluralists analyse the role of lobbying and the problems faced by even the most highly resourced groups, corporatism on the impact of highly integrated relationships and marxism on the exceptional nature of business and the importance of state structures.

Nevertheless, there are also fundamental problems. Pluralism, by concentrating on observable behaviour ignores the significance of structural arrangements, the context of group/government interaction and ideology. It overemphasises the significance of pressure groups and so underplays the importance of other factors in determining policy outcomes. Subsequently, it sometimes mistakes correlation for causality because it looks at the immediate cause of policy outcomes rather than the wider factors that might have influenced decisions.

Corporatism's main limitation is that it is concerned with a particular relationship which appears to be analytically useful but is in fact empirically rare. Corporatist theorists have attempted to overcome this problem by adapting the definition of corporatism. Consequently, corporatist fits a whole range of relationships and thus the theory has lost much of its explanatory power. In addition, corporatism seems only to have been appropriate to a very few policy areas, particularly areas of macro-economic policy and, hence, the theory has little to offer for the majority of policy sectors.

Similarly, marxism's main concern is with a small range of interests in particular areas of policy. Marxist analysis is economically determinist and tautological. Marxism sees the state acting in the long-term interests of capital but seems unable to explain how the state can know capital's long-term interests. Attempts to overcome these problems through creating a non-essentialist marxism seem to have little to offer that is not already provided by other theories.

Perhaps more importantly, these theories are all general theories. Each theory contains certain presumptions about the distribution of power within their initial assumptions. In marxism, it is assumed that capital will dominate and in pluralism it is presumed that power will be distributed. Therefore, each theory has difficulty in dealing with the subtleties of the relationships between groups and government in particular policy areas. They are concerned with understanding the state in general rather than the nature of specific group state interactions and how these might affect policy. They also fail to pay sufficient attention to the interests and resources of state actors. Both marxism and pluralism see the state as a condensation of social forces whether groups or classes. In doing so they underestimate the role of state actors in determining policy and the way in which social groups are often reacting to the state. Thus in the next chapter we will examine the concepts of state autonomy and policy networks in order to develop a more sophisticated view of state/group interactions.

Chapter 3

STATE AUTONOMY AND POLICY NETWORKS:
Reconceptualising State/Group Relations

The last chapter demonstrated that there are a number of problems with the traditional approaches to state/group relationships. They are reductionist, deterministic and they underestimate the importance of the state. In order fully to understand the impact that groups have on policy we need to be aware of the context within which they operate and the types of relationships that they develop with government. The influence of groups does not depend on their resources in terms of organisation, funds, leadership, knowledge and so forth, but on the type of relationships they have with the state, or more precisely, a particular part of the state. Group/state relations are strongly affected by the interests and capabilities of the state institutions. If state actors have an interest in a specific policy, they will build a relationship with a group that will provide the capabilities for developing that policy. Therefore state interests affect the type of relationships that develop, which in turn influences policy. As March and Olsen (1984: 747) highlight: 'Organisation makes a difference.'

To evaluate the impact of state interests and organisations, this chapter will examine two concepts: state autonomy and policy networks. It has been suggested that these concepts are mutually exclusive (Jordan 1990a) with policy networks being a development of pluralism (Richardson and Jordan 1979; Jordan and Richardson 1987). However, this chapter will demonstrate that political actors have the potential to act autonomously and can use this autonomy to develop distinctive policy networks with interest groups. These networks then affect the capabilities of state actors and organisations to develop particular policies. Therefore the organisational form of state/group relations influences policy outcomes. This chapter will demonstrate that group/government relationships take many forms and these relationships can be conceptualised as different types of policy networks. It demonstrates that these networks affect the abilities of state actors to act autonomously and so policy networks affect both the interests of the actors involved in the policy process and the final policy outcomes. The chapter will begin by examining the concept of state autonomy. It will then outline the development of policy network theory. Finally it will indicate how these theories can be integrated to provide a fuller understanding of group/government interaction.

State autonomy

The notion of state autonomy maintains that the state/state actors have interests of their own and, in certain circumstances, the ability to transform these interests into policy. Rather than society determining the interests of the state, it is the state that constructs society (Cerny 1990). For Nordlinger (1981: 1), in determining public policy 'the preferences of the state are at least as important as those of civil society'. Often the state will act according to its own preferences 'even when its preferences diverge from the demands of the most powerful groups in civil society'. Nordlinger outlines three types of autonomy: Type I is when state and society preferences diverge and state officials act according to their own preferences. A British example of type I autonomy is the introduction of the poll tax or community charge which was introduced by the Conservative government in 1989 despite the opposition of most interest groups, local authorities, many Conservative MPs and, according to opinion polls, the majority of voters.

Type II autonomy is when society preferences are originally divergent but public officials bring about a shift in societal preferences to make them the same as their own. An example in Britain is entry to the European Community. The decision to join the EC was made by the political elite. Once the decision to enter the EC was taken, government and media propaganda swung public support behind the decision. When there was a referendum in 1975, 66 per cent of the voters supported remaining within the community.

Type III autonomy is where the preferences of the state and society are non-divergent and the state acts upon its own preferences. This is an important type of autonomy. Often groups are seen as influential in persuading government to adopt particular policies. However, it is not always clear that the government adopted a policy because of the action of groups. It might have been the result of the preferences of state actors coinciding with those of interest groups. Therefore, policy analysts have often mistaken correlations for causality and thus focused on the wrong explanation for a particular policy. It is thus a central argument of this book that even though policies may appear to be the result of group pressure, they are often developed because of the interests of state actors. The farmers and British agricultural policy in Chapter 5 and the doctors and US health policy in Chapter 7 are examples of type III autonomy.

This raises two important initial questions. What interests does the state have, and how is it able to translate these interests into policy (or how much autonomy does it have)? First, there is a tendency for some state-centred theorists to see the state as a unified actor (Mann 1984). The state is neither unified nor does it have an ability to act. The state is nothing but a collection of institutions and rules. The term state actions is shorthand for individuals within particular agencies or institutions acting. These agencies, like departments, sections of departments and other state agencies, have particular roles which constrain how actors operate. Roles are 'clearly articulated bundles of rights, duties, obligations and expectations' (Knoke 1990: 7), but individuals are also intentional actors and knowing subjects who can analyse, recreate and make choices about their institutional roles (Giddens 1986). It is ultimately individuals within these agencies, acting within their institutional roles that make decisions and take actions.

It is not the state that acts but state actors within particular parts of the state. The state does not have a unified set of interests. Different state agencies have various interests, and individuals within those agencies may also have conflicting interests. Jessop (1990: 339) informs us that 'any actually existing state comprises a more or less distinct ensemble of multifunctional institutions and organizations which have at best partial, provisional and unstable political identity and operational unity. . . .' The state involves numerous changing institutions, often with unclear boundaries. Consequently state policy often derives from conflicts within the state – between different agencies and departments – rather than from the conflicts between the state and groups. As we will see, in the development of policy the role of groups is frequently to support its patron department in interdepartmental conflicts rather than to be involved in a group/state conflict.

Yet it is necessary to establish that state actors/agencies do have distinct interests. Weir and Skocpol (1985: 118) emphasise that both elected politicians and officials, 'have organisational interests of their own'. 'This formulation assumes that state managers collectively are self interested managers, interested in maximising their power, prestige and their wealth' (Block 1980: 229). The specific interests are obviously related to the department and policy concerned, but it is possible to highlight the broad parameters of the interests of state actors. First, the interests of state actors vary between those who are elected and those who are appointed – between bureaucrats and politicians. Politicians have interests in their re-election, their own careers, their departments, committee, agency and ideological goals. Bureaucrats have interests in their careers – which might conflict with the career interests of politicians – increasing their power *vis-à-vis* politicians and other departments, reducing the problems and surprises of policy-making, and in the development of policies which might increase their power, make life easier or solve problems. Bureaucrats are frequently concerned with what they see as the long-term interests of the department whilst politicians are more concerned with achieving political goals.

The interests of officials and politicians might conflict but within a department or agency they may have shared goals. In particular, with the development of a consensus, or shared perception of problems, they can come to share a similar world-view (see below). There are also some interests which do belong to the state as a whole. These include internal order, legitimacy, external security and economic growth. These goals can often conflict with the demands of civil society and can produce conflicts within the state on how they are to be achieved and who is responsible for achieving them. Therefore, actors within the state have interests which are to some extent determined by their institutional roles.

The interests they pursue are not purely individual interests but are partly determined by the organisational culture, the nature of the policy-making institutions and the relationship of these institutions to other parts of the state and groups in civil society. The policies that emanate from the state do not always reflect the demands of groups or classes but are the result of how state actors perceive their interests, how they perceive particular problems and their solutions, and how they think they can solve the problems of national interests such as security and economic growth. Consequently, state actors can propose policies which counteract the interests of powerful groups in society even in the long term. Although capital and other groups have resources which provide them with influence, the state, or state actors have their own resources and these can be used to achieve, or try to achieve, state-determined goals.

There is, then, no essential reason why the state must act in the interest of capital or respond to groups. State power is not reducible, even in the last instant, to class power (Block 1980). Frequently, the state will take actions that contradict the interests of the capitalist class. As Skocpol (1980) points out, although many of the policies associated with the New Deal were opposed by business, marxists could still argue that they served the interests of capital by ensuring the long-term economic success of capital and by dissipating dissension within the working class. However Skocpol (1980: 172) goes on to demonstrate that:

> the NIRA (National Industrial Recovery Act) blatantly failed to bring economic recovery, and it deepened conflict within the capitalist class, between capitalists and the state, and between capitalists and labour. Poulantzian theory predicts functional outcomes of state policies and interventions. It offers little direct theoretical guidance to why and how the failures of state policy could occur. . . .

State actors can have interests of their own and can act in a way that counters the interests of business. For Skocpol, the failure of the NIRA was the due to the state lacking capabilities rather than the power of business. Block (1980: 230) maintains that in order to pursue their own interests, state managers will 'seek to appropriate, or at least, place severe restrictions on the property of dominant classes'. Block, however, still operates within a marxist perspective and suggests that the economic context – the need to maintain economic growth within a world economy – ensures that state actors are constrained to act in the interest of business. He suggests that in exceptional periods – war, depression, and post-war reconstruction – there is a change in the political context and this provides state managers with more room for manoeuvre. This is an important point. It is recognition that both the state and business (and other groups) have resources, and that the balance or value of these resources change. At specific times the state has the ability to act in its own interests. This means that ultimately the state is not a capitalist state.

What resources does the state have? How is it able to ensure autonomous state action and how does the state overcome resistance within civil society? The ability of the state to act autonomously depends on its capabilities – the extent to which it can intervene in society, to achieve its policy goals without the support of societal actors. Weir and Skocpol (1985: 118) highlight how:

> politicians and officials are also engaged in struggles among themselves, and they must pursue these struggles, along with any initiative they take in relation to the economy or the mobilisation of social support, by using - or taking into account – the coercive fiscal, judicial, and administrative capacities of the state structures within which they are located.

If the state structures do not provide policy instruments for a particular policy then that policy is unlikely to be proposed.

Mann (1984) distinguishes between the state's *despotic* and *infrastructural* power. Despotic power is the state acting 'without routine, institutionalised negotiations with groups in civil society' (Mann 1984: 188). This is the ability of state actors to act directly to achieve their own goals without taking account of the interests of groups within society. Despotic power usually refers to ancient empires or authoritarian regimes. However, even within liberal democratic regimes, state actors have the ability, through their authority, control over legislation and control over coercive apparatus, to act without negotiation. In a democratic regime, the cost of such an approach might be very high in terms of vocal/physical opposition, the difficulty of implementing the policy, or loss of an election, but it is sometimes an approach that governments are prepared to take. In particular, Presidents and Prime Ministers are in the position to use their political authority and their formal (if not actual) control over the governmental machinery to use despotic power and attempt to adopt policies without consultation. In this way they can often break up or bypass the traditional state/group relationships, which was the strategy of Mrs Thatcher in challenging health policy (see Chapter 7).

However, in liberal democracies it is more usual for states to use their infrastructural power. This is 'the capacity of the state to actually penetrate civil society, and to implement logistically political decisions throughout the realm' (Mann 1984: 189). It is the capability of the state to intervene in society through its administrative machinery and its relationship with groups in society. The state has the ability to develop these capabilities because the resources that it has, and the functions it delivers, are necessary for society and specific groups (Mann 1984).

If the state is to act autonomously it needs both the ability to intervene and resources which it can exchange with groups in society. Atkinson and Coleman (1989) outline the conditions necessary for sectors of the state to act autonomously:

1. The bureau or agency needs a clear conception of its role and strong political support.

2. The bureau needs to be able to retain a distance between itself and its client groups.
3. There will be greater autonomy if there is 'a corpus of law and regulation that defines the responsibilities and those of societal groups'.
4. The bureau has the ability to generate its own information.

However, this suggests a particular notion of autonomy where state and societal actors can be very clearly defined and the state is acting in direct opposition to society. As we will see, the notion of state autonomy is much more complicated and it is necessary to understand the state's infrastructural power and the impact that this has on state intervention. If the state is to intervene in civil society:

> sheer sovereign integrity and the stable administrative–military control of a given territory are preconditions for any state's ability to implement policies. Beyond this, loyal and skilled officials and plentiful resources are basic to the state's effectiveness in attaining all sorts of goals (Skocpol 1985: 16).

The state's infrastructural power is based on its ability to raise taxation, to control the economy through financial and monetary levers, and to build a bureaucracy that can effectively carry out administrative tasks. Ikenberry *et al.* (1988) suggest that the state has the ability to build these institutions because it 'is situated at the intersection of the domestic and international political economies and is the principal national actor charged with the overall conduct of defense and foreign affairs'. The state can also mobilise inactive groups as a means of supporting state policy. In other words, state actors have clear advantages over groups within civil society. The state's ability to build administrative structures which operate over a whole nation means that it has a degree of centrality unavailable to other organisations (Ikenberry 1988a).

However, another source of capability is the types of relationships that exist with groups. It is clear that in the modern state the boundaries between the state and civil society are blurred (Richardson and Jordan 1979). The state intervenes in all areas of civil society and groups have regular and institutionalised access to the state. Atkinson and Coleman (1989) suggest that close relationships between states and groups limit state autonomy because the groups dominate the policy process. Likewise, it is often suggested that the state will have more autonomy if there is a high degree of conflict between groups, and the state can achieve its own goals by playing the groups off against each other (this is Marx's view of Bonapartism).

Nevertheless, in the second half of this chapter we will demonstrate that a close relationship with government can actually increase state autonomy. If the state establishes a closed-policy community, mutual dependency develops between the group and the state. Policy is developed through negotiations and any groups involved in the policy process can then assist in implementation. The state agency is able to achieve its goals through the incorporation of the pressure group. Policy networks are a means of extending the infrastructural power of society by establishing mechanisms for negotiation which allow greater intervention in civil society.

State autonomy is not a zero-sum. It is not something that belongs either to the group or to the state agency. By working together, a group and a state agency can increase each other's autonomy in relation to other parts of the state. Within a policy community the policy process can be sealed off from other state actors, pressure groups and networks. In a pluralistic policy arena, it is difficult for the state to control the development of policy. Without a consensus, it is hard for a single state agency to control the final policy outcome and, once policy is determined, implementation is harder to achieve because of the lack of assistance from groups. Therefore, the degree of state autonomy available often depends on the type of policy network.

The coercive, administrative and financial resources of the state and the existence of policy communities enable the state, or state agencies, to achieve a degree of control in civil society which is unavailable to other groups, and if we assume that the state is not essentially capitalist, then it can intervene to pursue interests of its own rather than of other groups. Yet more importantly, the 'state is inherently centralised over a delimited territory' (Mann 1984: 198) and therefore has a strategic position and reach unavailable to other groups (Cerny 1990). Other groups, 'exist in decentred, competitive or conflictual relations' (Mann 1984: 199) and so they are unable to control a specific territory. These groups therefore rely on the state to provide services over that area. The state has to provide: internal and external order; maintenance of communications; infrastructure; and maintenance of the economic system. Therefore groups in society are dependent on the state and this dependence means that the state has resources to use against groups.

The ability of the state to act autonomously depends on the nature of the state – the sort of administrative and financial resources available – and the relationship of the state to other groups. If it is well resourced, in terms of capabilities and can extend its infrastructural power through policy networks, it has the potential for autonomous action. For instance, the United States is often seen as a weak state (Dyson 1982). 'The American State tends to be decentralised and fragmented along bureaucratic or institutional lines, and state officials lack the range of policy instruments available to their counterparts in stronger states' (Ikenberry *et al.* 1988: 11). The many centres of power, the relatively small size of the central state, its inability to develop a large administrative machine, and the large number of conflictual interest groups are seen as making it very difficult for the US state to act autonomously. Some even refer to it as a stateless society (King 1990).

However, this view is too simplistic. Skocpol (1985: 14) avers that 'state autonomy is not a fixed structural feature of any society. It can come and go.' In fact, the state level is the wrong level of analysis for determining state autonomy. Atkinson and Coleman (1989) point out that state structures change from policy sector to policy sector. Even the US state, which appears weak, has the ability to act autonomously in certain sectors and at particular times. For example, Skocpol and Finegold (1982: 257) demonstrate that whilst the National Industrial Recovery Administration failed, the New Deal's 'agricultural program became successfully institutionalised'. Skocpol and Finegold maintain that the reasons for the differences in success were a result of different state capabilities in the industrial and agricultural sphere. In agriculture, there was sufficient administrative machinery, information, and contacts with farmers to enable the state to develop an agricultural policy. In industrial policy the state was too weak to intervene and the policy process was dominated by business interests and so failed.

Sectors and departments within the state have the ability to act autonomously in particular situations. The degree of autonomy is not pregiven but depends on the resources available at a particular time, and the form of relationships that exist between state agencies and interest groups.

The state autonomy approach has been subject to a number of criticisms. It has been suggested that other approaches to the state have always taken account of the power of the state (Almond 1988; Cammack 1989, 1990). Whilst this is undoubtedly the case, the state-centred perspective is demanding a change of emphasis. Marxist perspectives ultimately see the state as reflecting the balance of class forces in society, and pluralists see policy as the result of state/group interactions. As Nordlinger (1988) argues, Dahl and other pluralists see power as being dispersed throughout society. Statist theorists believe that state actors and agencies determine the behaviour of groups in society, and the role they play in the policy process. The state actually constitutes the role of groups (Cerny 1990) and uses them to pursue its own goals. Power often lies within the state rather than groups or individuals in society.

A second criticism is that in reality the division between the state and society is too blurred to make such a clear distinction. State interests are not developed in a vacuum but within the context of civil society. They do not come from nowhere but result from interactions and daily contacts with civil society. Politicians and bureaucrats live in society and their perceptions of state interests are influenced by their everyday social interactions. It cannot be denied that state/society boundaries are not clearly defined. The notion of policy communities and networks is concerned with examining the interrelationships between groups and society. Hence, the notion of state autonomy is not a zero-sum. Autonomy develops through relationships with groups, and it is not always achieved in opposition to groups.

It is important not to oversimplify the relationship between the state and society. At certain times and in particular policy areas state actors are dominant whilst in others it might be groups. In some ways the important point is not whether or not the state is autonomous but the need to recognise that the state has the potential to act autonomously and to pursue its own interests. The state/ state sectors have particular interests which they wish to pursue, and in making policy, they confront groups which want to have alternative interests. State interests are influences that have to be understood in the policy equation – they are a clear input into the policy process. However, the state is often not an equal partner in the process; it has a degree of authority and territorial and administrative control which enables it to override groups. States can go for the Tiananmen Square option and literally destroy the opposition. But the costs of ignoring groups could be high, and therefore state organisations prefer developing institutional relationships with groups as a means of extending autonomy. This chapter will now examine the forms of relationships that can exist between groups and government, and the impact that these relationships have on state autonomy and policy outcomes.

Policy networks

It was suggested in the last section that state autonomy has to be examined within the context of state/group relationships. This section will examine the nature of the potential relationships, analyse the types of policy networks that exist, and examine their impact on policy outcomes.

Within modern government, policy-making 'tends to fragment and specialise as a result of two fundamental trends, the expansion in the scope of governmental responsibility, and the increasing complexity of public affairs' (Campbell *et al.* 1989: 86). This leads some analysts of public policy to suggest that policy-making is becoming increasingly pluralistic as the policy process fragments and an increasing number of groups are admitted into the policy arena (Heclo 1978). However Campbell *et al.* (1989) maintain that this fragmentation is leading to policy being made within increasingly specialised arenas with a limited number of participants. The reality seems to be that in different policy arenas a range of group/government relationships exist.

Policy networks are a means of categorising the relationships that exist between groups and the government. Policy networks occur when there is an exchange of information between groups and government (or between different groups or parts of the government) and this exchange of information leads to the recognition that a group has an interest in a certain policy area. The exchange of information can be minimal – a group's name being placed on a consultation list, a group sending in a submission on a green paper – or it can be very intense with groups having institutionalised access to government and being involved in the detailed development of policy and, consequently, constantly exchanging a very high level of detailed information. According to Laumann and Knoke (1987: 13), 'The greater the variety of information and the more diverse the sources that a consequential actor can tap, the better situated the actor is to anticipate, and to respond to, policy events that can affect its interests.'

The state can be divided into a distinct number of policy domains. 'A policy domain is . . . a set of actors with major concerns, whose preferences and actions on policy events must be taken into account by other domain participants' (Laumann and Knoke 1987: 10). The number of participants, the degree of their integration into government and the degree of influence they have depend on the nature of the policy network within the particular domain. Potential policy networks can be arranged along a continuum from an issue network to a policy community (Hogwood 1986). This section will review the different types of networks and the impact that they have on state autonomy and policy outcomes. It will begin by examining the concept of policy networks.

Policy networks, and their importance for understanding group/government relations, derive from the notion of subgovernment in the United States (Ripley and Franklin 1980) and the work of Jordan and Richardson in Britain on policy communities (Richardson and Jordan 1979, 1985; Jordan and Richardson 1987) (see Jordan 1990b and Rhodes 1990 for a full discussion of these developments). In both cases, the development of these concepts was a recognition that there were problems with the pluralist view of the world. In particular policy areas, policy-making is not open but is made within subgovernments which are 'clusters of individuals that make most of the routine decisions in a given substantive area of policy' (Ripley and Franklin 1980: 8). Most decisions on non-controversial issues are made within small groups which include the key congressional subcommittees, government agencies and interest groups.

Richardson and Jordan (1979) likewise suggest that policy-making is segmented and that policy is made between a myriad of interconnecting and interpenetrating organisations. 'It is the relationship involved in committees, the *policy community* of departments and groups . . . that perhaps better accounts for policy outcomes than do examinations of party stances, of manifestos or of parliamentary influence' (Richardson and Jordan 1979: 74). Accordingly, the distinction between the governed and governors becomes blurred and the dominant style in policy-making is cooperation and consensus (Jordan and Richardson 1982).

The notion of policy communities and subgovernments as used by Richardson and Jordan tends to describe relationships between groups and government rather than explain how these affect policy outcomes. Moreover, they make little attempt to distinguish between types of communities and so the term policy community is used very liberally as a means of describing all types of group/government relations. No real distinction is made between the integrity and intensity of different relationships. In addition, they to some extent undermine their own notion of a closed and regularised relationship by seeing most policy communities as being relatively open. They stress that departments in Britain are always willing to consult a whole range of groups; that there is a tendency for policy communities to break down into issue networks and that often policy communities have numerous linkages and overlapping membership (Jordan 1981; Jordan and Richardson 1987: 145). This approach to policy communities is used as a description of a range of relationships and is very much within a pluralist framework by continuing to emphasise access and fragmentation.

Recently there have been attempts to make the concept of policy networks more theoretically informed. Rhodes in his work on local government and sub-central government has significantly extended the use and usefulness of the notion of policy networks (Rhodes 1986, 1988). Rhodes, from Benson (1982), sees a policy network as a 'complex of organisations connected to each other by resource dependencies and distinguished from other complexes by breaks in the structure of resource dependencies'. Rhodes (1988: 77–8) suggests that networks vary across five key dimensions:

1. Constellation of interests – the interests of those involved in a network vary according to service/function/territory or client group.
2. Membership – who are the members, are they public or private groups?
3. Vertical independence – to what extent is a policy network dependent or independent on the actors above or below it?
4. Horizontal independence – what are the interconnections between networks?
5. The distribution of resources – what resources do participants have to exchange?

Using these criteria, Rhodes identifies six types of communities: policy communities and issue networks, which will be discussed below; professionalised networks where a professional group is dominant; intergovernmental networks where the local government is represented at national level; territorial communities which include the major territorial interests of Scotland, Wales and Northern Ireland; and producer networks where economic groups play a key role. Rhodes then uses the concept to analyse a number of policy areas. He mainly restricts his use of these concepts to policy areas which involve aspects of the welfare state and hence he is largely dealing with interaction between different government actors. Rhodes admits that 'the utility of policy networks for analysing relationships between producer groups is yet to be demonstrated' (Rhodes 1988: 371). The aim of this book is to use the concept of policy networks to examine the relationship between groups, not just economic groups, and government. The remainder of this section will extend Rhodes's notion of policy networks to interest group intermediation.

Policy networks and pressure groups

Policy networks demonstrate that relationships between groups and government are segmented, and that relationships vary from policy sector to policy sector. In addition, as Rhodes has demonstrated from his study of local government (Rhodes 1981; Marsh and Rhodes 1992c), relationships between groups and government cannot be seen as zero-sum. It is not a case of pressure groups outside the system lobbying government in order to achieve specific goals. Rather, the relationship is one of dependency: 'Any organisation is dependent on another organisation for resources.' This of course applies more readily to intergovernmental relationships than in group/government relationships where each side can survive without the other. However, in particular situations when the government wishes to achieve specific policy goals, and groups wish to influence policy, groups and government are mutually dependent. In order to achieve goals, resources have to be exchanged (Rhodes 1981). If the government does want to achieve a particular policy goal with the minimum of conflict, it needs the assistance of groups in the development and implementation of policy. Government can exchange access to the policy process for cooperation and thus establish a policy network.

Moreover, the dominant coalition retains discretion, determines the rules of the game and regulates 'the process of exchange'. The government/government agencies remain, as we have seen, dominant. It has resources which are much greater than those of other groups and is therefore able to determine what resources should be exchanged and how. It is ultimately the government which calls the shots. 'The relationship is asymmetric'; it is government which creates the network, controls access to the network and the rules of the game (Rhodes 1988: 82). Finally, the impact of the network on policy depends on the 'relative power potential of interacting organisations', i.e. the resources that they have and the way they are exchanged. So for Laumann and Knoke (1987: 13), 'an organization's power and influence in a system is a function of its position or location in the overall resource exchange networks generated out of dyadic resource exchanges.'

Because power is the result of dependency based on an exchange of resources, governments and groups have an incentive to build networks. Despite Rhodes's insistence that the government creates and controls access to the community, the type of network that develops is not always determined by the government. The government has an interest in developing closed policy communities. Nevertheless, the type of network that develops often depends on the groups involved, the interests of various actors within government, the nature of the policy and the institutional arrangements that are available. Consequently, a whole range of networks which integrate groups and governments to varying degrees develop.

Marsh and Rhodes (1992c: 251) have outlined a number of dimensions which determine a network's position on the policy community–issue network continuum (see Table 3.1). First, a network depends on the number of participants. In a policy community the number of participants will be limited. It will usually involve one government agency or section within that agency. Occasionally a policy community will involve more than one department, for example the trade policy community in the United States (see Chapter 6) or the food policy community in Britain. However, if this policy community is to remain closed, one of the government actors must accept the lead of the other. In Britain, both the Department of Health and the Ministry of Agriculture were involved in the food policy community but Health was prepared to accept the leadership of Agriculture (Smith 1991; Mills 1992). The departmental role in a policy community is usually played by a department but on many occasions

Table 3.1 The characteristics of policy networks

Dimension	Policy community	Issue network
Membership		
Number of participants	Very limited, some conscious exclusion	Large
Type of interest	Economic/professional	Wide range of groups
Integration		
Frequency of interaction	Frequent, high quality	Contacts fluctuate
Continuity	Membership, values, outcomes persistent	Fluctuating access
Consensus	All participants share basic values	A degree of agreement but conflict present
Resources		
Distribution of resources within network	All participants have resources. Relationship is one of exchange	Some participants have resources, but limited
Distribution of resources within participating organisations	Hierarchical leaders can deliver members	Varied and variable distribution and capacity to regulate members
Power	There is a balance among members. One group may be dominant but power is positive-sum	Unequal power. Power zero-sum

Source: Marsh and Rhodes (1992c).

individual politicians will become involved. The community will also include one or two interest groups. These interest groups will be perceived as representative of a particular interest and have a near monopoly of membership. If there is more than one pressure group, those involved will not be competing but represent different interests within the policy arena. Food producers, farmers and doctors were involved in the food policy community but a single organisation represented each group.

Certain policy communities involve ' "experts", inside government, in universities or other institutions, who research and think about policy' (Campbell *et al.* 1989: 86). Often this is the case in very technical areas such as nuclear power where the role of scientist and technicians is central to the development of policy (Saward 1992). In the US, the particular role and resources of Congress mean that there is also a legislative role. This does not mean that Congress has a major input into policy. Congressional input is likely to come through the committee system. In addition, 'a concerted effort is made to insure that the membership of the subcommittee is supportive of the goals of the subgovernment' (McCool 1990: 282).

Therefore access to a policy community is highly restricted. As Laffin (1986: 6–7) points out:

Those within the community generally operate quite stringent entry criteria, these vary among issue areas but include such criteria as possession of expert knowledge; occupancy of a senior position in a relevant organisation; what civil servants call 'soundness', meaning that the person can be trusted to observe the norms of the community; and a reputation for getting things done.

There are a set of 'rules of the game' which actors have to abide by in order to gain entry to the policy community. The 'rules of the game' govern how participants have to behave if they are to gain access to the network: they will act constitutionally; they will accept the final decision of government; they can be trusted; the demands that they make are reasonable (Rhodes 1986). If a group wants to have access to a policy community it must forgo conducting high profile campaigns and become an insider developing policies in private (Jordan and Richardson 1987; Grant 1989a). Consequently, it is easy for a policy community to exclude radical groups. In order to attract attention they have to take overt action like demonstrations but in doing so they are breaking the rules of the game and so are excluded (Saunders 1975: 38).

Policy communities also have an institutional basis that provides a further means of exclusion. Within most policy communities there are particular institutions which are central to the policy process and membership of these institutions ensures access to the policy community. Often this will involve an advisory committee, an *ad hoc* committee created to deal with a particular problem or a particular section within a department which provides the focus for group/government interaction.

However, even exclusion is not simple. Within policy communities there are usually degrees of exclusion. Laumann and Knoke (1987: 229) suggest that the

global network structure contains a few central positions occupied by actors that maintain close ties with many others ... and a larger number of peripheral positions occupied by actors with lower visibility, fewer ties and generally tenuous involvement in the system.

A policy community tends to have a core and periphery (Laumann and Knoke 1987) or, in other words, a primary and secondary community. The primary/core contains the key actors who set the rules of the game, determine membership and the main policy direction of the community. They are continuously involved in the policy process on a day-to-day level. In the secondary community are the groups which also abide by the rules of the game but do not have enough resources to exert a continuous influence on policy. Therefore, the secondary community tends to involve groups which are important on particular issues and who have occasional access to the policy process. In agriculture, the core policy community involves the NFU and MAFF with groups like the CLA and NUAAW involved in secondary communities. These groups are consulted when specific issues such as landownership or pay affect them. There is also a third layer of groups which are completely excluded and have no access at all to the policy community.

Whilst membership in a policy community is limited, in an issue network it is extremely large. There are likely to be several government departments, agencies or subcommittees. The range of interest groups could be in the hundreds, and constantly changing, with groups continuously entering and leaving the policy arena. Heclo believes that in many areas of policy-making in the US there are 'a large number of participants with quite variable degrees of mutual commitment' and so 'it is all but impossible to identify clearly who the dominant actors are' (Heclo 1978: 102). An issue network contains a large number of actors with relatively limited resources. There are several government agencies and access to the network is fairly open, which enables groups to move easily in and out of the policy arena.

This leads directly to the second dimension of a policy network: continuity. The limited number of actors in a policy community means that the participants tend to be stable over a long period of time. The groups involved do not change frequently. In an issue network, as we have just seen, the membership is constantly changing as groups move in and out of the arena. The third dimension is frequency of interaction. In a policy community, the government agency and the key interests will be constantly involved in the policy process and so interaction is daily and of high quality. In an issue network interaction is erratic. The degree and importance of interaction will constantly change and who has contact with whom will also vary.

The fourth dimension is the degree of consensus. If a network is to develop into a policy community there has to be a high degree of consensus on policy aims and the rules of the game. 'Where there are no such shared attitudes, no policy community exists' (Jordan 1990b: 327). In fact a policy community often has more than a consensus; it actually has an ideology which determines the community's 'world-view'. Ideology is a way of making sense of the world by defining and ordering it (Therborn 1980: 15 and 18). Ideology defines not only what policy options are available but what problems exist. In other words, it defines the agenda of issues with which the policy community has to deal. Therefore members of a policy community agree on both the range of existing problems and the potential solutions to these problems. Laffin maintains that a policy community has a 'cognitive order', which is agreement on what passes as accepted knowledge in the community and a 'normative order' which is agreement on the values that underpin the community (Laffin 1986: 12).

The ideology thus privileges certain ideas within the policy process. In doing so it ensures that the interests of the dominant actors within the policy community are served and it acts as a further means of exclusion. By maintaining agreement on accepted problems, groups which try to raise new problems or suggest alternative solutions are automatically excluded. The policy community can suggest that new problems either do not exist or are the responsibility of a different network. Alternative solutions are defined as extreme or demonstrating a lack of knowledge about a problem and as such are again excluded. Therefore, within a policy community, power is exercised through Lukes' (1974) third dimension. By determining what problems and solutions are acceptable, it ensures that other alternatives are not even conceived of within the community (and sometimes outside the community). An attempt to conceive of them would destroy the consensus and thus the community.

In a policy community there is a consensus or ideology which limits 'the range of arguments that are permissible, legitimate and likely to be accepted as valid forms of controversy' (Laumann and Knoke 1987: 315). As a consequence, issues within a policy community are often depoliticised. They are seen as technical issues to be resolved by insiders because no conflict is perceived over the potential policy options. Therefore, there is no need to include other groups in the discussion of an issue. If the ideology is fully effective groups outside the community will not even claim the need to be involved in the policy community. The consensus on policy will be accepted by all. Hence groups which possibly could have opposed the policy community will remain potential groups (see Gaventa 1980).

In an issue network, it is unlikely that there will be a consensus – the sheer number of groups means that consensus is practically unachievable. Policy is likely to be highly political because so many groups with various different problems and solutions exist within the policy domain. There is often conflict between the various government agencies and departments. There may be conflict over who is responsible for a policy or an issue, who should be involved and what action should be taken. This conflict between government agencies is often a key reason why an issue network develops. The conflict between agencies makes the problem political and subject to debate. Agencies attempt to attract pressure groups into the arena in order to strengthen their position against other agencies and to increase their legitimacy. Consequently, the arena becomes increasingly political and further groups are drawn into the arena. This makes the possibility of consensus even more remote.

The fifth dimension which determines the nature of a policy network is the nature of the relationship. In a policy community it is likely that the relationship will be an exchange relationship. In other words, the groups involved will have resources that they can exchange. Groups with this level of resources have information, legitimacy, implementation resources, which can be exchanged for a position in the policy process, and some control over policy. In an issue network, although some actors have resources, they are likely to be limited. Most of the interest groups are likely to have little information to exchange and little control over the implementation of policy. Consequently, they are forced into overt lobbying activities. Likewise, government agencies, which do not have a monopoly of the policy area, cannot guarantee that an interest group has a role in the policy process.

Sixth, it follows from the nature of the relationship that resources also affect the nature of interaction. If groups have resources to exchange the interaction is likely to involve bargaining and negotiation over the direction of policy. If the government agencies want some of the pressure groups' resources, they have to offer some input into policy, and if the group is to stay within the policy community it is likely to want policy that favours its interests. In an issue network the relationship will be based on consultation at best. This consultation might involve a simple exchange of information and is unlikely to have much effect on policy outcomes (Jordan and Richardson 1987).

Seventh, in a policy community power is a positive-sum. In other words a policy community does not involve one group sacrificing power to another. It could involve each group in a mutual expansion of power as each increases its influence over policy. In an issue network power is unequal and there are likely to be losers and winners. As the losers have few resources they can do little if their interests are sacrificed in the development of policy.

The final dimension is the structure of participating organisations. The type of network that develops depends to some extent on the nature of the pressure groups involved. If a policy community is to develop, the leadership of a pressure group has to ensure that once agreement is reached, the membership will accept the policy. If the leadership cannot, there will be disagreement within the group and the policy consensus will collapse. In an issue network control over group membership is not an important factor.

In a policy community there are a limited number of groups which are stable over time and agree on the parameters of policy. They have resources to exchange which results in a process of policy-making that is based on negotiation and presumes that once an agreement is reached a pressure group can ensure that the membership will abide by the decision. A policy community involves the conscious and unconscious exclusion of particular groups. Groups are excluded through conscious decisions not to involve a particular group. They are also excluded through ideologies, rules of the game and the structure of policy-making. Policy communities involve particular informal and formal institutions. Informal institutions could be *ad hoc* committees, regular meetings between officials and interest group leaders, or informal day-to-day contact. Formal institutions include advisory committees, and other such committees, established to ensure the representation of particular interests in government. These institutions enable officials to determine who will be the insiders and the outsiders.

Issue networks generally lack formal institutionalised contacts between groups and government. There is little agreement on the nature of policy problems or how they should be resolved. There is little exchange of resources, and almost no exclusion, and as a result groups are constantly moving in and out of the policy arena. Issue networks can occur in areas of great political importance where it is difficult to establish a consensus (see industrial policy in Chapter 6) or where the issue is seen, in Lindblom's (1977) term, as a 'secondary' issue and so not one where a government agency feels the need to develop a monopoly and exclude certain groups (for example abortion issues).

Issue networks also develop in new policy areas where no groups have established dominance or where there are no established institutions to enable exclusion. It is important to note that issue networks are not completely open. They are relationships that are distinguished from the general pressure group universe. In order to be an issue network, groups have to be recognised as having some interest in the area and minimal resources to exchange (Marsh and Rhodes 1992c).

It must be emphasised that these terms are ideal types at either end of a continuum. It is seldom, if ever, the case that a network will exist which conforms to the eight dimensions outlined above. Often relationships will vary across each of these dimensions and so the number of networks is practically infinite. Nevertheless, these are dimensions that have important empirical relevance and as such help us to understand the types of relationships that exist between groups and government. The clearest example of a policy community which has many of the features outlined above is in British Agricultural Policy (see Chapter 5). Rhodes provides a useful example of an issue network in British inner city policy. Rhodes (1988) demonstrates the difficulty of establishing an inner city policy due to the number of actors involved. The network involved several Ministries, the Treasury, the Departments of Employment, Education, Industry and Social Security, and the Home Office. It also included several agencies within the Department of Employment, and a number of subnational government bodies such as different tiers of local government, area health authorities and a range of interest groups. The failure to achieve agreement between these bodies resulted in 'the continuing failure of innercity policy' (Rhodes 1988: 359). The most fundamental failure of the network was the inability to define the problems it faced.

It is also important to point out that policy networks can develop at different levels of government and can involve vertical integration. For example, a policy community concerned with the issue of agricultural prices and agricultural policy in general can exist at the departmental level whilst within the Ministry of Agriculture a policy community concerned with land drainage and sea defences exists at the level of a specific section of the department (see Cunningham 1992). Rhodes demonstrates how policy networks can link subnational bodies to national bodies. In addition, policy networks can also include an international element. With Britain's integration into the EC, a large number of policy areas now involve EC institutions and groups in the network. Likewise, trade policy is made in an international context with GATT being a key institution within the policy network. It is also possible for networks to exist with little or no key government actors. Grant *et al.* (1988) demonstrate that in the chemical sector, the central role in the network is performed by the key chemical companies.

Hence a policy network can exist at varying levels of government (national or local); in different policy areas (agricultural, industrial or health); or a subsector of policy (land drainage, chemical policy, community care) or even around particular issues. For example, in the case of food and agriculture, on issues of agricultural policy the community involves MAFF and the NFU. If it shifts to an issue of food policy the community expands to include DoH, food producers and retailers, food scientists and the BMA. If it is a particular issue concerned with food, the community can expand again to include the egg producers, environmental health officers and food scientists with particular interests. A network is a fluid concept. The food example demonstrates how the primary community can open in certain situations to allow members of the secondary community access on a specific issue. Although a policy community has a high degree of stability, when issues and levels of analysis change, the relationships between actors within the networks change.

Policy networks and state actors

This section will consider the impact that these networks have on the state and policy-making. Why do particular types of relationships develop? What do networks mean for state autonomy and how do they affect policy outcomes?

Jordan and Richardson (1987: 181) claim that there is 'a natural tendency for the political system in Britain to encourage the formation of stable policy communities'. Why should it be the case that government agencies want to create highly stable and well integrated relationships with particular interest groups? Policy communities have a number of advantages for government over other forms of networks. First, Jordan and Richardson (1982) believe that in Britain the style of policy-making is consultative, and regular, and institutional discussion is a means to ensure that consultation takes place. Second, consultation has advantages for government. It means that policy-making is consensual rather than conflictual. Through establishing a policy community government can depoliticise a policy area and so it is less likely to be politically dangerous. Third, a policy community makes policy-making predictable and therefore does not present government with new problems (Hogwood 1987). With a policy community the government agencies know the groups likely to be involved, the demands they will make and the potential solutions that exist. It reduces the likelihood of overload and the chances of failing to find a solution. Hence policy communities provide stability:

> Based on a limited constellation of interests with restricted membership, the communities routinize relationships by incorporating the major interests into a 'closed' world. Policy communities are a means of creating stability and hence they institutionalize the existing distribution of power (Rhodes 1988: 390).

Fourth, British government is highly departmental (Jordan 1981; Jordan and Richardson 1982). Policy communities are a means for a department to extend further the barriers against other departments becoming involved in policy-making. By segmenting and depoliticising a policy arena, a department is excluding other actors who are likely to interfere in policy and thus make the policy process more difficult. A policy community, by supplying a department with information and political support, can also assist Ministers in inter-departmental battles.

Despite the advantages of policy communities, they do not occur automatically or in all policy areas. The right range of circumstances has to exist for a policy community to develop: a degree of consensus; the single decision-making centre within government; and interest groups that can deliver members. Heclo (1978), Gias *et al.* (1984) and Salisbury (1990) suggest that in the United States the tendency is towards policy communities or iron triangles breaking down and becoming issue networks. Heclo avers that many of the traditional iron triangles are being opened up as new groups enter the policy process. Indeed a number of features of the US political system make it prone to issue networks. First, the separation of powers and the numerous regional divisions within government mean that there are many access points and so it is much easier for groups in the US to gain access to the political arena. Second, this ease of access and large number of decision-making centres make it difficult to establish a consensus in policy-making. Often there are substantial conflicts over who is responsible for a particular area of policy. Third, the power of Congress makes it difficult to exclude the legislature and this makes policy-making much more likely to become highly political. There is a tendency in the United States for the political arena to be much more open than in Britain and for issue networks rather than policy communities to exist. However, this book will demonstrate that despite this tendency, nothing is inevitable and the type of network that develops in Britain and the US depends on the policy area.

An important aspect of these relationships is the impact that they have on state autonomy. Often it is suggested that close relationships between groups and government result in the government department losing autonomy as it is captured by the interest groups. However, this is only the case if state autonomy is seen in zero-sum terms; i.e. that an increase in group influence is seen in the reduction in state power. The notion of policy networks is a way of coming to terms with the traditionally stark state/civil society dichotomy. As we saw earlier there are great problems in defining state autonomy because it is unclear where society ends and the state begins. The interests of the state do not develop in a vacuum but are determined within the context of civil society and the state's relationship with civil society. State actors are also actors in civil society, they live in society and have constant contact with groups which represent societal interests. Therefore the interests of state actors develop along with the interests of group actors and the degree of autonomy that exists depends on the nature of policy networks.

Rather than groups and state actors working in opposition and restraining each other's autonomy, autonomy can develop within particular policy networks relative to other networks. Autonomy, rather than belonging to states, exists within policy communities and 'exists to the extent to which a policy community resists penetration' (Campbell *et al.* 1989: 92). In other words, the agricultural policy network can increase its power in relation to other departments by being a closed policy community.

Policy networks are, in Mann's terms, a means of increasing the infrastructural power of state actors. Policy communities increase state autonomy by establishing the means through which state actors can intervene in society without using force. By integrating state and society actors, they increase the capabilities of the state to make and implement policy. They create state powers that would not otherwise exist and, more importantly, they increase the autonomy of actors in a policy area by excluding other actors from the policy process. Within a policy community, state actors and societal actors work together in order to increase their autonomy in relation to other groups. Hence, autonomy is not something that the state has in relation to society, but is something that state and society actors can develop in relation to other actors. Policy communities increase autonomy by establishing infrastructural power and by isolating the policy process.

If there is a loose network, even though the pressures on government actors to adopt a particular policy might not be very great, the autonomy of government actors is, in fact, less. First, state actors lack infrastructural power. Without a policy community there is no mechanism to intervene in particular areas of policy. Second, with the involvement of several government actors, no single agency or department is likely to be able to act on its own. Third, if the area is political, then the department will be operating in a political situation and is less able to take actions unobserved by the public, legislature or media.

Therefore, if a department wishes to achieve a particular policy, it is useful to establish a policy community as the means of creating the infrastructural power through which to achieve it. This involves giving an interest group a privileged position in policy-making that results in a mutual enhancement of autonomy rather than a loss of autonomy for one actor.

This does not mean that states cannot act without policy communities. It is clear, as we saw before, that states have greater resources than interest groups and that power is asymmetrical (Rhodes 1988). It is state actors who determine the rules of the games; the parameters of policy and the actors who will have access to the policy community. Particular state leaders – especially Presidents or Prime Ministers – can choose to ignore policy communities and impose policy against the wishes of the network. However, political actors have to realise the costs of such an approach. In tackling policy this way they are having to rely on despotic rather than infrastructural power and whilst this is acceptable and possible occasionally, there are few politicians in democratic systems who can continually choose to ignore the traditionally privileged interest groups. Moreover, by using despotic powers, state actors have to develop alternative means of implementation; if they ignore interest groups and policy communities they have to develop their own means of administration.

In this way the threats to state autonomy do not come from society but from political leaders and other political networks which might try to interfere in an already existing policy community. They might attempt to break it up, insert new members, change the policy agenda, or bypass it completely.

Policy networks affect the degree to which state actors achieve their goals. Rather than policy communities preventing state autonomy, as public choice theorists suggest, they actually increase the infrastructural power of state actors. However, it is important not to preclude the possibility of pressure-group capture within particular policy communities. There might be occasions when pressure groups dominate a policy community. Particularly in continental Europe, where the view of society is less adversarial than in Britain and the United States and corporate interests are accorded more legitimacy, opportunities for pressure-group domination of a policy community are high. Likewise, there is also a possibility that state autonomy is greater where there is an issue network. Therefore it is necessary to see policy networks and state autonomy as different dimensions (see Table 3.2).

Situation 1 in Table 3.2 represents the situation where a policy community increases the infrastructural power of state actors by establishing the means for policy-making and intervention. The policy community increases state autonomy. In situation 2 an issue network exists and, although state actors might lack infrastructural power because they cannot establish institutionalised relationships, autonomy is still high because there is conflict between groups who lack resources. Therefore state actors can impose their own policy goals without high costs. In 3 there is a policy community but it is dominated by the groups, and so its policy goals are determined by group interests. This is a rare situation but it does exist at particular times. Finally, in 4, the issue network reduces the infrastructural power of the state by making the policy process difficult and so it reduces the control of state actors over policy implementation.

Table 3.2 demonstrates the difficulty of state autonomy. Interests are not predetermined but develop within the context of social and economic arrangements and relationships between groups and state actors. Therefore, both the interests of the state and of groups develop within the context of networks. Often they cannot be clearly defined as state interests or group interests. Moreover, there are also levels of autonomy: actors within a network can have

Table 3.2 Policy networks and state autonomy

Level of autonomy	Policy network	
	Policy community	*Issue network*
High autonomy	1. Closed relationship producing infrastructural power	2. Many actors in conflict, high state of freedom
Low autonomy	3. Closed relationship pressure-group capture	4. Many actors, limited state control of policy

degrees of autonomy; the autonomy of networks in relation to other networks varies; and Presidents and Prime Ministers can have variable levels of autonomy over networks. Hence, autonomy varies according to the types of relationships, the structures of dependency, the resources available at a particular time, the perceptions of various actors and the degree to which actors are prepared to bear the costs of autonomous action. Thus, the concept of state autonomy is meaningless unless it is disaggregated to the policy level and particular relationships are examined.

Policy does not depend on the power of pressure groups and the way they try to influence the state. Rather it depends on the types of relationships that exist between groups and state actors. The nature of these institutions has an impact on policy. As March and Olsen claim (1984: 739), 'The bureaucratic agency, the legislative committee, and the appellate court are arenas for contending social forces, but they are also standard operating procedures and structures that define and defend interests . . . .' These institutional structures and standard operating procedures (SOPs) define what groups should be involved in policy, how they should behave, what options are available and who should be excluded. In doing so they have an important impact on policy outcomes. Hall (1986) suggests that organisations are important for four reasons:

1. The impact that interest groups have on policy depends on 'the organisation of the structures within which they are expressed'.
2. The interests of the actors are affected according to the structures within which they operate.
3. The structure of organisations affects the policies they produce.
4. In order to implement policy the state needs organisational resources.

Therefore the interests of state actors are to some extent determined by the organisations of the state, and the types of relationships that state organisations have with societal groups affect the nature of policy outcomes. This means that policy outcomes are the result of much more than the actions, tactics and resources of pressure groups, policy is:

> more than the sum of countervailing pressure from social groups. That pressure is mediated by an organisational dynamic that imprints its own image on the outcome. Because policy-making in the modern state is always a collective process the configuration of the institutions that aggregate the opinions of individual contributors into a set of policies can have its own effect on policy outcomes (Hall 1986: 19).

Policy is made within institutions that structure the interests of the state and pressure groups. Policy networks are to some extent the structuring institutions and so, as Rhodes (1988: 83) confirms, 'the analysis of policy networks presupposes that they have a key impact on policy content . . . . policy is both a dependent and independent variable.' Where a policy community exists it is much more likely that policy will reflect the goals of state actors (of course modified by their relationship with the integrated group). In a policy community, state agencies have greater control over the issues that are raised and the response to them. As we have seen, an important part of a policy community is a consensus on the policy options and so when a particular problem arises a limited range of solutions will be made available. Policy is limited to what is acceptable to the consensus within the policy community. The policy community is effectively a means of excluding certain policy options by making the option unacceptable to the policy community.

The food policy community in Britain determined that the government's role in food policy was to intervene when there was a direct danger to individuals from food. Therefore, when the issue of salmonella in chickens developed, the policy community did not see that the government had to deal with the general problem of salmonella but saw it in terms of providing information that chickens should be cooked properly by individual consumers. The problem became one for consumers rather than one that the producers had to solve. The policy community thus produced solutions that protected the interests of the dominant actors within the community.

Policy networks also include certain mechanisms for intervention. These mechanisms are structures which in Giddens' terms both enable and constrain. They might allow certain policy options but they do not ensure that others can be followed. Rhodes (1988: 253–4) demonstrates that the Conservative government in the 1980s failed to control local government expenditure because while central government attempted to implement a system of hands-on control it failed to develop the mechanisms to control the local government network. The government did not believe in the effectiveness of the local government network and thought that just by desiring to, it could thereby control local government expenditure. However, the centre depended on local government for the mechanism of control and therefore could not achieve its goal without local government support.

Issue networks mean that the potential policy outcomes are likely to be more varied and that it is much easier for groups to get alternative policy options onto the agenda. However, the downside is that it is much more difficult for these policy options to be implemented because government actors have less control over the policy process. Agreement is difficult to achieve between various government actors who have their own interests. There are no pressure groups which have the resources, or control over their membership to provide assistance in implementation, and there are likely to be groups within the network who will attempt to resist the implementation of policy. The consequence of an issue network is policy inertia, a policy mess (Rhodes 1988), or constantly changing policy as different actors gain the upper hand and attempt to implement a policy that suits their goals.

Policy networks are about more than understanding group/government relations. They are an attempt to understand the policy process and the impact that interest-group intermediation has on policy outcomes. These interactions affect both the autonomy of state actors and ultimately the final decisions. This approach therefore has important implications for power. Within this framework, power is not simply behavioural and observable. The policy network approach accepts that power is structural and operates through exclusion and non-decisions.

With the notion of policy networks, power is seen as being based on resources and dependencies. Actors have power if they have resources that can be exchanged and so actor A is dependent on actor B for particular resources. However, this dependence is likely to be mutual. As we have seen, state actors depend on pressure groups for certain resources and pressure groups depend on the state (Rhodes 1981). It is also clear that the state can make policy without groups but groups have great difficulty in exercising any influence if the state chooses to ignore them. In this sense power is both perceptional and relational. Often groups only have power if the state perceives them as important for particular goals and in doing so becomes dependent on the groups' resources. Consequently, factors which lead to the development of particular policies are not group pressures but are often external factors, like the economic situation, war, relations with other nations, social change. The government, in reacting to these problems, draws in pressure groups in order to increase infrastructural power, to reduce surprises, to limit societal demands and to ease implementation.

This is not to say that groups lack any inherent power at all. It is frequently the case that the costs of developing a policy without the involvement of particular groups is so high that state actors have little option but to involve the groups. In certain circumstances the state can be very weak and groups can be relatively strong, and hence have a large number of resources to exchange. In the case of health policy it is difficult to imagine the government developing an interventionist health policy without involvement of the doctors. Nevertheless, even here it is the decision to develop a health policy that makes the doctors important.

Policy communities, in particular, are also important as a means of conceptualising structural power. Knoke (1990: 9) maintains that power 'is a function of the position [actors] occupy in one or more network' and it 'emerges from . . . prominence in networks where valued information and scarce resources are transferred from one actor to another'. The establishment of a policy community creates a particular structure which privileges certain interests within the policy process. 'Once established . . . structural patterns tend to be reproduced, whether because of biases built into the structures themselves, or the expectations held by agents, or the linkages built into structural fields' (Cerny 1990: 27). The structures are sets of rules, standard operating procedures and formal and informal institutions which result from the continual repetition of routine activities (Giddens 1986) and thereby create certain choices. These are structured choices; they involve a certain range of options – sets of expected behaviour – and as such they represent the interests of the key actors within the policy community. Thus certain policy options become routinised within the policy process and so only particular decisions will be made. Consequently, power is structural. Policy outputs do not derive from the behaviour and choices of individual actors but are the result of actors within structural locations making choices from a range of structurally determined options.

In addition, certain groups and policy options are routinely excluded from the policy process. The exclusion of a particular group or particular policy option is repeated continually until it is habituated and then enstructured into the policy community through ideology and institutions (Berger and Luckman 1967; Giddens 1986). Frequently, groups are not excluded by the decisions of individuals but by the processes of policy-making. For example, in the agricultural arena during the 1950s and 1960s, individuals made a conscious decision not to consult consumers. The perception after the war was that there was no need for formal consultation of consumer interests and no mechanism was established to involve them in the policy process. They were structurally excluded. The day-to-day activities of actors within policy communities reproduce the structural features of the system (Giddens 1986: 24). Thus, through policy communities, power relationships are institutionalised and therefore reproduced without the conscious decision of the actors involved.

This does not mean that power is always structural. Even with the existence of policy communities, powerful actors (as we will see in the next chapter) can choose to break them up and thus remove the structural power. In other less integrated networks power is likely to take more observable and individualistic forms. In a loose issue network the power of the groups is almost completely expressed in terms of visible resources which are used in an attempt to influence government. In more integrated networks, and even in policy communities, there is often conscious exclusion of particular groups and issues.

Therefore types of networks can be related to Lukes' three dimensions of power. In an issue network power is exercised through the observable activity of interest groups and government agencies. In a more integrated network power is exercised through observable means and through conscious exclusion. In a policy community there is also observable power and conscious exclusion but in addition there is unconscious exclusion where power is also exercised through the structures of policy-making.

This demonstrates that the notion of policy networks is multi-theoretic (Dunleavy and O'Leary 1987; Marsh and Rhodes 1992c). Although Chapter 1 criticised the traditional theories, and this chapter has argued for using networks with a state-centred theory, policy networks need a wider macro-theory to explain the sorts of relationships that develop. Policy networks can be used in conjunction with a range of theoretical frameworks.

The traditional theories can use network analysis. Table 3.3 demonstrates that particular theories focus on certain aspects of networks. For marxists the

Table 3.3 Macro-theories and policy networks

	Macro-theory			
	Marxism	*Elitism*	*State-centred*	*Pluralism*
Policy network	Policy communities dominated by capital	Policy communities dominated by privileged interests	Various networks dominated by state actors	Issue networks no dominant group

networks would be closed and dominated by interests that represent capital. For elitists, networks would be closed and dominated by a small number of interest groups and state actors as in a corporatist model. For state theorists, networks could take different forms but would exist in order to pursue the interests of state actors. For pluralists, networks are continually breaking down into issue networks which makes it increasingly difficult for a small number of groups to dominate policy sectors. However, this book will demonstrate that no single view of networks should be taken. State/group relationships are highly variable. The interests that dominate vary and change, and need to be understood in an historical and political context. We cannot, therefore, prejudge the nature of policy networks before empirical investigation.

Conclusion

The traditional approaches to pressure groups have focused on the nature of groups or the activities of classes. Whilst accepting a role for the state, and the importance of state/group interaction, it has not been their main focus. The concepts of state autonomy and policy network demonstrate that in order to understand how policy is made, and the role of groups in its development, it is important to understand the interests of the state and the type of relationships that exist between groups and the state.

The state-centred literature often presents a division between the state and civil society which is too stark and ignores the fact that state actors operate within the context of civil society. What we have to accept is not that the state is autonomous, but that the state has the potential to be autonomous and that state actors have interests which derive from their position within the state. This is not the determining feature of policy but is a key variable in affecting policy outcomes. The interests and potentials of state actors are an important element in the equation which determines policy outcomes.

A second key variable is the type of policy networks that exists. Networks are important because they affect state autonomy and policy outcomes. Policy networks demonstrate that the power of pressure groups does not depend on their resources in terms of their ability to lobby government but derives from the types of relationships they have with government. From this perspective, state autonomy is not something that belongs to the state or groups but is a positive-sum which can be increased for mutual benefit in a specific type of relationship. Therefore, policy communities are an important source of infrastructural power. They allow government to intervene in particular policy areas without using force or even legislative and state administrative procedures. If a government agency wants to work in a particular policy area, there are great advantages to establishing a particular type of relationship.

This relationship then affects policy outcomes. In an issue network the lack of state capabilities and absence of consensus creates a tendency towards inertia as no group/agency has the ability to take decisions and implement them. In a policy community the ability to make policy exists but policy is likely to be conservative, protecting the interests of those within the policy community. A policy community is also underpinned by ideological and institutional features. The ideological features limit the range of policy options available and so subsequently affect outcomes. The institutional features determine which groups will be involved in the development of policy and this again affects the potential outcomes.

In understanding policy it is essential to recognise that state actors have interests and the potential to fulfil these interests. Yet, to do so against the interests of societal groups is often high in costs. It would require the use of despotic powers which is rare in liberal democratic regimes. States have an interest in developing integrated relationships with groups as a means of increasing infrastructural power and these relationships affect policy outcomes. Thus the notion of policy networks is explanatory as well as descriptive. The next chapter will examine explanations of how policy networks change.

Chapter 4

SOCIAL CHANGE, IDEOLOGY AND PRESSURE GROUPS:
How Policy Networks Change

The literature on policy networks is concerned with institutionalised relationships between government and pressure groups. In that sense its focus is on stability rather than change. However, it is becoming increasingly apparent that policy networks, and political regimes, do change. Indeed, a number of studies suggest that economic, political and social factors are increasingly forcing transformations in policy networks (see for example Mills 1992; Richardson *et al.* 1992; Smith 1991). Increasing numbers of actors are entering the political arena and consequently policy communities are breaking down into more open issue networks (Heclo 1978; Jordan and Richardson 1987; Salisbury 1990).

However, the policy networks literature actually says very little about why networks change (Marsh and Rhodes 1992c). In particular, the notion of a policy community is very static. The role of a policy community is to prevent change by excluding threats to the dominant interests. Nevertheless, it is the case that policy communities do change. Yet, there is no satisfactory explanation of why change occurs in particular networks. The role of this chapter is to examine the existing theories of change, to demonstrate the problems with these theories and to offer an alternative. The existing theories of change can be divided into three types – the economically/socially based general theories of post-industrialism and post-Fordism; the political accounts of change and the more specific pluralist accounts of change. I shall begin by examining post-industrialism and post-Fordism.

Post-industrialism and post-Fordism

Post-industrialist and post-Fordist theories provide an almost economically determinist view of change. They see change in political organisation as a reflection of the transformation of power relations which has resulted from economic and social change in industrial nations in the post-war period. It is undoubtedly the case that Britain and the United States have gone through a number of major economic and social changes in the last thirty years. Until the 1950s Britain had a largely manufacturing economy and 60 per cent of the population was in the manual working class. In the 1950s manufacturing employed 35 per cent of the employed total and produced 30 per cent of the GDP (Harris 1988: 15). Manufacturing also tended to be mass production in large firms which were concentrated in certain areas (Meegan 1988; Lash and Urry 1987).

In most of the post-war period there have been important changes in manufacturing. Between 1970 and 1986 manufacturing as a share of GDP has fallen from 34 per cent to 19.5 per cent whilst manufacturing's share of exports has fallen from 11 per cent to 8 per cent of value (Maynard, G. 1988). As a result (Allen 1988a: 185) 'fewer people today ... work in giant industrial workplaces. Many of the larger factories have disappeared and along with them certainty ... that a job means lifetime employment.' As well as a decline in manufacturing there has been a decline in the size of manufacturing units. There has been an increase in the number of enterprises employing under 100 employees from 78,676 in 1958 to 99,303 in 1981. There has also been a rapid increase in part-time and female employment (Allen 1988b: 100).

Throughout the twentieth century there has been a growth in service employment but for the first time in the 1960s more than 50 per cent of people were employed in the service sector and Britain's share of output of GDP by services reached 56 per cent in 1960–7 and 59 per cent in 1968–73 (Elfring 1988: 33 and 109).

This change has had a major impact on the occupational structure. The percentage employed in white-collar work has increased from 7.6 per cent in 1861 to 41.7 per cent in 1975 (Pollard 1979: 21). There has been the rise of what Goldthorpe calls the service class and an increase in professional employment. Lash and Urry argue that the twentieth century has seen the growth of professional groups in new areas like the manufacturing sector with trained managers, computer specialists and engineers taking a central role in the management of companies.

It is clear that the United States has also undergone substantial social change in recent years. According to Clarke (1984: 21): 'Since 1950, a major societal transformation has been unfolding which is gradually ushering America from the industrial to post-industrial era.' In 1950 the workforce was evenly balanced between service occupations and goods production but by 1980 two-thirds were employed in services. In addition, the level of education of the workforce has increased, the size of the technical and professional class has risen from 3.9 million in 1940 to 15.6 million in 1980 and the percentage of married women working has increased from 14 to 50 per cent between 1940 and 1980 (Clarke 1984; Issel 1985).

For post-industrialists and post-Fordists these economic and social changes have had a substantial impact on the interests and aspirations of societal groups. With increased income, consumer preferences have moved away from necessities to luxuries and services (Elfring 1988). With the change in employment patterns people's concerns have changed from production issues to consumption issues (Dunleavy and Husbands 1985) and according to Inglehart (1977) this has led to the development of 'post-material' values which emphasise the quality of life rather than economic issues.

There are two perspectives which try to evaluate the impact of these changes on society. First, Bell sees a society going through a number of stages until it reaches a post-industrial society. Second, some marxists have suggested that industrial society has changed with the transition from a fordist economic base to a post-Fordist economic base.

Both theories agree on some aspects of the transition but differ on the implications of this social change. They accept that there has been a decline in manufacturing industry; a move to a more service-based economy with the rise of a professional or service class (Bell 1974: 13–14; Murray 1988: 11–12; Lash and Urry 1987: 99); that to a certain degree society has become more fractured; and that the traditional class structure is changing.

Bell (1974: 14) identifies the United States as being closest to a post-industrial society with over 60 per cent of people being employed in the service sector. He also recognises that there is a change in the type of services provided. The existence of a large service sector is not new. In the nineteenth century there were a large number of domestic servants and a major business service sector has existed throughout the twentieth century. He argues that in a post-industrial society it is health, education, research and government services which become dominant and it is here that most people are employed.

According to Bell (1989) the transition to post-industrial society is assisted by the development of information technology. In this new stage it is knowledge that becomes the axial principle of society. Advanced industrial societies have seen a rapid increase in the role of information, with new technology and a major growth in knowledge (Steinfeld and Salvaggio 1989: 2). Many of the post-industrialists see information being spread more widely with the growth of information technology and telecommunications (Bell 1989: 96).

Marxist theories, concerned with the transition from fordism to post-Fordism, focus on changes in the economic base and the impact these have on production and politics. Advanced capitalist societies are increasingly characterised by diversity, differentiation and fragmentation, rather than homogeneity, standardisation and the economies and organisation of scale that were the features of mass society. Fordism was a system where products were standardised allowing mass production which was subject to scientific management (Murray 1988: 8). Changes in international markets, with the development of multinational companies and the industrialisation of many underdeveloped countries combined with recession, have forced the advanced industrial nations to change their production techniques (Lipietz 1987).

Post-Fordism is 'a new form of intensive regime of accumulation which will provide the basis for a new long wave of capitalism' (Bonefeld 1987: 114). This involves the increased use of new technology in production and storekeeping so that there is increased flexibility and economy of scope. As a result there is also flexibility in manufacturing with the production of a much wider range of products, smaller production runs and increased changes in design, and the workforce is divided between a skilled core which is multi-skilled, highly paid and permanent, and a peripheral unskilled workforce which is temporary and low paid (Murray 1988: 11). As a consequence the power of unions is considerably reduced, often to that of a company union (Bonefeld 1987: 115–17).

For Jessop *et al.* (1988: 129), post-Fordism is a useful 'heuristic device to uncover some powerful trends in society'. In the case of Britain, they argue, the Thatcher government accentuated the divisions between the core and periphery in order to change the balance of power so that the economy could be restructured: 'Thatcherism has an explicit strategy to restructure the British economy as part of a reinvigorated, post-Fordist international capitalism' (Jessop *et al.* 1988: 135). Thatcherism has produced (or at least encouraged) the move to post-Fordism rather than post-Fordism resulting in Thatcherism.

Thus, the post-Fordists and post-industrialists are suggesting that there has been major social and economic transformation which has changed the relative power of various groups in society and as a consequence group/state relations will change. Certain post-industrialists and post-Fordists see economic transformation reducing the power of the unions and subsequently see new social movements as becoming the motors of change in post-industrial society (Bell 1974; Gorz 1982; Hobsbawm 1979; Touraine 1976). In addition it is suggested that professional groups will develop a dominant position in the social division of labour and this will increase their political influence (Lash and Urry 1987: 162)

Finally, the implications for capital are complex. Post-industrialism/post-Fordism should favour multinational capital whilst disfavouring national capital which is unable to adapt to the increased demands of the market and flexibility in production. It should also result in less power for manufacturing capital versus service capital. At the same time it might redress the balance of power between capital and the consumer, as the demands the consumer can make become increasingly complex, intelligent and competitive. People's prime economic category will change from producer to consumer and so their main political interests will be as consumers rather than producers. This greater complexity and diversity of interests should also weaken the power of the state. The declining legitimacy and control of peak organisations will lessen the chances of making the types of corporatist arrangements indicative of the past.

If we were to use post-industrial or post-Fordist theory in relation to policy networks we would expect policy networks to adapt as social change introduced new issues onto the political agenda; as new/different groups gained power at the expense of other groups; and as new sources of information made control of the political agenda by policy communities increasingly difficult. This is a theme that is taken up in the literature on new social movements and by 'post-marxist' theory. For post-marxists, class-based explanations of politics are essentialist and reductionist. Social change means that class is no longer the key determinant in politics (see McLennan 1989; Pierson 1986). The establishment of a well-educated, affluent, new middle class (Rootes 1991) has led to the creation of non-class-based new social movements that are interested in cross-class issues of peace, race, gender and the environment. As a consequence of electoral dealignment, class dealignment and increased affluence, a new form of participatory politics has developed which is pluralistic and prepared to challenge the traditional order of politics. The new social movements undermine the existing policy networks by 'actively intervening in the ongoing processes of policy formation and decision-making' (Kuechler and Dalton 1990: 297). For Kuechler and Dalton (1990: 298):

> the new social movements have left their mark on the political arena in restructuring the issue agenda, in pushing for more direct citizen participation, and in redefining the 'boundaries of institutional politics'. Their ideological challenge was clearly successful across all nations.

According to post-industrialists and post-Fordists, social and economic change has created new interests and new forms of politics. These new interests generate an alternative set of issues that result in challenges to the existing policy networks and may lead to the creation of alternative networks.

A critique of post-Fordism and post-industrialism

Despite the fact that there has been significant social change in the industrial world, there are a number of problems with these theories in explaining social change. It is clear that both post-industrialism and post-Fordism suffer from a degree of teleology in that they see society moving to a predefined stage. In particular, Bell outlines the path that societies follow from pre-industrial, industrial to post-industrial. As such they:

> involve propositions about what outcomes are beneficial to social systems as a whole, and posit those effects as the very rationale for social change. This functionalist approach diminishes the sense in which human struggles, motives and actions determine how a 'system' muddles through in the first place (McLennan 1989: 206).

Kumar suggests that although there have been changes in society, it is far from clear that they indicate a move to a new social order. He maintains that the expansion of services has occurred since the beginning of industrialisation and that Britain is the only society where industrial workers have at any time constituted the majority of the population (Kumar 1978: 201–2). Rather than the service sector being the power house of a new professional class, work in the services is 'on the whole less skilled, lower paid, less unionised and less secure than in manufacturing'. Moreover, in recent years many of the areas where Bell saw the major expansion, education, health and government, have contracted whilst the services which he saw as part of industrial society, like banking and commercial law, have expanded. Even when there has been growth in health and education, it has tended to be at the lower end of the occupational scale (Kumar 1978: 216).

Gershuny also disputes the extent of growth in services. He argues that the consumption of services has actually fallen whilst the proportion employed in manufacturing has stayed within 3 per cent of its 1841 value. Although there has been an increase in service employment this does not mean more services are consumed, but rather that these services are concerned with the manufacture of goods (Gershuny 1978: 60–70). As Callinicos (1989: 124–5) highlights, with industrialisation in the Third World there has been a 'considerable growth of the industrial working class on a global scale'. There is also a lack of evidence that the benefits of a post-industrial society, outlined by Bell, such as less work, more leisure, increased information and greater participation, are occurring (Hamelink 1986).

The post-Fordist model is also problematic. First, in the version outlined by Aglietta (1979) it is functionalist and deterministic (Bonefeld 1987). It suggests that a crisis in Fordism leads to changes in the economic base which transforms the economic and political organisations of a society. Hirst (1989: 322) reminds us that it is a mistake to think that: 'the features of the production system can be used to characterise the wider society.' Second, the evidence to support the development of post-Fordist production in Britain is patchy to say the least. The notion that a dual labour force is a new feature of production is highly questionable. It is clear that women and ethnic groups have always provided a flexible, part-time low paid and temporary labour force and this group has grown in recent years whilst most men are still employed in full-time permanent work (McInnes 1987: 117; Pollert 1988).

In addition, there has been resistance to flexible techniques by workers and management in Britain. Where new technologies have been introduced it has been as part of a fordist strategy (Lane 1988: 159). According to Lane (1988: 160) 'the Taylorist thrust has intensified and employment conditions have significantly deteriorated.' The introduction of flexible production is very uneven. Some sectors like fast food are just adopting Fordism (Gamble 1989), others have never been Fordist, and never will be (Jessop *et al.* 1988). There is little indication that mass markets are breaking up and the introduction of flexible production is limited and generally used for the production of specific models (Callinicos 1989: 136). For Rustin (1989: 309):

> Post-Fordism is better seen as one ideal-typical model or strategy of production and regulation, copresent with others in a complex historical ensemble, than as a valid totalising description of an emerging social formation here and now.

Undoubtedly, the post-industrialists/post-Fordists identify important changes in advanced industrial societies. It would also seem correct to assume that these changes will have an impact on the influence of particular groups within society. First, the growth of an international service economy changes the problems that policy-makers face and the possible solutions. Economic development might no longer depend on regional aid to ailing industries but attempts to make the economy competitive on the world market by concentrating on certain specialisms. Second, the aspirations and interests of individual workers change as their role as producers declines. With this transformation, their fundamental political axis could be as consumers and not in the workplace. The pursuing of consumption issues requires alternative forms of political articulation to those of production issues. Third, the resources and importance of groups change with the transformation of the economy. Groups will have resources if they have a strategic place in the economy. The rise of the service sector and the internationalisation of the economy change which groups are central and, therefore, have the most economic power. Fourth, the growth of professions will mean that there are more groups which have the resources to influence government. Their impact might increase as the importance of manual workers declines. Fifth, these changes have implications for the power of the state. According to Luhmann (1982), the growth of new interests, new groups and information society has increased the complexity and diversity of society. This makes society more difficult to control or direct, or even difficult for it to achieve consensus as a basis of legitimate action. Consequently, the state is less able to implement policies because it has less influence over non-state groups. Further, the increased internationalisation of the economy means that the options available to the state have become much less.

However, in suggesting that social change will result in changes in the power of particular groups, post-industrialists/post-Fordists exaggerate the degree of social change; they overemphasise its importance for the distribution of power and they ignore the extent to which the political context will limit or vary the impact that these changes have on state/group relations. Social and political change do not take place in a vacuum. They take place within existing political structures which affect the impact that change has on group intermediations. There are two factors in particular which will affect the impact of social change: new right ideology and the existing policy networks.

Political explanations of change

The relations that groups have with the state are not just the result of social and economic factors but they depend on the perception that the government has of particular groups and the structure of the relationships that the groups have with the state. The social democratic consensus that existed in Britain for thirty years from 1945 also had implications for the power of groups. Keynesianism with its mix of increased expenditure, government intervention and full employment resulted in an increased role for the state and therefore increased contacts with pressure groups particularly in the welfare and social services, and the economy. Many groups developed an important political role through institutionalised relationships which provided stability, legitimacy and assistance in implementation. Moreover, Crosland (1974) argued that the consequence of full employment was to increase the power of the unions in relation to business. Panitch (1977), from a marxist perspective, concurs with this view, arguing that corporatism was the result of the need to emasculate the power of labour in the face of its increased power as a consequence of full employment. In the United States there was also an acceptance of Keynesianism and full employment. In addition, the New Deal Coalition ensured the representation of certain interests – labour, the poor, ethnic groups, Northern liberals – in the centres of government.

New right ideology, in challenging the post-war consensus has challenged the social democratic and New Deal views of pressure groups and their role in the policy process. Both Ronald Reagan and Margaret Thatcher were influenced by new right thinkers who saw pressure groups as malign forces that distort the political and economic market, reduce individual liberty, overstretch the resources of government and reduce economic performance (Barry 1987; Brittan 1975; Hayek 1979; Olson 1982). One of the Conservatives' main platforms in the 1979 General Election was a rejection of the corporatism which they argued had developed in Britain in the 1960s and 1970s. On many occasions Margaret Thatcher declared her distrust of organised interests and even rejected the concept of society. She believed in extending the area of individual rights and the range of individual choice.

As a consequence, the government embarked on an attack of what it saw as corporate and other intermediate institutions. Trade unions have faced a long-term diminution of their rights, the sponsorship divisions of departments were abolished (and reintroduced again in 1992 by Michael Heseltine), the tripartite National Economic Development Office has been abolished and other tripartite institution like MSC and wages boards have been abolished or threatened with abolition. Likewise in the United States, Reagan stressed the need to reduce the influence of 'special interests' and in particular to lessen the power of the unions (Kreiger 1986).

The view of the new right, and of journalistic accounts of the last ten years, is that Thatcherism, in particular, has transformed British society and changed the power of groups in society. As Edgell and Duke (1991: 21) point out:

> Between 1979 and 1989, the Conservative policy to restructure British society by enhancing the primacy of the market profoundly affected social and political divisions. The overall direction of this policy represented an attempt to alter the balance of class and sectoral forces in the Thatcherist Britain . . . .

It is argued that Mrs Thatcher substantially changed the relationship between the state and society. It is claimed that she rolled back the frontiers of the state (Young 1992), thus increasing the sphere of civil society and reducing the role of agencies which integrated groups with the state. One of the clearest examples of this reduction in the size of the state is the privatisation policy. As Marsh (1991: 463) indicates:

> The scale of privatisation is immense. In fact, by 1991: over 50 per cent of the public sector had been transferred to the private sector; 650,000 workers had changed sectors, of whom 90 per cent had become shareholders; 9 million people were shareholders, which represented 20 per cent of the population, as compared with 7 per cent in 1979; the nationalised sector accounted for less than 5 per cent of the UK output as compared with 9 per cent in 1979; about 125,000 council houses had been sold, most to sitting tenants under the right to buy provisions; and contracting out was well established in the NHS and the local authority sector.

Related to the goal of rolling back the state, was a rejection of Keynesianism in an attempt to reduce public expenditure. A major part of the Thatcher government's policy was aimed at reducing spending in the public sector, abandoning the commitment to full employment and cutting taxation. This, in principle, had important consequences for the power and relationships of particular groups in society. A further important feature of Thatcherism was direct challenges to the power of 'special interest groups'. The Thatcher government's greatest challenge was to the trade unions through legislation, privatisation, economic policy and direct confrontation as in the 1984–5 miners' strike. But the government also, to varying degrees, challenged the power of teachers, doctors, the Church of England and even barristers. Kavanagh, amongst others, has suggested that Mrs Thatcher has been highly successful in reducing the power of the unions (see Marsh 1992a). Kavanagh (quoted in Marsh 1992a: xvii) states that:

> The government's legislation on industrial relations and trade unions has taken hold. Here is an area where the balance of advantage has changed since 1979, from unions to employers and managers and from the consultative role granted to the unions to one in which they are virtually ignored by government.

Hence, through legislation, economic and social policy and direct confrontation it is claimed that the Thatcher government changed the balance of power in Britain from corporate public sector groups to individuals in the private sector. For Peter Jenkins (1988), not only did Mrs Thatcher destroy the power of the trade unions, she also buried the socialist-dominated post-war consensus. Consequently there is a new common ground in Britain:

> Its assumptions are individualist rather than collectivist, preferring private to state

ownership, putting the rights of the member before the interests of the trade unions and sound money above priming the economy (Jenkins 1988: 374).

In establishing this new consensus, the Thatcher government challenged the existing power structures and increased the power of the central state and the individual over the intermediate institutions of local government, pressure groups and the schools.

However, such an explanation of change is too simplistic. It exaggerates the degree of change and it pays little attention to the context within which new right governments have operated. This approach suggests an instrumentalist view of a unified and neutral state which the new right was able to win control of, and use, to change the power structures within Britain and the United States. Yet, it is increasingly clear that although Thatcherism, and to an extent Reaganism, changed much, many policies remained the same. This raises the question of why they were successful in some areas and not in others.

For instance, to take a simple measure, although public expenditure decreased between 1978/9 and 1990/1 as a percentage of GDP from 44 per cent to 39 per cent, it increased in real terms by 26 per cent (McKie 1992). Some of the largest increases were in the areas of the welfare state which Mrs Thatcher had initially been strongly committed to cutting. Rose (1990) has highlighted how most of the policies which were undertaken by Mrs Thatcher's government – at least up to 1985 – were policies introduced before 1946. 'Of the 118 different programmes that constituted the inheritance of the 1945 Labour government, more than five-sixths are still in effect more than four decades later; only nineteen have been terminated' (Rose 1990: 273). Of the policies continuing in 1985, 84 per cent were introduced before 1946 and this accounted for 99 per cent of expenditure. Only nineteen new programmes had been introduced which accounted for only £1.1 billion of expenditure. Even where the government introduced new legislation, the government still:

> failed to achieve many of its aims it set itself. In addition, as is always the case, the policies sometimes had unintended consequence which undermined the effect of the policy or the achievement of some other policy objectives (Marsh and Rhodes 1992d: 174).

Even examining the government's role with the trade unions has to be treated with care. As Marsh (1992a: 110) points out, 'It is clear that the unions' political role has reduced significantly since 1979.' Although the absolute number of contacts between government and unions might not have declined, 'the pattern and quality of those contacts has changed significantly' (Marsh 1992a: 112). However, it is also the case, as McInnes (1987) and Marsh (1992a) show, that there has been much less change at the shopfloor level in relations between unions and employers than the government might have expected. Moreover, the new Conservative legislation has been little used (Marsh 1992a).

It is also important to recognise that much of the change in trade union power was not the result of Thatcherism but, as the post-Fordists and post-industrialists might suggest, of social and economic change. With the decline in manufacturing employment reducing the number of trade unionists and the rise in unemployment affecting the willingness of trade unionists to strike, it seems that the power of trade unions would have been weaker in the 1980s with or without Thatcherism. Indeed, as Marsh and King (1986) indicate, the power of the trade unions decreased substantially during the second half of the 1974–9 Labour government.

In many areas the Conservative government did not achieve what it wanted, or claimed, to achieve (Marsh and Rhodes 1992b). This demonstrates that purely political explanations of change fail because they do not take account of the context within which politicians and bureaucrats act. Politicians come to power and face the pre-existing relationships between groups and the state and numerous internal and external constraints. Political ideologies, policy goals, or social and economic change for that matter, do not occur within a vacuum. The nature of the existing policy networks affect the ability of politicians to achieve policy goals (Marsh and Rhodes 1992d). The impact of both new right thinking and social change has been limited by the type of policy network that exists in a particular arena (Marsh and Rhodes 1989).

Within a policy community, the relationships between the groups and officials have existed over a long period of time, there is a broad consensus on policy options, groups are involved in detailed policy-making and there are institutional means of excluding 'outsider' groups. It might be reasonable to expect that with social and political change these relationships will change. The development of a closed policy community is to some extent the result of the government perceiving particular groups as politically, socially and economically important. In industrial society certain groups are perceived as being important and these groups tend to develop institutionalised relationships with government.

However, policy communities have the ability to survive social and political change. A group might become less politically and socially important but policy-makers can decide to continue its privileged position in the policy process despite the political rhetoric. Or the government could decide to change policy but, because of the existence of the community, be unable to control the implementation of that change. This has occurred to some extent with local government where the central government relies on local authorities to implement change (Marsh and Rhodes 1989). Marsh and Rhodes (1992d: 181) point to the difficulties of actually implementing new policies:

> the major cause of the Thatcher Government's failure to deliver more radical policy change, and more specifically greater change in policy outcomes, is the 'implementation gap'. The Government experienced major implementation problems. Some of these problems are common to all governments: conflicting objectives, insufficient information or limited resources. However, some problems

were clearly exacerbated by the Thatcher Government's approach to policy-making. In particular, their rejection of consultation and negotiation almost inevitably led to implementation problems, because those groups/agencies affected by the policy failed to co-operate, or comply with the administration of policy.

Hence, following Sabatier, Marsh and Rhodes (1992d) point out that the government's success or failure in regard to change depended on a number of factors such as: the nature and clarity of their objectives; their theory and information; the existence of appropriate tools; control over officials; the nature of the relevant policy network and socio-economic situation.

Political explanations fail to analyse the subtleties involved in changing policy and policy networks. They see the state as neutral and thus pay little attention to the constraints policy-makers face. They do not deal with the question of why certain policy networks are changed relatively easily and others are not; or even why politicians sometimes choose to challenge certain policy communities and not others.

The impact of post-industrialism and new right ideology on state/group relations depends on the extent to which the existing policy communities can be changed. Often this is very difficult either because the community has resources that the government needs, the groups are useful for implementation, or the existence of the community is outside government control (Smith 1989b). Life is much easier for policy-makers if they have an established policy community in which expectations are stable, and therefore often at the departmental level it is expedient to continue well-established policy communities (Jordan and Richardson 1982).

The implication of this approach is that the impact of social change on pressure groups will vary from policy sector to policy sector and from nation to nation. Where there is an issue network or looser network the effect of social and political change is likely to be greater than where there is a closed policy community. In a policy community, unless the government is prepared to face the political cost of challenging established interests, old relationships are likely to continue despite external pressure for change. Even if social and economic factors do challenge policy communities, they might still fail to achieve policy objectives because they also lose the mechanisms of implementing policy goals; they reduce their infrastructural power (Mann 1984; Marsh and Rhodes 1992d).

Consequently, more specific theories of change are required. As Anthony Giddens suggests, it is necessary to deconstruct theories of social change because they are mistaken about the accounts of change that are possible. For Giddens it is not possible to formulate 'theorems of structural causation which will explain the determination of social action in general' (Giddens 1986: 227). A general theory of social change is not possible. This is not to say that political and social change is unimportant. The impact of these changes is profound but it is mediated through existing structures. This means that change in networks and policy will depend on the nature of the networks, the policies and the degree to which the political actors have the resources necessary to achieve changes. It is necessary to seek explanations of why certain networks change and others do not. The following section will examine pluralist theories of change.

Pluralist explanations of change: Downs and the issue-attention cycle

Pluralist theorists, whilst accepting the existence of policy communities and subgovernments, recognise that policy networks and communities can change through new issues coming onto the political agenda. For instance, although Richardson and Jordan (1985: 83–4) see that access to a policy community is not completely open, they claim that it is increasingly difficult for a community to prevent access to policy arenas. It is their contention that the increasing number of pressure groups have the ability to '*force* issues onto the agenda' (original emphasis). They argue that groups can identify issues and through political action can ensure new issues are accepted onto the agenda. The role of groups might be supplemented by the media, political parties and government actions (Richardson and Jordan 1985: 89). Therefore, for Richardson and Jordan, it is political actions which lead to new issues being imposed on the agenda and so policy communities breaking down.

Hogwood (1987: 36–40) acknowledges the importance of political factors but also suggests that issues can be helped onto the agenda by non-political factors. Hogwood and Gunn (1984: 68) concede that the political pressures for change are likely to be more effective if: there is a crisis so the issue can no longer be ignored; a particular issue dramatises a larger issue; the issue has an emotional appeal; the issue has a wide impact; it 'raises questions about power and legitimacy in society'; and it is fashionable. They maintain that if one or more of these factors combine with the agenda-setters like interest groups, parties and the media, then the issue is more likely to get onto the agenda.

Yet, Hogwood alleges that there are less and less areas where new issues can arise and so policy succession, rather than a radical change in the agenda, is the more likely outcome (Hogwood 1987: 35; Peters and Hogwood 1980: 1–3). This in some ways corresponds to the view of Downs that there is an 'issue-attention cycle'. According to Downs (1972: 38) a problem, 'suddenly leaps into prominence, remains there for a short time, and then – though largely unresolved – gradually fades from the centre of public attention'.

Downs (1972: 41) sees issues going through five stages. First, the problem exists but is not discovered. In the second stage there is '[a]larmed discovery and euphoric enthusiasm' and political leaders attempt to take some action to solve the problem. Third, the costs of solving the problem are realised and this leads to the fourth stage, the gradual decline in public interest. Finally, the problem 'moves into a prolonged limbo'. Nevertheless, this is different to the pre-problem stage because at the height of enthusiasm new institutions are sometimes created which continue to give the problem attention even after the public interest has declined and so it may occasionally attract public attention again.

Lastly, Solesbury (1976: 383) asserts that:

> Issues finally evoke responses from government when they have become powerful enough to capture public resources, when they become the subject of political debate, when they come to dominate the media, when organisations grow around them conducting campaigns both for and against responses and they begin to be used to gain influence and money. They have then entered a field of competing political forces in which there are governments needing programmes, candidates needing election platforms, parties needing manifestos, executive agencies needing work, legislators needing specialisms, interest groups needing campaigns, newspapers needing editorial lines.

For Solesbury (1976: 382) issues and institutions are intertwined. New ideas are the result of 'the everyday concerns of institutions'. In their routines and practices they come across new issues to put forward. When these issues receive wide attention they reach the political agenda. Issues are more likely to receive attention if they 'can be clearly emphasised by particular occurrences' and are highly visible. Moreover, issues also need legitimacy – it has to be accepted that they are of 'proper concern to government' (Solesbury 1976: 384–7).

It would appear from the preceding summary that issues are likely to make it onto the agenda if there is a clear problem or crisis that is taken up by an institution, be it party, pressure group, or department, which then pressurises the government to accept it as a legitimate area of concern. Often these issues are only likely to receive public attention for a short time and are now less likely to be new issues. As a result no group is able to maintain a monopoly over a policy area for a long time because these factors will ensure new issues reach the agenda (Richardson and Jordan 1985: 13).

Although these explanations may prove useful in certain policy areas, there are several problems in applying them to areas where there is a closed policy community and stable agenda. For instance, in the case of British agriculture, the policy community mobilised issues off the agenda and prevented new groups and issues having access. The theories of agenda change outlined above have a number of failings. First, they continue to accept the pluralist assumption that if a problem is severe enough, and an interest group or institution makes enough noise, the issues will get onto the agenda. This view denies the ability of the policy community to control the issues which have access to the agenda and fails to recognise that the fixed agenda defines certain problems out of existence.

This leads to the second problem. The activities of pressure groups might lead to issues being raised on what Cobb and Elder (1983: 85) call the systemic agenda. These are issues subject to widespread general political debate. However this does not mean they become part of the institutional agenda; 'items explicitly up for the active and serious consideration of authoritative decision-makers'. In other words, that an issue receives media attention and public debate is not enough to threaten the policy community or change the agenda. It is only the first stage in a very long process which might not get any further – like the debate over unilateral disarmament.

Another possibility is that the actors within the policy community, recognising the pressure for action, will take this issue on board and make superficial changes in policy to protect the policy community and prevent new groups coming aboard. This appears to be the case with the agricultural policy community. Thus, the policy community can argue that there is no need for new groups to have access to the community because the existing one is taking account of all views. Policy communities will often follow strategies of damage limitation.

Third, the above explanation is too dependent on groups and institutions for explaining changes in policy. Pressure groups and other political factors are only part of the process of raising new issues and in many cases not even a very important part. If the agenda is to change, the government's perception of the problem has to change. Pressure groups are frequently unable to change the government's perception of central planks of policy.

It is necessary to look to external or structural elements which might cause the changes in perceptions and policy. These external factors can take several forms. They can be world events – like drought or war; economic events – depression or changes in commodity prices; institutional events – foreign governments or institutions can make demands on domestic government; human events – changes in world population or demands. Any of these factors or combination of factors can change the climate within which domestic governments operate without their control and not as a result of individual action. Therefore government perceptions change not because a pressure group demonstrates but because it is faced by a new set of problems. If pressure groups are unable to gain admittance to the policy community by definition they are unlikely to have much impact on the policy.

Fourth, the problem with Downs' theory is that it only really explains why issues are subject to public attention and not why they should be considered by the policy community. Often issues are dealt with by the policy community without becoming the subject of public attention. Public attention might be important if there is pluralism but it is not important in defining the agenda. Again, it might raise issues to the systemic agenda but only rarely will it define a new agenda – precisely for the reason that Downs gives; public attention cannot sustain the issue for long enough. A closed policy community will aim to keep issues from the public sphere but can still choose to ignore it even if there is widespread debate.

Finally, Solesbury's theory suggests that new issues derive from the operation of political institutions. If this is the case, the issues will be defined by the policy community that makes and implements policy and it will not raise issues that threaten its own existence. In their everyday routines institutions only look for issues within the confines of the existing agenda or otherwise they would threaten their own community. Consequently, they are unlikely to be the source of any radical change that would reduce their power or alter their composition.

This is not to say that the above theories offer nothing in the way of explanation. Pressure groups are important in raising issues but they are only one of the factors and, where there is a fixed agenda and a closed policy community, their influence is likely to be slight. They may provide a theory of agenda change in situations where the agenda and policy community are relatively open but not when they are closed. If there is a closed community the government and the legitimated interest groups have control over the interests that enter the policy community.

How do policy communities change?

The problem with the above explanation is that it fails to acknowledge the difficulties that pressure groups often face in gaining access to the political agenda. What we need to explain is how closed policy communities change if access is limited; if groups which can challenge the existing agenda and interests within the policy community are excluded.

Hogwood and Gunn (1984) focus on external factors in explaining agenda change and so it is clear that it is important to consider more than political resources. According to Dunleavy (1981: 3) as well as using political resources to win political battles: 'it may be important to win a rational argument, to undermine a policy paradigm intellectually to solve a technical problem, to demonstrate a shift in the intellectual technology of the policy area.' The problem is determining how the 'policy paradigm' is undermined when 'the bias of the system can be mobilised, recreated and reinforced in ways that are neither chosen nor the intended result of particular individual choices' (Lukes 1974: 21).

The concept of 'policy paradigm' provides a clue to how agenda change can be explained. There is a parallel between Lukes' concept of a fixed agenda and Kuhn's idea of a paradigm. Lukes' third dimension sees agendas as fixed by 'socially structured and culturally patterned behaviour' which prevents the conception of problems and concepts that might lead to the questioning of the agenda. Kuhn (1970: viii) defines paradigms as 'universally recognised scientific achievements that for a time provide model solutions for a community of practitioners'. By substituting scientific achievements with policy achievements and extending the community of practitioners to all those involved in policy-making the parallel between Lukes and Kuhn becomes apparent. With Lukes the ideological and cultural constraints provide solutions to problems and prevent new or radical solutions being considered. Likewise a paradigm provides model answers to problems and policy-makers or scientists do not see beyond these solutions.

Consequently, Kuhn's schema of paradigm change can help in understanding agenda change. Kuhn (1970: 35) proposes that in a period of normal science (when the agenda or paradigm is unquestioned) problems have known solutions. Problems that cannot be solved are rejected as being metaphysical, the concern of other disciplines or too problematic. A paradigm starts to be questioned when the problem that should be solved by the known rules and procedures is not. An anomaly is revealed which cannot be aligned to professional expectations (Kuhn 1970: 35). When the number of anomalies increase there is a crisis and this leads to an investigation of new solutions, commitments and rules for science – this is a scientific revolution (Kuhn 1970: 7 and 70).

Thus, we saw in the last chapter that policy communities not only have set problems but set solutions. They face difficulties when they are threatened either by new problems for which they have no available solutions or they have solutions which no longer work. In the 1930s, Britain was faced with a situation of long-term economic depression and unemployment which according to the dominant paradigm should only have lasted until equilibrium was re-established. However, the classical economics solution of cutting public expenditure and controlling the money supply did not solve the problem. This led to the questioning of the traditional agenda and the search for new alternatives and this allowed Keynesian economic theory to be taken seriously for the first time.

Despite questioning of the old agenda, it is not the case that a new agenda automatically arises. The crisis might not result in a period of pluralism. As Kuhn (1970: 156–9) warns, there is often resistance to the new paradigm from the old scientists. The established policy community, in other words, will try to prevent new issues being raised. The collapse of an agenda or policy community is not likely to be sudden. They have the resources and mechanisms to prevent new groups and ideas having access. Yet the possibility of change does exist. Change in a policy community is most likely to happen, in the first place, at the ideological level. The first threat will be to the sets of beliefs that protect the agenda by excluding from the community those who do not share the dominant beliefs. Ideology is the most difficult aspect of the policy community to maintain because there are no physical means for enforcing it on the population and there is often competition from alternative ideologies. The problem of maintaining ideology is even more arduous when the distinction between ideology and reality becomes too diverse. Saunders (1975: 55) maintains that: 'dominant ideologies reflect (to some extent) the life experiences of all classes and they only make sense because they are grounded in the form of life of the society as a whole.' When the political situation changes ideologies soon fail to reflect that 'form of life' and so they no longer make any sense. Hence they lose their legitimacy and so a space is created for new ideologies to try to become dominant.

Even so there is still no guarantee that a new ideology will gain predominance. The dominance of a new ideology can usually be achieved only through what Gramsci called a 'war of position'. Gramsci (1971: 235) argued that in modern society, 'civil society has become a very complex structure' and so the relationship between the state and civil society has become very intricate. If a full frontal attack was made on the state by dominated classes (a war of manoeuvre) it would fail because 'when the state trembled a sturdy structure of civil society was revealed'. The dominant moral and intellectual ideas of the society (the hegemony) would ensure that the existing order was protected despite the attack on the state.

So for Gramsci (1971: 57), 'A social group must already lead (i.e. be hegemonic) before winning governmental power.' To achieve this position the group has to engage in a protracted war of position. It must try to make its ideas dominant in society. It has to change the agenda so that its ideas become the dominant world-view. After accomplishing that task it can make a frontal attack on the state and gain state power.

Of course, this theory cannot be applied literally to specific policy arenas, but it can help in understanding how new ideas become dominant in a policy area. If a pressure group wants to change agricultural policy there is no point in just demonstrating against the government. If the government does not accept any of the group's arguments, the demonstrations will be ignored. If new problems arise it allows the pressure group to embark on a war of position to try to change perceptions and beliefs so that its ideas become more acceptable. Those within the policy community will try to maintain their dominance and so the possibility of a long campaign exists. However, once the pressure group has undermined the dominant ideology its ideas will become legitimate and it can then attack the policy community.

If we are properly to understand change, it is necessary to go back a stage. The important question is: Why do these new problems arise which lead to a questioning of the agenda and a war of position? This is where the previous theories do have a role because they focus on the external factors – economic, social and political – which can affect policy communities. However it is important to realise that these factors occur within the context of existing political arrangements and so the outcomes of external pressures are likely to be highly variable.

The potential factors likely to lead to threats to policy communities include:

1. *Changes in external relations.* Changes in the international order can have a major impact on domestic politics and the interests and policies that are seen as important. Two most obvious areas are defence policy and areas related to the EC. The end of the Cold War has changed the nature of the defence policy community. It has changed the relative power of various actors within the community and resulted in the community facing new threats and problems.

Likewise developments within the EC have created new threats and possibilities for various networks. In certain areas policy-making has shifted to the European stage and consequently networks have become multinational (see Peterson 1992a, 1992b). In some cases this gives the network greater autonomy from domestic political pressures but it also means that there will be more actors involved in the policy network. For instance, an EC policy network will generally involve national governments working through the Council of Ministers and the

Council of Permanent Representatives; it will involve at least one interest group from each country, and possibly more; it will include the respective directorate-general from the Commission which will have further contacts with national governments and Euro-level interest groups, and it could involve the European Parliament and certain advisory committees and the Economic and Social Committee. In this sense, the European Community corresponds much more closely to the US system of policy-making with many access points and a whole range of groups rather than the closed, elitist and executive-dominated British system. This, of course, makes the establishment of consensus much more difficult, and so the maintenance of a closed policy community less likely.

2. *Economic and social change*. The post-Fordist and post-industrialist theorists emphasise the importance of social and economic change. Whilst it is important not to overestimate the impact of such changes, it is clear that social and economic changes both affect the relative power of various groups and raise new problems and influence the attention that is paid to problems. One area where this has been important has been in the development of new social movements. Inglehart (1977, 1990) argues that increased prosperity has resulted in the development of post-material values. These values have led to the creation of groups interested in new issues such as peace, the environment, racial and sexual equality. Although these groups, initially at least, operated outside the traditional political institutions, through raising new issues they have confronted established networks with new problems. This is especially true in the area of the environment where general public concern has led to politicians having to take environmental issues seriously.

More recently, new social movements have achieved some access to established networks. Certain groups have established ties with existing mainstream parties and this is especially true of the environmental and peace movements. In Germany, the peace movement influenced SPD policy by establishing links and working with constituency parties (Rochon 1990: 113). In addition, through overlapping membership and building coalitions, groups have been successful in building alliances with traditional social movements and thus achieving access to established networks (Klandersman 1990: 134). Perhaps, even more importantly, as Rochan points out, 'contacts between the peace movement and West European governments have been more fruitful than one would expect':

> Among movement leaders, the relationship with government was frequently one of intensive consultation and negotiations. Most peace movement leaders maintained regular contact with political figures who were willing to help, who could provide information, or who might be persuaded to support the movement (Rochon 1990: 118).

In Britain, the Secretary of State for the Environment was prepared to consult environmental groups such as Friends of the Earth quite extensively when he was developing his environmental policies. So new social movements have raised new issues and increased their access to government, but the extent to which they have challenged existing policy communities is open to question.

3. *New problems*. One of the reasons why new social movements have had increased access to established policy networks is because governments have been confronted with new problems to which traditional interests have not had solutions. Mrs Thatcher became concerned with environmental issues when she was presented with scientific evidence that there was a hole in the ozone layer over the Antarctic. When governments are presented with new problems, which the traditional networks have difficulty in solving, the government might turn to alternative groups and so provide access for a new set of interests.

4. *New technology*. Changes in technology can create new problems. For example, the development of biotechnology and genetic engineering has presented networks with new issues and problems. Again this has allowed different groups access to the policy process. New technology has also allowed the detection of problems that were not previously visible.

5. *Internal divisions*. The development of new problems, new groups and new external pressures can lead to internal tensions within policy communities if the various interests within a community disagree over the options for dealing with new issues. In other words, the new issues can lead to a politicisation of a particular policy area and this leads to the breakdown of the consensus. If a consensus breaks down and a policy area becomes one of political controversy there is then a tendency for other groups and actors to become involved in the policy community. As a result the policy community is likely to be threatened or destroyed.

If controversy develops, highly resourced political actors like Presidents or Prime Ministers can become involved in the policy arena and thus remove decision-making from the community. There is also a likelihood that the interests within the policy community will attempt to draw in other actors that support the position thus diluting the community. In addition, controversy might lead to media attention which again can raise new issues and increase the pressure for various interests to become involved in the policy community.

6. *Despotic power*. In the last chapter it was argued that although groups could on occasions dominate policy communities, it was ultimately political actors that determined the rules of the game within a community. Consequently, political actors can use their despotic power to break up a policy community. They can decide that different or new groups will have access to a policy community; that new decision-making centres can be involved or that the issues a community deals with will be completely different. This demonstrates the importance of party in explaining change (Rhodes and Marsh 1992c). Party ideology can provide new ideological initiatives for challenging existing policy networks.

There are two ways in which this can occur. First, a political actor within the community can decide to break up the network, to give access to new actors or exclude a certain group of actors. For example, the Conservative government in

Britain has changed the nature of the Youth Training Policy network by changing the network from one where trade unions were involved on an equal basis to employers to one where they are almost completely excluded (Marsh 1992b). In education policy, the Secretary of State for Education, Kenneth Clarke, was prepared to impose changes on education without consultation with teachers. The problem with such a strategy is that the costs can be very high. The result can be a substantial loss in infrastructural power if the political actor loses the cooperation of groups who are necessary for the implementation of policy. But if politicians are prepared to bear the costs then they can change a community.

However, the costs are likely to be lower if it is a political actor outside the community that can change the policy community. In Britain and the United States, the Prime Minister and the President have the authority to break up existing policy communities. They can force new issues onto the agenda, they can take decisions themselves, they can give access to different groups, or they can change the institution which is responsible for making a decision. The cost could still be great because high-level executive involvement can make a policy area controversial and conflictual, and the chief executive still needs to retain support within and outside of government. A political colleague may not be very happy about losing his/her policy community. But again, if the President or Prime Minister is prepared to bear the costs this may be a very effective way of achieving policy change. Perhaps the clearest example of this is President Reagan's sacking of all air traffic controllers on strike in order to break the union. The costs were high financially, in terms of short-term air traffic control, and politically, but it was a cost the President was prepared to bear. If the chief executive can cope with the costs he or she can effectively change policy communities. However, there is clearly a political and physical limit to how often this can be done. Few leaders are going to want to challenge all policy communities and are likely to choose their targets carefully.

7. *Challenges between networks*. Frequently there are horizontal challenges to policy networks from other networks. Often conflicts occur over territory as different communities contest responsibility for particular policy areas. These disagreements threaten policy communities because they can make a policy area political and so undermine the consensus. In certain circumstances horizontal conflicts can result in a change in the decision-maker. In Britain there are frequent territorial battles. The agricultural policy community centred around the Ministry of Agriculture and the environmental policy community centred around the Department of the Environment have clashed over issues of land use and environmental protection concerning agricultural land (Lowe *et al.* 1986).

8. *Challenges within communities*. It is sometimes the case that interests within a policy community accept the agenda/consensus because they are in a subordinate position. They either accept the agenda or they are excluded from the policy community. However, external changes – shifts in economic resources, the increased salience of particular issues – can change the relative power of

members of policy communities. If this occurs groups which were once subordinate can develop the ability to change the agenda and change the relationships within the community.

There are great difficulties with general theories of change in relation to explaining changes in policy communities. Undoubtedly, policy communities change because of social, economic and political developments but how this change is going to affect the community often depends on the nature of that community. Certain policy communities, because they are very closed, highly resourced or have a very strong consensus, might have the ability to withstand a great deal of pressure to change. Any attempt to change a community involves a high degree of political risk and it is frequently the case that political actors are not prepared to bear the costs. It is often easier for them to retain the community because it makes administration easier. By destroying a community, state actors have to create new mechanisms for the development and implementation of policy.
    However, as we will see in this book, change does occur but the causes of change are many and complex. They can be internal or external, political or economic, or they can be a combination of many. Moreover, policy communities are well-established institutions. They have mechanisms for dealing with external threats. They can directly resist change or they can coopt certain groups or issues. It is unlikely that change occurs immediately. There will be a war of position as the established community attempts to deal with the external threats either by assimilating or diverting them. There does come a point when new groups or issues enter policy communities and so the communities are forced to change, or more dramatically, political actors force changes by giving access to new groups or by establishing new decision-making centres.

Conclusion

The notion of a policy network – particularly when concerned with the policy community end of the continuum – is generally a static concept. There has been little discussion of how and why policy communities change. They are seen as organisations that prevent change through exclusion. They exist to prevent threats to the interests of the included actors. Nevertheless, it is apparent that policy communities do change and it is therefore necessary to develop a theory of change. Explanations of change hitherto have either tended to be very general or highly voluntaristic. The general theories see change occurring because of macro-level developments in society and/or the economy. Such theories tend to be highly teleological and fail to specify the mechanisms through which change occurs.
    The voluntaristic theories tend to see change occurring as a result of either the will of political actors or of pressure groups. They overestimate the ease with

which political actors can change policy or the ease with which pressure groups can gain access to the political arena. If groups do change policy communities it is often because of wider changes that have occurred.

This chapter has not denied the importance of social, economic and political factors in changing policy communities. Indeed it has demonstrated that these factors are vital in understanding change. Nevertheless, it has pointed out the need to be specific in understanding the factors that cause change. These can be many and varied. Policy communities are subject to both internal, external and horizontal pressures. Moreover the ability of a community to withstand these pressures depends greatly on the nature of the community. A policy community can survive a great deal of pressure for change if it contains a very few actors with a strong consensus and has a high degree of control over the implementation process. If there are a number of actors with a weaker consensus then external pressure can create internal tensions and this can lead to change within the community. If a community contains more than one actor with political authority then the ability of the community to withstand external threats is likely to be less. In this situation conflict can develop between the decision-making institutions and this leads to conflict over territory, the politicisation of the issue area and the inclusion of an increasing number of groups. Consequently the community is destroyed.

In accounting for change, it is essential to examine the pressure that a community faces in terms of external political pressure, or social and economic changes, and how these forces affect the relative power of groups. We then have to examine the reaction of the policy community to those pressures. Is it able to withstand them through winning a war of position? Does it have the ability to coopt new issues and groups? Will external pressures result in internal conflict which threatens the community? The form and degree of change is greatly affected by the nature of the community and the relationships within it. The remainder of the book is concerned with examining the development and nature of policy networks. It will examine how they change and the impact they have on policy outcomes and state autonomy.

Part II
Case studies

/ *Chapter 5*

AGRICULTURAL POLICY:
The Paradigm Policy Community

In both Britain and the United States, agricultural policy is seen as the paradigm case of a closed policy community, or in the American arena, an iron triangle. In each country farming organisations have established institutionalised relations with the agricultural policy-makers and policy has been characterised by a high level of agricultural subsidy. However, it has been suggested that the network in the United States has, over the past ten years or so, disintegrated into an issue network (Browne 1988). In Britain, whilst the policy community has been subject to external threats and there have been significant changes in policy; the policy community is basically intact. The US case suggests that even the paradigm policy community is not as closed as has been suggested and thus supports Jordan's (1981) argument that closed networks can be opened by persistent pressure groups. However, this chapter will demonstrate that there were fundamental differences between the British and US agricultural networks. Although the US policy network was relatively closed, it was not as well integrated as the British agricultural policy community. The chapter will begin by examining the development of the British agricultural policy community.

The British agricultural policy community

According to the criteria outlined in Chapter 3, the agricultural policy community is a highly integrated community. It has a very restricted membership with shared interests; it has limited horizontal articulation being largely isolated from other networks; and although it lacks vertical interdependence, the absence of sub-central administrative units results in resources being distributed between the Ministry of Agriculture, which makes and implements policy, and the National Farmers' Union (NFU), which can provide information, cooperation and assistance in implementation.

The agricultural community also has a number of specific features. It has two important internal structures – the ideological and the institutional. The ideological structure is the dominant set of beliefs which are shared by members of the agricultural policy community. All those involved in agricultural policy-making between 1945 and the late 1970s (and to a large extent in the 1980s) held a common view of the goals of agricultural policy. Governments, officials, ministers of agriculture and NFU representatives believed that the state should intervene in agriculture, provide price support and increase production. Therefore, the issue faced by those within the agricultural community was not whether prices and production should be increased but by how much they should be increased. Groups or individuals who raised questions about subsidies or production were not given access to the policy-making process. For example, in 1951 Stanley Evans was sacked as Junior Minister in the Ministry of Food for questioning the level of agricultural subsidies (Smith, 1990a).

The institutional structures are the second means of excluding unwelcome groups from the agricultural policy community. There are four important institutional structures. First, is the Ministry of Agriculture, Fisheries and Food (MAFF). MAFF provides the community with a single decision-making centre with the authority to make agricultural policy. It has an interest in maintaining good relations with the farmers and in increasing agricultural expenditure. Agricultural policy is made in the Agricultural Commodities Division. Within this division, EC I and EC II set the broad lines of agricultural policy. They ensure that it is in line with European policy and are responsible, with the Economics and Statistics Division, for the organisation of the Annual Review. The development of detailed policy, and the provision of information for the Annual Review, and to the Minister, is carried out within the individual commodity sections. In developing policy these committees have frequent contact with the NFU. In fact, the union has a shadow commodity structure which means close and long-term contacts develop between, for example, the cereal sections within the Ministry and the NFU's cereals committee.

Second, until Britain joined the European Community (EC), the Annual Review surveyed the state of agriculture and determined agricultural prices for the coming year. It gave the farmers a statutory right to consultation and excluded other groups from the process. Moreover the goal of the Annual Review machinery was to see the extent to which prices should increase. It therefore lacked a mechanism for changing agricultural policy or creating new goals (Smith 1989a). After joining the EC, the Annual Review was a statistical exercise which provided the basis for Britain's negotiations in Europe until it was abolished in 1992. Third, there are 'the rules of the game' (Saunders 1975) which determined how groups should act in order to obtain access to the community. They are, of course, determined by the policy community (Rhodes 1988).

Latterly, a fourth institutional structure has been created with Britain's membership of the EC. It covers the Council of Agricultural Ministers and Directorate General (DG) VI of the Commission. In the EC agricultural policy is developed by DG VI which has very close contacts with national and European farmers' organisations. It also has very poor relations with non-farm groups such as consumers and environmental groups. According to one British MEP, 'DG VI sees its role as that of a farm support organisation' (Smith 1990a). Once DG VI makes proposals on agricultural prices the final decision-making body is the Council of Agricultural Ministers. It is composed of the agricultural ministers from the twelve member states all of whom have close relations with their national farm organisations and see it as their role to win the best possible deal for their own farmers. This situation partly accounts for the rapid rise in the cost of the Common Agricultural Policy in the 1970s and early 1980s.

A second feature of the agricultural policy community is that it has an inner and outer circle – a primary and secondary community. The primary community involves groups which are intimately involved in policy-making on a day-to-day basis whilst the secondary community includes groups that only have access to the department when an issue which specifically affects them is being considered. For example, at the Annual Review the NFU would be involved in all stages of the Review including detailed bargaining over prices, whilst the Country Landowners' Association (CLA) and the National Union of Agricultural and Allied Workers only had the occasional meeting to give their views on the Review. So the NFU is in the primary community; groups like the CLA and the food processors are in the secondary community. Lastly, there are excluded non-community groups like the Friends of the Earth who have little contact with the Ministry of Agriculture (Smith 1989b).

The existence of this two-track community might explain some of Jordan's (1981) confusion. Undoubtedly, there are many groups involved in the agricultural policy process but few have access to the primary community. Access to the secondary community often involves consultation but little else. When it does involve more, the groups are often acting under licence from the primary community. They have to follow the rules of the game set by the primary community and share their values on the direction of agricultural policy. So although the Poultry Farmers' Association may represent chicken farmers to the Ministry of Agriculture, they do so within a framework set by MAFF and the NFU, and are regarded as a responsible group. The primary community knows that these groups will not question the established agricultural agenda and if they did they would be ejected for being too extreme.

Another important question is how the community dealt with groups which were affected by agricultural policy but did little to influence its outcome. In other words, how did the community deal with the ordinary consumer rather than organised consumer or environmental groups? The consumer was excluded by the policy community which allowed access only to groups which the community saw as acceptable. As Grant (1983) highlighted, the perimeter fences around the agricultural policy community have been particularly high and groups or individuals which lacked official sanction or technical knowledge were excluded. More important, the community was able to ensure the absence of any demand for entry into the agricultural policy community through depoliticising agricultural policy. By excluding groups which disagreed with agricultural policy, the community was able to say that there was a consensus on agricultural policy. Consequently, the consensus demonstrated that there was only one possible agricultural policy and so there was no need for consumer representation as the community ensured that agricultural policy was in their interest (Smith 1988). In this way, issues which might have politicised agricultural policy – like land nationalisation – were excluded from the political agenda because of fear that they would have broken up the community (Smith 1989c).

Wilson (1977) rejects the claim that the close relationship between the Ministry and the farmers destroyed pluralism. He maintains that pluralism was retained by interdepartmental conflict and oversight of the agricultural policy process by various departments. Undoubtedly, the relationship between a closed community and other departments is interesting, especially in the case of the Treasury's relationship to the Ministry of Agriculture. The Treasury was in a position to question (and reduce) the cost of agricultural policy, and its role is to be critical of projects especially when they involve increases in agricultural expenditure (Heclo and Wildavsky 1974). Indeed Brittan (1964: 38) suggests that the Treasury's guiding philosophy is one of 'suspicion that the projects of other departments will cost much more than appears at first sight'. Certainly until entry to the EC the Treasury was closely involved in various stages of the Annual Review. When the Ministry of Agriculture's officials were negotiating with the farmers' union they could not accept a NFU proposal without consulting the Treasury (HC 254 1958: 115–17 and 123). Although the Chancellor did not place an upper limit on the money that would be available (HC 77 1962: 14), the final price determinations were very often the result of a mutual process of negotiations between the Treasury and the Ministry of Agriculture (HC 254 1958: 126).

The critical role of the Treasury, and the fact that it did have a formal input into the policy process, suggests that there was 'Whitehall pluralism'. However, there are a number of reasons for questioning such a conclusion. The Treasury accepted the shared values that operated within the policy community. The Treasury did not question the view that agricultural production should be increased and that government money should be used to achieve this goal. Indeed it was the Treasury which initiated the high production and high support agenda in 1945–7 as a means of saving dollars and improving the balance of payments, and in the 1950s and 1960s the Treasury actively supported the agenda by providing the finance to increase farm prices. In 1951 and 1952 the Treasury agreed to a higher price award for farmers than several Cabinet Ministers wanted (CAB 128/19; CAB 124/24), while in 1953 the Chancellor declared that he wanted to see agriculture supported in order that more food be produced at home (*The Times* 11 December 1953). This support was the basis of government agricultural policy up to the 1980s and so obviously had Treasury approval.

Although the Treasury wanted to contain the costs of agricultural policy and did press for the 'lowest possible payment' (Wilson 1974: 92), it did not threaten or question the high production and high support policy. These aims were supported by the Treasury. All the Treasury wanted, according to Selwyn Lloyd, the Chancellor in 1961, was exchequer payments brought down to the lowest possible level consistent with the government's aims (*The Times* 25 January 1961). The Treasury wanted what the Treasury always wanted, a policy at the lowest possible cost. It was not demanding an alternative policy.

Even if the Treasury wanted to limit payments to farmers it was constrained in what it could do. A 1958 Select Committee reported that, although there were limits on particular items of agricultural expenditure, 'there was no real control of expenditure' (HC 254 1958: x). Usually, the level of expenditure depended on world prices which the Treasury could not influence. In addition, the 1957 Agriculture Act limited the degree to which the Treasury could reduce support prices; they were not allowed to fall below 97 per cent of the previous year's guarantees.

Once Britain joined the EC, Treasury control over agricultural expenditure was almost eliminated because price increases are determined by the Council of Agricultural Ministers. The Treasury could insist that the Minister hold a certain line on what price increase there should be but if he was in a minority of one there was very little he could do. Barnett (1982) claims that when John Silkin was Minister of Agriculture, from 1976–9, he would ring in the middle of the night asking for authority to go above the agreed figure knowing at that time there was very little chance that it would be refused.

There is little doubt that the agricultural policy community was a very closed policy community which was protected by a widely accepted ideology and excluded many other groups from the policy process. This position was further facilitated by the fact that within and outside government the goals of the community went largely unquestioned. The depoliticisation of agricultural policy created a consensus which excluded certain issues from the policy process.

Why did various governments accept the continuation of this closed policy community? The existence of a closed policy community with limited participants has a number of advantages for government. It can increase state autonomy by creating the capabilities for the state to intervene in new policy areas (Smith 1989d). Once the state decided it was going to have an agricultural policy it was much easier to achieve with the cooperation of the farmers. Furthermore, in developing an agricultural policy it was easier to deal with one group rather than many. The process of establishing close relations with a single group simplifies the policy-making process by limiting demands and making outcomes more predictable (Jordan and Richardson, 1982). The NFU performed a useful task for the government by aggregating the demands of farmers from many different commodity sectors. The NFU has been very successful at accommodating the conflicts between the various branches of farming in order to create a single 'farmers' view'. Incorporation, as Offe (1981) has pointed out, is a means of limiting demands. In order to retain their position the farmers had to act 'responsibly'. As a result they have been prevented from making excessive demands and have consequently limited their political activity.

In addition, the Ministry could (and does) use the NFU to sell agricultural policy to farmers. An NFU official gave a useful insight into the process. If the farmers wanted a certain grant, say £100, the County Secretaries of the NFU would go to meet civil servants, and even the Minister. The Department would say how they understood the farmers' position but times were hard and the Treasury would not give the money so £50 was the maximum available. The County Secretaries, feeling very pleased with having met the Minister, would go back to try to convince the farmers how well they had done and how pleased their members should be. Consequently, it would be the County Secretaries who were blamed for the smaller grants rather than the Ministry.

The creation of a closed policy community also has more particular advantages for the Ministry of Agriculture. In the 1930s, agricultural policy-making was very pluralistic and state intervention was limited because the main concerns in agricultural policy were export markets, cheap raw materials and foreign relations. The Ministry of Agriculture was limited in what it could do and the demands of the farmers were often ignored. By establishing close relations with the farmers, the Ministry increased its political resources *vis-à-vis* other departments. Through containing agricultural policy within a policy community it increased its autonomy in agricultural policy-making by excluding non-farm interests. The chapter will now examine how this policy community was established.

The creation and maintenance of the
agricultural policy community

The fact that the agricultural policy community has so many advantages for the government in general, and the Ministry of Agriculture in particular, suggests that the creation of the closed community was not, as Self and Storing (1962) and Wilson (1977) seem to suggest, due to the power of the farmers. Rather, it resulted from a number of external factors which changed the government's perceptions of agriculture and the goals of its agricultural policy. Until the 1930s all governments were opposed to agricultural support (Cmd 2581). Even as late as 1938 the official line from the Ministry of Agriculture was that:

> Although it has been the policy of the Government to take steps to secure a reasonable return to the efficient producer whilst *maintaining* the present level of production, it would be a very different thing to employ the policy of guaranteed prices to secure a continuous expansion of production (MAF 53/ 134) (original emphasis).

During this period the NFU did not have privileged access to government. What they did achieve was through the normal lobbying techniques of a non-incorporated pressure group. They sent deputations to the Ministry of Agriculture; they lobbied MPs; they even held mass demonstrations; and threatened to stand against Conservative candidates in by-elections. During the 1930s the farmers were only one of the players in the agricultural arena and often a minor one. Other agricultural organisations like the CLA, the Central Chamber of Agriculture, the National Union of Agricultural Workers (NUAW), and the Royal Agricultural Society all had some access to government. More important, agricultural policy was largely dominated by industrial and foreign policy interests. Britain was, at this time, an exporting manufacturing nation which had a large empire (CAB 27/619). Baldwin, in a letter to the NFU, warned that Britain was predominantly an industrial society and, 'Industrial prosperity must always be an essential foundation for the well-being of home agriculture' (MAF 53/134). It was generally industrial and Foreign Office interests which were instrumental in ensuring that Britain did not support agriculture, the government feared that such support would damage overseas relations and trade.

What factors led to the creation of a closed policy community where the farmers obtained a privileged role in the policy-making process and other interests were largely excluded? The severity of the agricultural depression in the late 1920s and early 1930s forced the government to take certain actions. The depression demonstrated that the *laissez-faire* paradigm no longer worked. Agriculture's problems of falling prices, underproduction, poor quality and a lack of investment would not be solved if agriculture was left to the market and, as a result, the government's perceptions of its role in relation to agriculture changed.

An even more important factor was the fear of war with Germany. The government did not want a repetition of 1914 when British agriculture was unprepared for war. Therefore, in 1936 an interdepartmental committee suggested: the establishment of land fertility committees; the extension of drainage grants; the raising of deficiency payments; grants for lime and slag; and a campaign against animal disease (MAF 53/108). By 1937 the Minister of Agriculture wanted a 10 per cent increase in wheat production and he accepted the need to introduce a price insurance scheme for wheat and oats. The 1937 Agriculture Act provided price insurance for sheep, barley and oats, and this represented a significant change in agricultural policy.

At the same time there were important changes occurring in the NFU. The Union made a concerted effort to build up its membership, to become the sole farming organisation and to act responsibly. When the government increasingly began to intervene in agriculture it was the NFU that it looked to for advice and support. The relationship between the farmers and the Ministry of Agriculture became increasingly institutionalised. By 1939 the Ministry and the NFU were meeting weekly in order to discuss means of supporting agriculture and increasing agricultural production.

It took the events during and immediately after the Second World War to firmly establish the policy community and the unquestioned agenda that agriculture should be supported and production increased. During the war the government had no choice but to increase food production. In order to achieve this goal the government promised farmers high prices (*NFU Record* October 1939), and it incorporated them into the decision-making process. This arrangement worked for the first two years of the war. However, between 1942 and 1944 there were continual conflicts between the farmers, supported by the Ministry of Agriculture, and the government, in particular the Treasury, over the prices the farmers should receive (CAB 71/6).

The requirements of the war placed the farmers in a strong position. The government could not afford to lose their confidence. To solve the problem over price fixing the government announced that it would set up 'a better machinery for fixing prices' (HC Deb 397: c.726). Hence the Annual Review was established where the Ministry of Agriculture and the NFU would each year review the conditions of agriculture and the goals of agricultural policy. Subsequently, the Ministry would determine what price increase the farmers would receive (Smith 1989a). This arrangement established the institutional basis of the policy community. Agricultural policy-making was effectively removed from government and placed in the hands of the Ministry of Agriculture and the NFU who, in the 1947 Agriculture Act, were guaranteed consultation. This effectively excluded all other agricultural groups from the process.

Initially, the government did not intend the high level of expenditure and the production patterns established during the war to continue once the conflict ended (MAF 53/171; CAB 127/170). However, a world shortage of food and a British shortage of dollars forced the government to maintain its policy of high support and high production (Cmd 6879 1946: 9; Cmd 7072 1947: 3). In order to avoid a shortage of grain and to save dollars, the government had no choice but to abandon its commitment to livestock expansion (MAF 53/182).

This decision had a number of important consequences for the agricultural policy community. The programme was initiated by the Treasury and not the Ministry of Agriculture. Therefore, the Treasury was prepared to provide the funds necessary for expansion, and it accepted the NFU/Ministry view of the goals of agricultural policy. Because there was no disagreement about the need for agricultural policy, farmers and the Ministry could be left to develop agricultural policy without the representation of other interests. As a result, the powerful and important position of the farmers continued even though the war ended and so they further institutionalised their relationship with the Ministry. Finally, it established that increasing agricultural production was essential for the economic well-being of the country and thus was an unquestionable goal. Tom Williams promised that:

Expansion of net output by £100 million is not put forward as a temporary necessity. The Government is signifying permanency by substantially raising the price of livestock and livestock products up to 1950–52 (*NFU Record* September 1947).

In this way, the policies which were established during the war were strengthened in the post-war period. It was accepted that the farmers would have a privileged position in policy-making, and that they would receive a high level of state subsidy in order substantially to increase production. As a Treasury official informed a MAFF official:

> we are now in the position where agriculture will be under fire for not expanding enough. . . . In these circumstances the time may come when certain advances which have hitherto been regarded as visionary may become practical politics (CAB 124/572).

Britain's economic position improved considerably in the 1950s but the agricultural agenda did not change. The ideology of expansion became widely accepted within government, opposition and public. In June 1952 Tom Williams (HC Deb 498: cc. 2210–14), by then the opposition spokesman on agriculture, stated that, 'On the question of future production policy there can be no two opinions about the need for maximum production, for . . . the days of cheap abundant supplies seem to be gone.' This more or less remained the line of all governments during the 1960s and 1970s. For example, the 1961 Annual Review White Paper (Cmnd 1311 1961) proclaimed that, 'the objective of production remains the most that can be produced economically and efficiently with the market requirements, steadily increasing technical efficiency and diminishing unit costs.'

In addition to the productionist ideology, the policy community was protected by its institutional structure which enabled the farmers and the Ministry of Agriculture to exclude groups which could raise new issues. The Ministry of Agriculture was in a position to fight for the farmers' interests in the Cabinet. Parliament had almost no input into the agricultural price procedure, only formally approving the prices after they had been agreed (HC 138 1969: 4). Other agricultural interest groups, like the CLA and the NUAW, also had little input into the Annual Review. The CLA felt that the Annual Review was confined to the consideration of the farmers' interests and made no attempt to discover 'whether the landlord is receiving an adequate return on his capital' (HC 137 1969: 315–16). Non-agricultural interests were in an even more difficult position. The Ministry admitted that on the occasion of the Annual Review, 'We do not specifically consult consumer associations' (HC 137 1969: 225). Environmental concerns were even further from the mind of policy-makers. In MAFF the environmental aspects of agriculture were not examined because there was no environmental lobby and the environmental consequences of intensive agriculture were not immediately apparent. On the whole farmers were seen as the custodians of the countryside and environmental groups have had great difficulty in achieving access to MAFF (Lowe *et al.* 1986: 124).

When economic conditions changed, inertia was maintained by the closed policy community which ensured that policy was made within a small group who had shared values on the goals of agricultural policy. There were no means by which alternatives could enter the policy process. The ideology of the policy-makers was such that they did not consider other options and groups which might have suggested alternatives were excluded. However, in the 1970s, and particularly the 1980s, the agricultural policy community has been subject to increasing challenge. In the next section I will examine why these challenges have occurred and what impact they have had on the policy community.

Challenges to the agricultural policy community

From the mid-1970s at least there has been increased questioning of the agricultural policy that Britain has followed after joining the EC. In 1976 the Conservative MP Richard Body questioned the need to increase agricultural production further (*The Times*, 10 January 1976) and in 1978 a Labour MP moved a motion in the Commons which called for: 'the abolition of support prices, levies and taxes upon third countries, food taxes and intervention' (HC Deb 947: c.843).

In the 1980s this criticism has been even more intense. In 1982 Richard Body hit the headlines by producing a sustained criticism of the Common Agricultural Policy (CAP) and raised the issues of the cost of the policy and the level of production, which had been ignored since the 1930s (see Body, 1982 and 1984). He was joined by a diverse range of critics. The 1987 Conservative Party manifesto called for a 'radical overhaul of the CAP' (Conservative Party, 1987) and the British governments' line on CAP has been that prices should be reduced in order to reduce production and so bring the cost of CAP within strict limits. Labour MEPs have proposed that price support should only be used in the last resort and 'for the rest, prices should be allowed to find the level at which supply and demand come into balance' (HL 237 1984/85: 95).

In addition, consumers, food production companies, environmentalists and even farmers have recognised the need for change in agricultural policy. Consumer groups have questioned whether the high prices of the CAP should be paid 'regardless of need or efficiency' (Consumers in the European Community Group 1984: 11). Environmentalists have become increasingly concerned about the effect of increased production on the countryside. Even the European Commission has called for substantial reductions in prices, and tried to introduce measures to limit the level of production (Com (85) 333).

How is it that the policy community which was so successful after the war has been unable to keep these issues off the agenda in the 1980s? One major factor is that excluded groups have become more active and more involved in the agricultural arena. Both environmental and consumer groups have expanded their membership and become more active in their lobbying activity which has been helped by increased media attention. Cox *et al.* (1986) claim that the environmental policy community is very large and has mushroomed in the last twenty years and this, they suggest, 'has been the most serious challenge to the farmers in the last twenty years'.

However, it is important not to over-emphasize the role of groups in forcing change on agricultural policy. Any changes that have occurred have been the result of external pressures on the CAP. Three major structural pressures have provided the main motors of change within the EC. They are: the level of over-production; the cost of CAP; and the international agricultural situation. By 1984 most of the major products were in surplus (HL 153 1983/84: vi) and by 1987 the stores contained 1⅓ million tonnes of butter, 1 million tonnes of skimmed milk powder, 600,000 tonnes of milk and between 13 and 14 million tonnes of grain (BBC 1987). Over-production has led to a second problem, cost. By 1986 the Community was, on paper, bankrupt as the cost of the CAP had increased faster than the increase in the Community's resources and took up to 75 per cent of the EC budget (BBC 1986a). Third, there has been pressure from the United States, Australia, New Zealand and many Third World countries for the EC to reduce its production and, in particular, its export subsidies. The EC has moved from a net importer to become the largest agricultural exporter in the world. Most of these exports occur with the aid of export subsidies which means that the EC undercuts the markets of the traditional exporters (Wilkinson 1987). Recently, the United States has been using GATT and the threat of trade wars to force the EC to reduce the level of its export subsides with the goal of abolishing all such subsidies within ten years.

With increasing political pressures for change from environmental groups and consumers, and severe economic crises in the period after 1983, there was increasing recognition that major changes in the policy were necessary. As the House of Lords Select Committee on the European Communities recognised (HL 153 1983/84: v):

> The financial crisis of the community focuses attention on the Common Agricultural Policy in a way that has not happened before. . . . With the Community fast running out of money the need for financial reform in the operation of the CAP becomes imperative.

Agricultural Ministers of all European countries have realised the necessity to reduce costs (*The Times* 19 March 1984). The British government has called for policy change on three fronts. First, the level of production has to be reduced as a previous Minister of Agriculture, Michael Jopling acknowledged, 'we cannot go on and on producing more and more food which we can neither eat nor sell' (BBC 1986b). Second, the government is prepared to make it clear to farmers that 'the era of open ended guarantee prices is at an end' (HL 82-II 1982/83: 7). Third, in 1984 Mrs Thatcher ordered a review of policies on countryside protection with the intention of replacing, 'the policy of expanding food production – which has dominated the British countryside for forty years – with one that emphasises conservation of the countryside' (Lean 1984).

Perhaps most striking is the change of attitude within the European Commission. It has now recognised the need to reduce farm spending, cut the level of production and reform the CAP. In the Commission's paper, *Perspectives for the Common Agricultural Policy* (Com (85) 333), it acknowledged the constraints of market realities, financial limits and the international situation. It asserted the requirement to give 'market price a greater role in supply and demand'; to pay more attention to the 'demands of the consumer . . . [and] to the requirements of the food industry' and consider 'the role of the agriculture as the protector of the environment' (Com (85) 333: ii–vii).

Since 1983 the pressures to reform agricultural policy have become immense. There was widespread recognition of the problems both within and outside government. There was a growing consensus on the changes that needed to be made. The EC's financial position has meant that it had little choice but to change and the people who apparently could force change, the government and the Commission, accepted the need for reform. How then did the agricultural policy community respond to these pressures and to what extent has it survived the demands for change?

The response of the agricultural policy community

From the British perspective in the post-EC period, the agricultural policy community contained the NFU, the Ministry of Agriculture, the Council of Agricultural Minister and DG VI. Each of these responded to the pressures for change in different ways.

The NFU has followed a strategy of damage limitation by accepting the need for certain changes within agricultural policy without destroying the policy community nor the privileged position of the farmers. Initially the position of the farmers was directly to confront the demand for change by rejecting proposals and using the old arguments: that Britain needed to maintain production for economic reasons; farmers' incomes had to be protected to conserve the countryside; and the CAP had largely resulted in benefits to Britain. In the early 1980s, according to an NFU official, individuals within the union realised that if they maintained this position they would lose the argument because their position was so weak. So the NFU adopted a new approach. The leadership recognised that it had to move away from its productionist position. In order to manage the policy change the NFU ensured that it was involved in the initial stage of the development of agricultural policy. As an ex-President of the NFU admitted:

> we were trying to lead farmers and show that we recognised the need for change and to show that farmers are realistic. We felt that we would have less say in the future if we did not make new proposals for agriculture.

The new emphasis of policy was stated in a 1984 policy document:

> For several decades the expansion of domestic production has been a central feature of British agricultural policy. But increasing output throughout the European Community has made it harder to find commercial outlets and the need to dispose of surpluses of some commodities has put a heavy cost on the Community budget. The pressure to control spending calls for a *reappraisal of the expansionist approach* (emphasis added) (NFU 1984).

The NFU has acknowledged that prices and production have to be reduced and its goal is to achieve these reductions in a way that is least harmful to the farmers. In addition, in reaction to the pressures of environmental groups, the NFU has created front organisations in order to produce environmental material with an agricultural feel. It has helped create groups such as the Farming Wildlife Advisory Group, Rural Voice and the Agricultural Advisory Service. The union has also argued that if farmers are to protect the countryside they need to receive state support and so it has played a role in developing schemes which pay farmers to use environmentally sound methods. Such schemes have enabled many farmers to escape the chemical treadmill and to survive cuts in support prices. If all else fails, the NFU has advised farmers that when there is a great deal of pressure for change they should sit tight. The NFU has realised that the environmental lobby is not strong or rich enough to concentrate on more than one area and that the media will only sustain interest in a particular issue or area for a very short period. Therefore, if farmers withstand the pressure, in a short time a new issue will arise and the spotlight will move. What the NFU has done is to take the initiative to a certain degree in the environmental and price areas. This eliminates the need to allow new groups into the policy community.

The response of the Ministry of Agriculture has been in some senses similar to the farmers. It has had to accept demands for change, particularly in a government committed to reducing subsidies and limiting the cost of the CAP. The British government has been at the forefront of the European Community in pressing for reforms in the EC. The Minister of Agriculture has called for a price freeze or even price cuts for products in surplus (HL 112 1984/85) and at the Copenhagen Summit in December 1987, Mrs Thatcher refused to allow an increase in the EC budget unless agreement could be reached on reducing agricultural prices and production (*The Observer* 6 December 1987). More recently, the British government strived to persuade the Council of Ministers to accept a limit of 155 million tonnes for the amount of cereals that would receive support and opposed using set-aside as a means of avoiding these limits (*The Times* 8 January 1988).

To a large extent the policy community has managed to preserve its exclusive nature because of these tactics. The Ministry of Agriculture has not opened itself to environmental and consumer interests. On the environment the Ministry is still seen as being 'complacent and narrow in its approach with an overriding concern for the intensification of farming' (HL 247 1983/84: 2). There are many loopholes in the Wildlife and Countryside Act which either allow farmers to ignore the legislation or to receive large sums for participating (Lowe *et al.* 1986). The MAFF's overall strategy on the environmental issue has involved the acceptance of minor changes at the margins. Certain uneconomic farmers can be encouraged to try new forms of production but, for the majority of farmers, the continuation of intensive production is inevitable. High production should continue because the goal of agricultural policy continues to be self-sufficiency within the EC. As Michael Jopling said (HL 107 1985/86: 5–6): 'it is prudent in community terms in the market always to be thinking of producing a modest surplus because we all know the volatility of agricultural productivity.'

One consumer group official believes that the Ministry of Agriculture is taking more notice of their case but the feeling is still that, although the Minister's head was telling him to reduce prices, his heart was still very sympathetic to farmers. The MAFF continues its role as the advocate of the farmers and still goes to Europe with the goal of protecting their interests.

In protecting the farmers the Ministry is assisted by DG VI and the Council of Ministers. DG VI still allows little access to consumer groups and environmentalists, arguing that they do not really represent the interests of their constituents. At the Council of Ministers the majority of member countries continue to believe that farmers should receive a high level of support. Despite the Commission's call for a restrictive price policy, the Council of Ministers rejected drastic price cuts for cereals for several years, regardless of the over-production (HL 153 1983/84: xii; HL 112 1984/85: x; HL 83 1985/86: 10). In 1988, France and Germany resisted Britain's call for a drastic cut in the amount of wheat which would receive support. Most European countries retain faith in high price support, high production and the CAP. Consequently, 'The idea that the whole machine might need scrapping and redesigning is ... automatically excluded from policy options offered ...' (Gardner 1987: 172).

Nevertheless, it would be wrong to say that nothing has changed. In Britain all grants which encouraged increased food production have been abolished (*The Times* 29 November 1988). The EC has recognised the need to reduce costs and production and so stabilisers for most produce in surplus have been introduced. In addition, community milk quotas are to be extended and there have been real price cuts. The agreement on the limit of the agricultural budget reached in 1988 means that the constraints on agricultural expenditure are much greater than before (HL 83 1987/88). There has also been recognition of the impact of agriculture on the environment and grants are now going to environmentally friendly farming.

However, the 1988 reforms had a limited impact on agricultural costs and surpluses. The main features of CAP were still in place, with producers continuing to receive artificially high prices in order to maintain production. The level of cereal production at which price penalties came into play was higher than the level of cereal production at the time. Prices were still double world prices, the cost of export refunds remained high and production was well above demand (HL 34 1988/89; HL 34 1989/90). As a consequence, the stocks which greatly declined in 1989, largely as a result of drought in the United States, returned in 1990. In 1990 beef stocks tripled, the store of skimmed milk powder rose from 5,000 tonnes to 333,000 tonnes, the butter stock increased by 450 per cent, and there was a large rise in cereal stocks (*The European* 9–11 November 1990).

By early 1991 it was clear that the 1988 reforms had not had the desired effect. It seemed that the budget would increase by a further 7.9 billion ecus by the end of the year and 4 billion ecus by the end of 1992. However, the greatest pressure for reform came not from within the EC but from the United States and GATT. During the Uruguay round of GATT, the US proposed a 75 per cent reduction in European internal support and 90 per cent cut in export subsidies. Yet, EC farm ministers rejected proposals for a 30 per cent cut in farm prices (Palmer and Wolf 1990). The US increased pressure on the EC by announcing a 25 per cent reduction in farm support over the next five years and increased protection if no GATT agreement was reached (Palmer and Wolf 1990). They also said that the failure of the talks would lead to a trade war in agricultural produce (*The Guardian* 14 November 1990).

In December 1990, the failure of the EC to accept large cuts in subsidies resulted in the GATT talks grinding to a halt. However, the fact that GATT seemed to be on the brink of collapse had a salutary effect on the EC. The majority of countries are industrial nations and have a more immediate interest in maintaining free trade rather than agricultural subsidies. The combination of US pressure and a world-wide pressure started to crack the EC farm alliance. Perhaps most importantly, Germany with its high dependence on international trade shifted its support from France and Ireland, who opposed compromise, to the British and Dutch positions, who recognised the need to look for some type of compromise (*The Guardian* 5 December 1990).

The consequence of these events was that the EC commission proposed a radical plan for the reform of the CAP. The plan outlined by the Agricultural Commissioner, Ray MacSharry, involved a 35 per cent cut in cereal prices, cuts of 15 per cent for butter and beef and 10 per cent for milk. To protect small farmers, Mr MacSharry said there would be more set-aside, payments for early retirement and subsidies for environmentally friendly farming (*The Guardian* 12 December 1990; 19 February 1991). Yet these plans unleashed hostility within the policy community. Despite Britain's continual call for reform, Minister of Agriculture Selwyn Gummer said, the proposals for reform were 'preposterous and unacceptable' and he claimed they would fossilise small and inefficient farming (*The Guardian* 5 December 1991). Britain opposed a scheme for reform which it saw as harming the interests of Britain's farmers. Likewise, other countries opposed the size of the cuts with the French in particular objecting to cuts in export subsidies. Nevertheless, pressure continued to come from GATT which suggested that the EC reform package did not go far enough (*The*

Guardian 13 January 1992). Eventually in May 1992 the Council of Ministers did agree on a plan for radical reform of CAP:

> The reforms aim to slash over-production by reducing the price the EC pays the farmer and the land under cultivation. The price cut will be 29 per cent for cereals, 15 per cent for beef and poultry, and 5 per cent for dairy products, principally milk.
>
> As compensation for these cuts, there will be additional grants to farmers which for the next three years will cost an extra £3bn. To qualify for these payments arable farmers of all but the smallest holdings will be obliged to remove 15 per cent of their land from production. There are generous grants available to enable them to turn it over to forestry, and early retirement. (*The Independent* 22 May 1992)

This agreement has a number of interesting features in terms of network analysis and the agricultural policy community. Although the agricultural network was certainly impinged on by other actors like GATT, the United States, Trade Ministers and even Prime Ministers, it was the community which made the decisions on reform. The agricultural community has less control over the agenda but it still controlled the decision-making process and in that sense the community has not become any more open. In reforming agriculture, the community did its best to protect the interests of its own national farmers. For instance, the British negotiated long and hard to ensure that even the largest farmers received compensation for price cuts. Despite the free market rhetoric, the British agricultural minister wanted to ensure a fair share of the subsidies. Despite the reform and the fact that it has been seen as radical:

> The basic apparatus of CAP remains. There will still be guaranteed prices, albeit at a lower level, with export subsidies and Community preference. The cost to the Community budget will be no lower, and probably higher, in the short term. . . .
>
> It is also far from certain that lowering cereal prices and setting aside land will significantly reduce production. (*The Independent* 22 May 1992)

The farmers are still being guaranteed a certain level of income, and it is as yet uncertain how GATT will react to these reforms. The cuts in support prices are certainly relatively large, but the fact they have had general approval from the NFU seems to suggest that the policy community has ensured the most favourable reform package possible in the hostile circumstances.

The political agenda has changed. It is no longer one of increasing production and prices. New issues are on the agenda. The government and the EC are now concerned with limiting production, the impact of agriculture on the environment and the consumer, and the cost of CAP. However, any changes have largely occurred within the existing policy community. The community has attempted to limit damage by securing control over the reforms in policy. It has tried to ensure that the reforms that are introduced do as little harm as possible to the interests of farmers. The British policy community has been lucky in that it has been saved by membership of the EC. In most other member nations, farmers are still economically, politically and socially important. Consequently, other governments have been prepared to continue to pay the cost of agricultural support. It has only been when the costs of support became so great as to bankrupt the Community, and over-production led to increased criticism, that change has been accepted. Even so, change has been limited. It has not involved a complete overhaul of the CAP, but only an attempt to limit costs to an affordable level, and to bring supply and demand into line. Now that surpluses have been reduced, and world cereal supplies have fallen due to drought in the United States, the pressure for further reform will be reduced.

The agricultural policy community's ideology was undermined by increased costs and over-production. It could no longer justify its existence by stressing the need to increase production. However, it continued to use its institutional structures to exclude the groups demanding change and resisted their demands for access, by incorporating certain reforms. However, these reforms have ensured the continuation rather than the collapse of CAP. It has enabled the community to justify the continued exclusion of consumers by pointing to its ability to recognise problems and adapt. For the time being the MAFF/NFU policy community is safe, but with the opening up of the agenda, pressures for further change remain. Environmental groups have more influence than in the past and the Conservative government claims to be taking environmental issues seriously. Pressure from GATT and the United States will continue to change the international context of agricultural policy, and European social and economic change will erode the influence of the farming lobby.

The agricultural policy community and state autonomy

The agricultural policy process in Britain clearly demonstrates the complexity of the notion of state autonomy (Smith 1989d). Agricultural policy has always been seen as an area of pressure group capture. Yet it is clear from examining the development of British agricultural policy that the relationship between the state and farmers has been highly complex. The privileged position of the farmers derived, to a large extent, from the goals of government policy. During the war the government had to increase agricultural production. This was not a goal that could be achieved through despotic power, but had to be achieved through the cooperation of the farmers. Hence, the agricultural policy community was a state-created network established in order to increase the state's infrastructural power in the area of agricultural policy. The government needed the policy community to achieve its goals.

Likewise after the war, it was the Treasury which set the parameters of agricultural policy. At a time of economic and food crises, increases in agricultural production were seen as highly desirable, and so it was the Treasury which initiated and funded the long-term expansion of agricultural production. However, the policy and the interests became enstructured. They developed institutional structures, ideology, and rules of the game which made it difficult to change the policy when circumstances changed. Consequently, autonomy had shifted from the government level to the network level. The agricultural policy community managed to seal off the agricultural policy process. Again, this was not because of pressure group capture but because the NFU and MAFF had mutual interests in maintaining the community and autonomy. The farmers were ensured high prices and the MAFF had control over a simplified policy process because they did not have to adjudicate between conflicting interests or deal with other departments. This autonomy was increased with entry into Europe. Within the EC, agricultural policy was placed almost completely beyond the control of the national government which made the network even more autonomous. However, issues of international trade and relations with the United States have threatened this autonomy. Demonstrating that when agricultural policy impinges on wider economic and foreign policy goals, executive level actors are prepared to intervene in agricultural policy. It appears that autonomy is shifting away from the network to the state level but, as we saw with the latest reforms, this is only to a limited degree.

The US agricultural policy network: from policy community to issue network?

The British agricultural policy community highlights a paradox in the US agricultural policy network. As in Britain, the US agricultural community is frequently cited as a very closed network. It is seen, in American terms, as the classic iron triangle with policy decisions being made within a very closed network of the congressional agricultural committees, the United States Department of Agriculture (USDA) and key agricultural interest groups; in particular the American Farm Bureau Federation (AFBF) and the National Farmers Union (NFU) which were said to have captured the network (Browne 1986). Within this general network, a whole series of sub-networks existed. These sub-networks were concerned with particular commodities and linked together commodity interest groups with commodity sections of USDA, and commodity subcommittees within Congress (Lowi 1969; McConnell 1953).

Yet, despite the apparent closeness of this network, it has been argued that, unlike the British policy community, it collapsed fairly rapidly in the 1970s and 1980s into an issue network. This raises the question of why does a closed policy community in one country survive pressures for change largely intact whilst the other changes relatively rapidly? In this section we will demonstrate that despite the close relations between farmers and the state in the United States, and the farmers' success in achieving substantial support, there were major differences in the US agricultural network. It had certain weaknesses which made it very vulnerable to external pressures. In particular, there were significant conflicts within the community which did not exist in Britain, and the President maintained a degree of control over agricultural policy which did not exist within the British central executive. Consequently, the fact that it has disintegrated much more rapidly than the British community is not surprising.

Establishing the agricultural network

US agricultural policy in the 1920s was similar to that of Britain during the inter-war period. The dominant belief amongst policy-makers was that agriculture should be left to the market. However, in the period between 1920 and 1933, US agriculture was in crisis. Falling farm prices and demand led to a widespread debt crisis (Finegold 1981). The severity of the crisis did result in the government facing substantial pressure to take some form of action. The *laissez-faire* ethos of the US state and society initially limited the potential options. President Hoover did not want a bureaucratic solution to the farm crisis and believed that the way out of the crisis was through cooperation (Hamilton 1991). Nevertheless, the difficulty of establishing such intervention among disparate and poorly organised farmers meant that the 1929 Agricultural Act whilst being designed to encourage the formation of coops and improved marketing, also established the Farm Board. The Farm Board was given a $500,000,000 fund to make loans to coops, and to organise clearing houses and stabilisation programmes (Hamilton 1991). Hence, the Act did attempt to create a private sector solution but through using substantial state intervention. Yet, despite the efforts of the Farm Board, it could do nothing to cope with the fall in prices that followed the 1929 stock market crash. 'From 1929 to 1932, gross farm income declined by more than half, and the value of capital employed in agriculture dropped from $58 billion to $38 billion' (Finegold 1981: 5).

Finegold (1981), Kenney *et al.* (1989) and Hooks (1990) suggest that this financial collapse, combined with a severe industrial crisis, 'created a fundamental political crisis for American capitalism'. This forced the state to take a much more interventionist approach through the New Deal. Hence, the initiative behind the New Deal was state centred rather than deriving from pressure groups (Finegold 1981; Skocpol and Finegold 1982). It was the state-centred solution of the Agricultural Adjustment Act of 1933 which led to the establishment of the agricultural policy network and set the direction of agricultural policy for the following thirty or forty years.

In the early 1930s, agricultural pressure groups were not particularly strong. 'And perhaps even more important, competing "national farmers' Associations" were pushing quite different programs for farm recovery' (Skocpol and Finegold 1982: 261). Indeed, the major farm organisations were largely opposed to the system of production controls that was introduced with the agricultural Adjustment Act of 1938 (AAA) (Finegold 1981). Hence, the AAA was initiated by state actors concerned with the severity of the farm crisis and the impact that it was having on the general economic situation.

The goal of the AAA was to establish 'parity' in agricultural prices and income. This meant raising the market prices so that the prices of products had the same purchasing power as they did in the base period of 1910 to 1914. The AAA introduced a number of measures – production controls and price supports, export subsidies, subsidised credit and crop insurance – to achieve this goal (Pasour 1990). The central feature was the establishment of certain price supports in return for production controls. In addition, the Commodity Credit Corporation was established whereby the government would loan money using farmers' crops as collateral. If farmers did not repay the loan, the government retained the crops (Kenney *et al.* 1989). In other words, the government was directly buying the surplus produce of the farmers. As a result USDA expenditure increased from $129 million in 1929 to $1.2 billion by 1935 (Pasour 1990). USDA became the largest federal government agency and took the largest share (19 per cent in 1935) of the non-defence budget.

The AAA set the framework for the following fifty years of agricultural support. Despite the Supreme Court declaring the production control and tax features of the New Deal programme unconstitutional in 1936, the federal state was not thwarted from intervening. The 1933 Act was quickly replaced by the Soil Conservation and Domestic Act of 1936 which equally had the goal of increasing farm incomes to the parity level. However, it was the Agricultural Adjustment Act of 1938 which was to become the permanent replacement of the 1933 Act and which set the pattern for future agricultural support. The Act included loans for producers of certain crops if marketing quotas were accepted; crop insurance for wheat; price supports for particular commodities and systematic storage (Tweeten 1977).

During the war agricultural support increased even further with direct support for individual commodities becoming standard. 'In 1945, for example, price support was announced for 166 farm commodities' (Cochrane and Ryan 1976: 72). With the shortages of war, agricultural policy became concerned with increasing, rather than restraining, production, and so increased production and high guaranteed prices became the dominant feature of policy into the 1950s (Tweeten 1977). However, the 1950s saw the re-emergence of substantial surpluses. The government's solution was PL 480 which basically provided for the dumping of US surpluses on developing countries through accepting non-convertable currencies. In the 1960s, with continuing problems of over-production, the basis of policy remained attempting to control production in return for guaranteed prices. In the 1970s with the level of production and the cost of support continuing as a problem, the Nixon administration introduced set-aside whereby farmers would be paid for taking some land out of production. Nevertheless, the government did place a ceiling on how much individual farmers could receive in support (Cochrane and Ryan 1976; Tweeten 1977).

Thus from the New Deal, and in particular in the period after the Second

World War, US agricultural policy was defined by an agenda very similar to that of Britain. As Kenney *et al.* (1989: 140) maintain, 'farm price supports became the norm and congressional debates centred on adjusting these programs'. As in Britain, the issue of price support became a technical issue but there were important differences. First, concern with over-production was present much earlier in the United States and second, as we will see, the degree of consensus on mechanisms for increasing farm incomes was much less than in Britain. Agricultural policy was subject to greater debate and more conflicts than was ever the case in Britain.

Nevertheless, the development of support programmes from the early New Deal into the 1970s resulted in the establishment of an integrated network, or as several US writers claim, an iron triangle. The following section will analyse the nature of that network and highlight the weaknesses that made it substantially different from the British agricultural policy community.

The agricultural network

In establishing the agricultural programmes of the New Deal and after, the main general farm organisations, the American Farm Bureau Federation, the National Farmers' Union and the Grange, officials within USDA and the congressional agricultural committees established very close relationships. According to McConnell (1953: 75), Washington relied on the farm organisations for the development of policy and, 'The officers of the Department of Agriculture recognised the farm organisations as consultative organs in themselves . . . .' This consultation was so close that the Farm Bureau saw the programme that emerged in 1933 as its own (McConnell 1953) although certain authors (Finegold 1981; Skocpol and Finegold 1982; Wilson 1977) suggest that the policy adopted derived from the administration. Undoubtedly, the administration did negotiate closely with the farmers in developing the AAA (Talbot and Hadwiger 1968). Significantly, after the 1933 Act was struck down the Agricultural Secretary Wallace, 'called a conference of farm organisations to frame new "permanent legislation" ' and the act that finally passed 'incorporated most of what the Farm Bureau had asked . . . . With the passing of the 1938 Act, the Farm Bureau had accomplished its basic legislative program' (McConnell 1953: 78–9). In addition to developing close relations with the administration, the main farming organisations 'were able to cultivate responsiveness from agricultural committees who . . . continued to hold sway over a generally supportive congress' (Browne 1988: 16).

From the New Deal period, the agricultural arena was characterised by a relatively closed and integrated network. The network defined a distinct set of insiders which included, 'a small cadre of farm state legislators, ranking USDA officials and representatives of the Farm Bureau, the NFU and the Grange' (Browne 1988: 41). The outsiders were the White House, the Bureau of the

Budget, non-agricultural members of Congress, other agricultural interests and non-farm interests. Consequently, the central authorities had very little control over agricultural policy (Browne 1988).

It was also a network that had institutional and ideological structures. The institutional structures were the congressional committees and the USDA. The congressional committees basically determined agricultural policy. They were dominated by members of Congress from rural Republican constituencies and Southern Democrat constituencies who had very close relationships with the main farm organisations. Bills that were not reported by the agricultural committees were buried and therefore the committees were crucial in the passing of farm legislation (Hathaway 1963). According to Cochrane and Ryan (1976: 114):

> A combination of congressional characteristics – representation on a geographical basis, the committee system, and seniority – operates to produce farm price and income legislation that treats certain commodities with tender, loving care. Historically membership in the House Committee on Agriculture has been heavily weighted with Southerners who have much seniority; consequently the problems of cotton, tobacco and peanuts have received solicitous attention and through a friendly working relationship between southern farm Democrats and mid-western farm Republicans, feed grains have received generous support. The composition of the Senate agricultural committee has been such as to lend further support to the commodities listed above and in addition provide a friendly hearing to producers of wheat, sugar, and dairy products.

The committees were at the centre of a network which was able to exclude non-farm interests and to ensure that the interests of agricultural producers were protected. This congressional part of the network was very proficient in ensuring that agricultural policy was seen in terms of protecting agricultural prices for a whole range of produce.

In addition, an important administrative part of the network was provided by USDA. As a large bureaucracy in a relatively weak state, the Department of Agriculture was able to develop the capacity to make and implement agricultural policy with a high degree of autonomy from other state actors. In the period during and after the First World War, USDA was reorganised, 'to heighten its capacities for policy orientated research and for centrally coordinated policy implementation' (Skocpol and Finegold 1982: 272). In addition, the Bureau of Agricultural Economics was established within the department and this gave USDA the capability to develop agricultural policy.

Ideological structures existed in the sense that there was a degree of consensus over agricultural policy. There was at least agreement in the 1920s and 1930s that something had to be done to solve the farm crisis and in the post-war period there was agreement that a certain level of prices had to be maintained. However, there was not agreement over how these goals should be achieved.

Thus an important role of the network, and in particular USDA, was to establish a consensus. In order to obtain a certain level of agreement, 'practically everyone's scheme was included in the AAA' (McFadyen Campbell 1962).

A central feature of the network was that the farmers were integrated into the administrative as well as the policy process. The AAA required a high level of local involvement in the assigning of quotas and the checking of compliance. It was realised that there was only one organisation that could do this – the educational extension service – which had long been dominated by the Farm Bureau. Consequently, the Farm Bureau came to dominate the local committees concerned with administering the AAA. When the 1933 Act was struck down, the new scheme concentrated local administration into county agricultural conservation associations. This increased Farm Bureau domination because administration was organised along general rather than commodity lines. Of the 169 members of State Soil Conservation Committees where the Farm Bureau was organised, 117 were Farm Bureau members and 90 per cent of the county membership was made up of Farm Bureau members (McConnell 1953).

The Farm Bureau's role in local administration is indicative of a wider feature of the agricultural network – the dominant position of the AFBF in the network. Despite the inclusion of other interest groups and several government agencies, the US agricultural policy network provides probably the best example of a captured community of all the case studies in this book. Hooks (1990) suggests that despite the fact that USDA was fairly autonomous in the establishment of the New Deal for agriculture, towards the end of the 1930s the Farm Bureau became a larger and stronger organisation and it increased its support within Congress. Moreover, it established strongholds within USDA. Nevertheless, with presidential support, USDA remained dominant at least until the Second World War. However, during the war with the need to increase production, the AFBF managed to become much more dominant within USDA: 'Although the national interest was compromised, the narrow interests of elite farmers were well served – they made excessive profits producing unneeded and expensive goods' (Hooks 1990: 36).

The Farm Bureau also attempted to ensure its dominance over the other farm organisations. During the period of the New Deal, the Farm Bureau was very successful in overcoming the sectional and partisan division within the agricultural community. Hence, the role of the Bureau was crucial in unifying the various agricultural interests and regions, and achieving some agreement in the 1930s (McFadyen Campbell 1962). Browne (1988: 17) maintains that the Farm Bureau's electoral connections meant that it was increasingly difficult for Congress to listen to the rest of the agricultural lobby, 'agricultural pluralism did not return to the Washington lobby in the three decades after the early 1920s'. This enabled the Farm Bureau to attempt to seek a monopoly and it claimed that it represented all farmers, although its membership was made up of a very distinct group of farmers (McConnell 1953). The Farm Bureau was clearly dominant amongst the general farm organisations and had a privileged position in relation to USDA. It was frequently consulted and kept informed of policy decisions and it was involved in administration. This leads McConnell to suggest that agricultural policy from the 1930s onwards was Farm Bureau policy. But McFadyen Campbell (1962: 1) questions this view:

> whether the American Farm Bureau Federation was a central force in the making of the New Deal for Agriculture, or conversely whether the power of the American Farm Bureau was largely an outgrowth of the New Deal has been the subject of bitter controversy.

She suggests that although USDA listened to the AFBF, it was the Agriculture Secretary who made the decisions and, on occasions, was prepared to do so without consulting the farmers. Likewise, Hooks and Finegold suggest state interests were important in the development of policy. It could be that this was a case of type III autonomy where 'public officials translate their preferences into authorative actions in the absence of divergent state–society preferences' (Nordlinger 1981: 74).

From the 1930s until at least the 1950s, US agricultural policy can be characterised as being made within a very well integrated network which was close to a policy community. It had a limited number of actors – although clearly more than in Britain – and there were institutional and ideological structures which ensured the exclusion of interests which threatened the dominant agenda. The central concern of the agenda was the maintenance/achievement of parity prices for farmers through the support of the prices of a range of commodities. This provided a consensus throughout the community. Although there were a range of agricultural interest groups involved in the community, including the general groups and a range of commodity groups, the AFBF managed to ensure dominance through making concessions to both the national and commodity groups, and by establishing very good contacts in Congress.

Yet, despite the nature of this network, Browne suggests that it broke down relatively quickly. He points out that whilst in the 1950s the whole network might only have contained twenty-five farm organisations, agribusinesses and facilitating industries, by the 1980s there were many more actors. He suggests that there were eighty-four agricultural organisations alone and most of these had unique interests (Browne 1988). So unlike Britain, the US policy network has responded to changing circumstances by increasing in size. However, the US network was always fundamentally different from the British agricultural community and these differences made it much weaker.

Weaknesses of the agricultural network

Despite the apparent consensus and institutionalisation within the US agricultural policy network, it contained a number of deficiencies. It lacked the integration of the British agricultural policy community. Although there was some agreement between the farm organisations on the need to do something to help agriculture out of crisis, there were major differences between the farm organisations on what should be done. These differences stemmed from the significant ideological divergence which existed between the farm organisations (Talbot and Hadwiger 1968). The Farm Bureau, at least in principle, believed in the free market and a *laissez-faire* approach and established links with the Republican Party. The National Farmers Union was a strong supporter of the New Deal and developed coalitions with the Unions and the Democrats (Wilson 1977).

These ideological conflicts meant that the consensus on agricultural policy was not really a deep value agreement but more an uneasy coalition formed in order to achieve specific policy goals. It was constantly on the verge of breakdown, and frequently did. For example, it was relatively easy to reach agreement on emergency measures for the New Deal but 'agreement on more permanent programs was more difficult to obtain' (McFadyen Campbell 1962). Each of the farming groups tended to move out of these coalitions when it suited their interests. Although a degree of consensus was established in the face of the desperate depression of the 1930s, it became increasingly difficult to maintain as circumstances changed. As early as the Second World War, the Farm Bureau was beginning to side with the opposition to the New Deal and against the National Farmers Union (Talbot and Hadwiger 1968).

Unlike Britain, there was no fundamental ideological consensus on the nature of agricultural policy. Whereas in Britain there was a clear agreement on the goals, and a general agreement on how to achieve them, the US network disagreed on the goals and subsequently on the details of agricultural policy. The network was characterised by significant conflicts over policy with the farm organisations, Congress and the administration all proposing different policies at various times. Cochrane and Ryan (1976) believe that after the Second World War, 'two opposing camps emerged with respect to what shape farm legislation should take'. On one side was the Farm Bureau and the Southern members of Congress. On the other was the Secretary of Agriculture, Clinton, officials and economists within USDA and non-farm interests. There was not, as there was in Britain, an almost universal acceptance that farmers should be supported and production increased.

In the late 1940s, and the 1950s, when the problems of over-production were becoming apparent, a whole range of solutions were debated. In 1948 Secretary Brannen proposed a radical change in agricultural policy with an income standard to replace parity; income payments to replace price supports for producers of perishable goods; a new list of commodities and no price support on production over a certain limit (Cochrane and Ryan 1976). However, the Farm Bureau opposed this policy and it was defeated in Congress. This signifies major differences with the British network. It would be unthinkable for MAFF to have developed a major change in agricultural policy without consultation with the leading farm organisations. MAFF would not have proposed a farm policy that had the complete opposition of the leading farm organisation. More importantly, the fact that the policy was defeated in Congress demonstrates that the US network had more than one decision-making centre.

This conflict over policy meant that agricultural policy was a highly political issue. Agricultural policy was not just a technical issue of trying to decide how farm support and farm prices should be increased. The Republicans and Democrats took distinct policy positions on agriculture with the Republicans favouring a move to flexible support and a free market, and the Democrats favouring higher price support (Pennock 1962). Republicans, even from rural constituencies, frequently opposed farm subsidies (Wilson 1977). The United States failed to develop a bipartisan agricultural policy. In addition, this politicisation was exacerbated by the various farm organisations supporting different parties. Unlike the British NFU, the US NFU and the Farm Bureau were openly partisan.

The network was also distinctive because the President did play a role in agricultural policy. This limited the extent to which the network could seal itself off and depoliticise the policy process. From Hoover through to Reagan, the President frequently intervened in agricultural policy. Roosevelt strongly pushed the AAA, Truman supported the Brannen plan and attempted to win Congressional support, and Kennedy was involved in agricultural reform in the 1960s (Cochrane and Ryan 1976). As a large department in a generally minimalist state, it was difficult for the President not to have a role.

A further weakness of the network, particularly in the 1960s and 1970s, was that it increasingly relied on external support in order to pass legislation. As the farming population declined and increasing numbers of Congress members became concerned with urban rather than rural issues, the House Agricultural Committees, according to Porter (1978: 24), 'has faced the difficulty of finding enough votes to secure passage of agricultural legislation'. In order to pass agricultural legislation, coalitions have been developed with urban interests. Initially this was achieved by incorporating food stamp legislation into farm bills in order to build a rural–urban democrat coalition. More recently a rural–urban labour coalition developed over support for minimum wage legislation in return for support for farm legislation (Porter 1978). The need for such a coalition placed severe constraints on the agricultural network. Farm policy had to be made acceptable to urban interests and the coalition was rather *ad hoc* and weak.

The nature of the political system, the ideological opposition, the general view of the state and the belief in *laissez-faire* meant that agricultural policy always remained political in the United States. Consequently, there were many more groups involved in agricultural policy than in Britain and often very little compromise between the groups. Consumers wanted lower food prices, taxpayers less costly programmes, agribusiness wanted free trade and increased production; organised labour would support farm legislation in return for labour legislation (Cochrane and Ryan 1976). In addition, there was no single dominant farm group.

Even the Bureau failed to represent a large number of farmers and there were major ideological and policy differences between the various farming interests. Thus, the divisions were ideological, regional, economic and commodity-based. The farm organisations did not have the ability of the British farm organisations to coopt the various fractions within the farming community. Moreover, there were several decision-making centres, USDA, Congress and the President, and frequently a lack of policy agreement. They had the support of different interest groups and so ensured that there were a significant number of actors in the network. Consequently, the network was not built on consensus and depoliticisation:

> The policy and its program elements were the product of a prolonged struggle and a series of compromises. Many diverse interest groups participated in the struggle and compromises; the struggle many sided and the compromises many dimensional. Farm policy and the specific programs that took shape in the period 1948–73 might properly be viewed as an uneasy, continually evolving compromise among diverse and contending interest groups (Cochrane and Ryan 1976: 86).

Once circumstances changed, these compromises were very difficult to maintain together.

From integrated network to issue network?

Despite the problems and number of actors in the agricultural network, it was fairly well integrated. The integration was based on compromise rather than consensus but institutionalised relations did exist between farming groups and decision-makers. However, the compromise was uneasy and there was often open conflict. Accordingly, the network was relatively open to change. From the 1950s onwards the agricultural network was faced with a number of external pressures which, it is argued, have led to the network becoming an open issue network.

First, there have been important sociological and economic changes. Farmers have moved from being the largest group in the population to a relatively small group. The farm vote which was once a significant factor in agricultural policy has much less influence. The concerns of the majority of Congress members are urban, rather than rural, and so it is increasingly difficult for farmers to win the support of Congress for extra government spending. Subsequently, the farm bloc no longer has a majority in Congress. In addition, the difficulties of the agricultural lobby have increased because of the fragmentation within Congress as a result of the increasing number of subcommittees. This has disaggregated the process of making agricultural policy and forced increasing compromises on the farm bloc (Hardin 1978: 18). Fragmentation resulted in many more issues being considered within Congress which made it more difficult to predict policy outcomes. Farm legislation increasingly depended on detailed negotiations. 'As economic times worsened for farming and as farm legislation became harder to pass, farm protests rekindled within the domain' (Browne 1991: 364).

The conflict over agricultural policy has been increased by rising prices, and the growth of the consumer movement which has created an active questioning and opposition to farm policies which raise prices to the consumer. For instance, Guth highlights how milk pricing policy had always been made within a very closed network. However, in the 1970s, rising milk prices 'drew a number of consumer groups into dairy policy debates' (Guth 1978: 501). He points out that the:

> consumer activism of the early 1970s helped sustain widespread public concern over milk questions, translated into some legislative influence, and created a favorable milieu for administrators in consumer-orientated agencies. Generally, however, consumers' groups ability to capitalise on public concern was circumscribed by limited finances, expertise and lobbying manpower (Guth 1978: 502).

It is not only consumer groups which have increasingly challenged agricultural policy. There has also been increased pressure from the poverty lobby, farm workers and environmentalists. Even within rural areas migrant farm labour, poor and low production farmers, and blacks are beginning to organise and challenge the traditional interests of the farming lobby (Cochrane and Ryan 1976). The large increase in government expenditures for food stamps and other transfer programmes, and for safety, environmental, and civil rights legislation since the mid–1960s is a reflection of the effectiveness of these various groups in the public policy process (Pasour 1990: 50). It has been suggested that these groups are beginning to change the agricultural agenda so that its concerns are not those of the farm lobby alone.

There have also been important changes in the farm lobby. Agriculture has become increasingly specialised and this has created a feeling amongst farmers that they are not being adequately represented by general farm organisations. The response of farmers has been to join commodity groups rather than general farm organisations. The last twenty years has seen a rapid increase in the number of farm groups (Browne 1986). Many of these groups want access to the political arena and they increase the potential for conflicts within the farming community. These new commodity and single issue groups have become more active and have been establishing Washington-based representatives and using professional lobbyists (Browne 1986). As a result the Farm Bureau has to expend much effort in trying to build coalitions with various commodity groups. Consequently:

> it is no longer able single-handedly to dominate either the agriculture committees or the Congress via its widespread membership and, thus, has lost most of its control over positive policy formation that this influence once provided. As a result,

it also lost much of its former influence over the larger commodity interest groups (Hathaway 1963: 225).

During the 1980s these changes were consolidated by wider changes in economic and political priorities and concern with the growing cost of agricultural policy. President Reagan was elected with a commitment to reducing public expenditure, government intervention and the budget deficit. Agricultural policy sinned on all these counts. It was costly, involved a great deal of government intervention and, as a byproduct, increased the budget deficit. There was growing concern about the ever increasing cost of agricultural support and over-production (Infanger *et al.* 1983; Petit 1985). In agriculture, the government wished to reduce the cost of farm support, reduce government intervention and emphasise exports and productivity. The aim of the administration was to contain costs and to eliminate what it regarded as obsolete programmes (Moyser and Josling 1990). However, there was a great deal of opposition within Congress to such reform. The outcome was that:

> The President did not get the commodity program reform, but he did get concessions from the Congress to limit predicted cost. The House was unable to cut sugar and peanut programs, though it was able to get the Senate to go along with more spending on dairy and grain programs. The commodity groups achieved the minimum objectives in that all programs survived, though most had to settle for less than they wanted (Moyser and Josling 1990: 147).

Faced with the pressure of increasing deficit because of Reagan's tax cutting, Congress did cut price support for a range of commodities in the 1981 Farm Act (Infanger *et al.* 1983).

However, the problem for US agricultural policy-makers was that the environment changed considerably in the early 1980s. Throughout the 1970s, the government had encouraged increased exports. During the early 1980s world production grew and the market for exports became more difficult. In addition, the high value of the US dollar made US exports less competitive. As a result exports fell by 11 per cent between 1981 and 1983 (Galston 1985). The problems were exacerbated by many farmers borrowing heavily in the late 1970s in order to increase production. They were then badly hit by high interest rates and falling land prices (Harl 1990). Many farmers were unable to repay their loans and there was a 'significant increase in farm forclosures' (Moyser and Josling 1990: 110).

Therefore, despite the administration's desire for agricultural reform, pressure was mounting to actually take measures to protect farm incomes. With the costs of farm support soaring due to increasing production and farm incomes falling, the Reagan administration was forced to take some action. In January 1983 Reagan announced the Payment-in-Kind programme which paid farmers not to produce wheat, corn, cotton and rice with the aim of taking 50 per cent of land out of production. Although the programme temporarily reduced costs, huge surpluses were given away (Moyser and Josling 1990).

The most important attempt at reform came in the 1985 Farm Bill. The administration proposed making agriculture more market-orientated by lowering loan rates and reducing target prices to the market level. Nevertheless, Congress was strongly opposed to the level of cuts that the Reagan administration desired. In addition, there was a great deal of lobbying by commodity groups who were concerned with protecting their own particular programmes (Browne 1988). In the final Act there were some small cuts in target prices, loan rates were reduced and there were production limits on deficiency payments. The administration achieved something but there was no radical change in agricultural policy. Any reform that has been achieved has been largely incremental (Moyser and Josling 1990).

The pressure to reform agricultural policy in the United States has continued. President Bush remained committed to the abolition of agricultural support in order to achieve a settlement within GATT to the problems of agricultural trade. For the 1990 Farm Bill, the Bush administration called for cuts of $1.9 billion in agricultural expenditure. Most of these cuts will come through accounting methods, although there will be at least $600 million savings in the real budget (*Congressional Quarterly Weekly Report* 22 April 1989: 894). Moreover, Senate was prepared to support cuts in the Budget as long as it was not a result of depriving affluent farmers of price support (*Congressional Quarterly Weekly Report* 21 July 1990: 2303).

To some extent US agricultural policy has changed. Social and economic changes, in addition to ideological changes, have provided a challenge to a weak network. There has been the introduction of set-aside in order to reduce production, and agricultural price supports have been reduced. The important question is the extent to which this is due the changes that have occurred in the agricultural policy network. Browne (1986, 1988) demonstrates that the large increase in groups involved in agricultural policy means that the network can now be characterised as an issue network. There has been a vast expansion of groups involved in the policy process. In addition to the general farm organisations there are now the commodity groups, commodity user groups, agricultural academic foundations, congressional agricultural committees, appropriation committees, the Office of Management and Budget (OMB), USDA, the White House and environmental and consumer groups. Browne suggests that '215 organisations were identified as active in the wide-ranging related issues that constitute the agricultural policy domain' (Browne 1988: 348).

Despite this large increase in involved groups, it is not necessarily the case that agricultural policy has become pluralistic. Although many groups are involved in the sense of lobbying or expressing a view, many fewer actually have any influence. As Browne (1989: 373) points out:

Farm protest groups (such as the American Agriculture Movement), church groups (such as Catholic Rural Life Conference), public interest groups (such as Consumers Union), nonfarm research organisations (such as the Soil Conservation Society), generalist rural interests (such as the Rural Coalition), and labor (such as both the United Auto Workers and the United Farm Workers) have attempted to influence agricultural and rural policies for many years. Many of them participate in interorganisational coalitions with established farm and agribusiness groups, maintain active Washington offices, and regularly comment on US farm, rural, food, safety, and trade programs. Usually, however, they have a reform – or high decision cost – perspective that does not fit well with congressional decision-making. Quite significantly, none of these interests are seen by agricultural staffers as important players with either access or influence.

As these groups do not share the values of the network, they do not have any real access to the policy-making process. Despite the changes to the agricultural network and the conflicts of values that did exist, it was farm groups with the agricultural congressional committees which were involved in making agricultural policy in the 1980s. So for the 1985 Farm Bill, 'During the concluding conference committee markdowns, almost no other interests gained access, but major commodity groups were frequently called in for consultation, even assisting in drafting the final provisions days after the congress had passed the bill' (Browne 1988: 234).

The agricultural network had become larger, but in this instance, it is an issue network which does not have open access but one where access is given to certain interests who have particular contacts, resources and knowledge. Consequently, the actors within the network were still concerned with protecting their interests in agricultural support. Commodity groups replaced the general farm organisations but this did not provide access to non-farm organisations (Moyser and Josling 1990). The strength of these groups and this network can be demonstrated by the difficulty in achieving reform. Between 1980 and 1986 the cost of agricultural support increased from $3 billion to $26 billion (Thompson 1988: 243). Although the cost of support dropped to about $10 billion in 1990, this was due to changes in world agricultural trade rather than policy reform.

As in Britain, those most intimately involved in making agricultural policy have an interest in maintaining agricultural support. There have been reforms but these have been made because the network has realised that the external pressures to change are great and if some concessions are not made, radical change will be forced upon them. Similarly to CAP reform, the network has been concerned with cutting costs whilst protecting the main elements of the farm programme and ensuring that farm incomes are protected. Moyser and Josling (1990: 133) highlight:

> The commodity groups, though now joined by new actors in lobbying, still dominate the policy process. They are strongest in Congress, but still have significant influence with the Executive. Their greatest strength is that they are defending price support and other programs already in place. . . . Well financed,

they have continued to cultivate close ties with USDA and the House and Senate
Agricultural Committees.

With these committees still dominating the agricultural policy process and the
general immobilism and 'pork-barrelling' of Congress, it is relatively easy for the
network to prevent change.

The US agricultural network has never been highly integrated. Even at its
strongest point, during the 1930s, there was a lack of a monolithic farming
organisation and several competing perspectives over the direction of agricultural
policy co-existed. In addition, the decision-making process has been fragmented
with Congress, USDA and the White House all playing an important role in the
development of policy. The weakness of this network did not prevent the
development of a substantial support programme for agriculture. Although there
were many agricultural groups involved, the network was fairly successful at
excluding non-farm groups. Hence, the development of agricultural policy was
much more complicated than in Britain because it was necessary to reconcile the
interests of various agricultural groups. It involved the reconciliation of non-farm
interests only to the extent that their support was needed to get farm legislation
through Congress.

Conclusion

Agricultural policy in Britain has, since the Second World War, been made
within the confines of a closed policy community. This community has included
the Ministry of Agriculture and the National Farmers' Union who developed a
shared view of the goals of agricultural policy. They have used this consensus
and the institutions of the policy community to exclude other groups and issues
from the policy agenda. This community was created, not because of the power
of the farmers, but because the depression and the war meant that the
government had to intervene in agricultural policy. In order to develop an
agricultural policy the cooperation of the farmers was essential. Therefore, they
were coopted into policy-making. By using the NFU, the Ministry of Agriculture
simplified the policy process through reducing the number of groups involved.
The NFU performed the role of aggregating and limiting demands and then
helped to sell the agreed policy to its members. In return, the Ministry had to
offer the farmers guaranteed prices. The policy community, therefore,
substantially increased the Ministry of Agriculture's infrastructural power.

In recent years this policy community has been under increasing attack
because of increased concern over the cost, the level of over-production and the
environmental impact of the policy. However, the community has managed to
survive. Now that the decision-making centre is in Europe, it has become much
more difficult for excluded groups to break in, and the community has been
adept at accepting certain demands for change in order to reduce external

pressure. Although the agenda has changed in that it is much less productionist, the policy-makers remain the same and at least in the immediate future the continuation of the CAP seems certain.

The agricultural policy community is distinctive because of its degree of internal integration and isolation from other networks. Although other departments and interest groups have played a role in agricultural policy, they have done so on terms laid down by the community. This demonstrates the importance, within a community, of its structures and ideologies. These factors determine the options available, and the groups involved, within the policy community. Nevertheless, the agricultural policy community is not a completely isolated institution. It is clear from this study of agricultural policy that the establishment and success of the policy community was, to a large extent, due to the context within which it operated. It emerged as a result of depression and war, and was firmly established as a result of economic demands in the post-war era. Its success in the 1970s was reinforced by membership of the EC and threats to its position have been due to the problems of cost and over-production. It is its international context which has allowed it to survive domestic pressures for change.

The development and change of policy communities results, to a large degree, from external factors. To some extent, policy communities are an attempt to deal with new problems which develop beyond the control of government. Government tries to deal with these problems through creating new capabilities, and policy communities assist this task by simplifying demands and providing means for implementation. This does not mean, as Rhodes' definition suggests, that policy communities necessarily involve dependence by central government on sub-central actors for implementation. Rather, it is the case that the Ministry relied on the farmers for political support and legitimation but implementation of price policy remained with the centre. This indicates that policy communities are not necessarily the result of overpowerful pressure groups, as Lowi (1969) might aver, but of the demands on government. The government in Britain created the agricultural policy community when it wanted an interventionist agricultural policy. In doing so, they made the farmers a powerful group. This may also be the situation in other policy areas.

In the United States the agricultural policy was also highly integrated, at least for a particular period, but it took a very different form to the British network. There was neither a single dominant decision-maker nor a single dominant interest group, and so the value system that underpinned the network was based on uneasy compromise rather than consensus. Consequently, once circumstances changed, new groups could move into the network relatively easily. To an extent the network has become an issue network. Yet, this does not mean that the relationship has become pluralist. The US agricultural issue network demonstrates that an issue network is a distinct structure rather than the whole pressure group universe. The agricultural network in the 1980s and 1990s is an issue network because there are a large number of actors. However, these actors still have certain resources to exchange and exclusion continues. The network is more open but not completely open. The groups involved are agricultural groups concerned with maintaining agricultural support. Thus, an issue network can be seen as a network that is distinct from the general pressure group universe and still has some mechanisms for exclusion.

The nature of the networks in Britain and the United States had implications for state autonomy. In Britain, the network was originally created to increase the infrastructural power of the state in times of crisis, only for the autonomy to slip increasingly to the network and out of the control of other state actors. In the US, the network was also created by state actors at a time of crisis but the degree of autonomy has been much more variable over the long term. In the 1940s and 1950s, the network was captured by the Farm Bureau. Since the breakdown of the integrated network, it has been increasingly difficult for any state or group interest to control the direction of agricultural policy. The agricultural issue network seems to highlight the difficulty of state autonomy when there are many actors involved in the policy process.

It is interesting that in Britain and the US similar pressures to change policy have developed. Both countries have been faced with problems of over-production, of out-of-control budgets, of increased pressure from consumer and environmental interests. Each has faced pressure from new right governments for cuts in expenditure. In each case the networks have tried to respond in similar ways. They have attempted to coopt the pressure to reform by accepting some changes in policy whilst maintaining the fundamental features of agricultural support. In each case a strategy of damage limitation has been pursued and as a consequence change has been incremental rather than fundamental. Neverthe-less, the existence of different types of networks in Britain and the US has meant that the pressures for change have had different effects. In Britain, where the network was highly integrated and consensual, the community has managed to stay largely intact. In the US, where the network had some major weaknesses, relationships have changed much more rapidly highlighting the way that networks mediate change.

The case of agriculture also reveals that policy communities and networks can be used as explanations of policy outcomes rather than purely descriptions of government/pressure group relations. The existence of the agricultural policy community explains how, through the exclusion of issues and groups, agricultural support has remained so high in Britain in the post-war era. It was through the ideological and institutional structures of the community that change was prevented in agricultural policy. If agricultural policy had been made within an issue network which lacked a single policy-making centre with numerous groups moving in and out of the arena, agricultural policy would be much more pluralistic – as was the case in Britain in the early 1930s. It was only when the community's structures were placed under stress that changes threatened. Hence, the role of pressure groups in influencing policy is limited by external constraints and by the policy process. To understand policy outcomes we have to understand policy-making and this indicates the importance of policy networks and policy communities. In the United States, the nature of the network, and the fact it has been based on compromise, explains the complexity of the US agricultural policy process and the swings and changes in policy there have been in the post-war period. The fact that the network has managed to exclude non-farm interests has meant that despite the policy flux, the interests of farmers have been generally well protected.

Chapter 6

BUSINESS AND PUBLIC POLICY:
The Problem of Business Policy Networks

Chapter 2 highlighted how the traditional theories of interest group intermediation place particular importance on business/government relations. The resources that business has, and its importance to the overall health of the economy, place business in a special position. Despite these resources, the networks that develop between business and government are not always very well integrated. They vary greatly across sector and time and this suggests that the generalisations made by traditional approaches are too simplistic.

This chapter will examine business/government relations in two particular areas – industrial policy in Britain and trade policy in the United States – in order to indicate the difficulties of deterministic approaches to business/ government relations. It will show that interactions between government and business depend on the institutions involved in policy-making, the nature of the state in general, and the goals and capabilities of state actors. Comparison between these two areas will indicate that the types of policy networks that exist are likely to vary, and by focusing on a number of policy subsectors, it will show that networks can actually vary within particular policy areas. This highlights the variable nature of business power, and demonstrates the difficulty, which exists particularly in marxist and corporatist theory, of seeing particular trends in either state/interest group relations or the nature of the capitalist state.

Business policy networks

It has been argued that both Britain and the United States are weak states with limited capabilities for intervening in the economy and hence they seldom become involved in detailed industrial policy (Dyson 1982; Grant 1987). Although the US government is involved in industry, most of the intervention is '*ad hoc* [and] uncoordinated' with the demands deriving 'from society rather than state' (McKay 1983: 47). In addition, writers like Vogel (1989) and Grant (1987) have pointed to the political weakness of British and American business organisations. This would suggest that business/government relations in Britain and the US tend to be pluralistic and adversarial with business distrusting the state and the state lacking the ability or desire to play a major role in directing the economy (Marquand 1988; Vogel 1983; Gamble and Walkland 1984). In addition, the relationship between business organisations is competitive rather than cooperative (Coleman 1990: 240).

However, Wilks and Wright (1988a) and Atkinson and Coleman (1989) suggest that it is simplistic to talk of a weak state/strong state continuum because states can vary in their strength and capability according to agency or department. Even though the United States is often classified as a weak state there is:

> extensive government intervention in the US political economy. Much of this intervention is when the free market failed, or when circumstances are such that the government feels it has no option other than to take the initiative. Increasingly, the government has felt, or has been persuaded to take, a responsibility to correct market failures or assume roles 'in the national interest', in respect of which both major parties, with differing degrees of enthusiasm, have accepted the principle of government intervention (Edmonds 1983: 72).

This intervention creates the possibility for integrated networks to develop as relationships are established between state actors and the industries subject to intervention. If the state is to intervene it needs the assistance of trade associations, firms and individuals in order to develop particular policies. This can immediately create institutionalised relationships and dependency. The state requires cooperation and information from industry, and industry desires state assistance and some influence on policy. Nevertheless, the degree of integration can vary greatly according to how many actors are involved, the degree of consensus and depoliticisation, the length of the intervention and the degree of exclusion of the public and trade unions.

From the discussion of the pluralist and corporatist literature in Chapter 2, it is clear that a number of important networks exist between government and industry. Business has established integrated links through advisory committees and the Business Council. Domhoff (1978: 62) outlines a whole range of networks that link government to business in the policy process:

> the central units in the policy network are ... the Council for Foreign Relations, the Committee for Economic Development, the Business Council and the American Assembly, which are best characterised as the policy planning and consensus seeking organisations of the power elite.

Particular examples can be found in sectors such as tobacco. Fritchler (1983) describes the nature of the tobacco policy community in the United States pre-1964. This community included:

> the paid representatives of tobacco growers, marketing organisations and cigarette manufacturers, congressmen representing tobacco constituencies, the leading members of four sub-committees – two appropriation sub-committees and two substantive legislative committees in each house – that handle tobacco legislation

and related appropriations; and certain officials who were involved with the various tobacco programmes of that department (Fritchler 1983: 6).

This was a small group of people who knew each other and shared similar values on the nature of tobacco policy. This community managed to make policy with relatively little interference and although the issue of a health warning was on the agenda for forty-five years, the tobacco community was able to keep it a low priority for thirty-five years (Fritchler 1983). This community had a degree of integration which allowed it to exclude groups and individuals who might threaten its agenda and interests. By depoliticising the policy area, to a degree, and controlling the institutions of policy-making, the tobacco community was fairly well insulated.

Nevertheless, such a well-integrated network would appear to be rare in both Britain and the United States. In fact after 1964, the tobacco policy community had great difficulty in depoliticising policy and preventing threats to its interests. Similarly in Britain, the tobacco network has found itself constantly under threat from the medical profession and the health lobby (Read 1992). Certain sectors, such as coal in Britain, have not even established integrated networks despite high levels of state intervention (Taylor 1989). Despite the resources and the economic importance of business, the types of networks that develop are highly varied. Contrary to the marxist position, state and business interests are not always compatible and sometimes close relationships do not develop. This raises the questions of why in some sectors business is able to form policy networks at particular times, why they disintegrate, and why some do not form at all. To examine these issues the chapter will contrast US trade policy and British industrial policy.

Trade policy in the United States

Trade policy in the United States provides a useful example of how integrated networks can develop, but can also quickly disintegrate into looser issue networks. This is a particularly interesting example. The United States lacks strong business organisations, the political system is particularly open to interest group pressures, and consequently, Krasner argues, this results in the state being weak. Moreover, trade policy is particularly suited to the pork-barrel politics associated with the United States. It has the potential for a myriad of interests to fight for special protection for their industries from overseas trade. The United States also has a long history of protectionist policy.

Despite the nature of pressure group politics, the weakness of the US state, and the tradition of protectionism, the 1950s and 1960s in the US saw the development of a fairly closed community dedicated to the pursuit of liberal trade which largely represented the interest of state actors rather than interest groups. As Destler (1986: 143) emphasizes, throughout most of the post-war period US trade policy 'operated within a national political environment that was unusually conducive to liberal trade policies. . . . There was an overwhelming elite consensus in favor of market openness and trade expansion.' However, by the end of the 1960s this community was already under threat, and by the 1980s policy was made in a fairly open issue network. This chapter will outline the development of this community.

The development of the trade policy community

Until 1934 and the Reciprocal Trade Agreement Act, trade policy was to a large extent dominated by Congress (Lake 1988). As a consequence, trade policy was subject to the pressure of various interest groups, and so was highly conflictual, with a tendency towards protectionism. The result was the Tariff Act of 1930 – Smoot Hawley Act – which amended 20,000 tariffs mainly upwards (Destler 1986). This act, introduced at the height of the depression, resulted in a massive drop in US trade as other countries retaliated against US protection.

By 1934 this protectionist policy had already been largely reversed. The Reciprocal Trade Act of 1934 allowed the President to negotiate tariff reductions of up to 50 per cent without recourse to Congress. Congress no longer gave 'priority to protecting American industry. Instead, its members would give priority to protecting themselves: from the direct one sided pressures that had led them to make such bad trade laws' (Destler 1986: 11; Goldstein 1988: 188). With the 1934 Act, the influence of interest groups was greatly reduced in the policy-making process (Pastor 1983).

The Act was important because it transferred power to the executive which enabled the President to make trade policy that favoured national goals rather than sectional interests. Accordingly, the State Department became pre-eminent in the field of trade policy (Schaetzel 1986). The importance of the shift to executive dominance only really became apparent in the immediate post-war period. After the Second World War, the United States had the resources to establish itself as the hegemonic power; where 'one state is powerful enough to maintain the essential rules governing interstate relations and is willing to do so' (Keohane 1984: 34). The US – because of its economic strength and the post-war weakness of its competitors, the fear of a return to the inter-war depression and the strength of liberal ideology within the US – wanted to create a liberal world order. The Marshall Plan, GATT, and Bretton Woods were established to provide the institutional framework for this policy (Krasner 1978). The United States intended to ensure its own economic prosperity and to appear as a benevolent power helping Western Europe recover from war. European recovery entailed access to the United States' markets (Destler 1986). Free trade suited both the economic interests and the political goals of the US government. Consequently, a consensus could be established over the direction that trade policy could take:

The ideological consensus proclaimed that foreign trade was a good thing, that high tariffs were to be avoided, that we should be helping or drawing closer to our free world allies, and that we should not sell abroad without buying abroad. Protectionists, on the defensive, rarely denied these principles (Bauer *et al.* 1972: 465).

With the acceptance of the principle of liberal trade and executive policy-making, further legislation was passed such as the 1955 Reciprocal Trade Act which gave greater discretion to the President in removing trade barriers. The apotheosis of the free trade policy was the early 1960s. In 1962 Kennedy passed the Trade Expansion Act which gave the President the authority to reduce tariffs by 50 per cent over five years across the board rather than product by product. This provided the President with substantial autonomy to pursue multilateral negotiations through GATT (Pastor 1983). Trade policy-making moved from Congress to an executive-dominated policy community that accepted the free trade consensus, and largely excluded protectionist interests. This change established a trade policy that limited the impact of societal demands and increased the autonomy of state actors.

In a congressionally dominated system how was the executive able to reassert its control over trade policy? First, it was clear, even to Congress, that the legislature could not make trade policy in the national interest. If there was to be liberal trade, which many members of Congress, the executive and business believed to be desirable, the policy process had to be controlled by the administration. Second, because various interests had historically lobbied hard for protection, the executive was prepared to buy off certain industries with special concessions (Krasner 1978). Third, there was little opposition to such a policy. Trade policy was not a salient issue amongst voters and most business people, whatever their direct material interests, preferred a liberal trade policy to protection (Bauer *et al.* 1972). Fourth, in the post-war period, liberal trade was sold as necessary for the fight against communism and so became part of a wider Cold War ideology. Consequently, questioning of liberal trade became even more unacceptable (Krasner 1978). Finally, Congress was not cut out of the policy process. Trade policy was still based on negotiation between the White House and Congress and channels for congressional influence remained. The 1934 Act was the result of a process of consultation between Congress and President and escape clauses were built into the 1934 Act and subsequent legislation (Pastor 1983). Moreover, as we will see, through the House Ways and Means Committee and the Senate Finance Committee, Congress had access into the policy community.

In the immediate post-war years the role of interest groups in the trade policy community was important but limited. State actors within the executive had a clear ideal of the sort of trade policy that they wanted. However, there were a large number of interests that continued to press for protection. Since the 1920s particular industries have pressed for protection on the grounds of difficult economic circumstances or dumping by overseas competitors. Many of the high tariffs which survived into the post-war era resulted from 1922 and were 'retained by industries with sufficient political strength to guard their ancestral ramparts against the erosion of seven tariff cutting rounds conducted under the General Agreement on Tariff and Trade' (Hufbauer *et al.* 1986: 6). Whilst US Presidents have advocated the benefits of free trade, they have prevented these interests damaging the overall direction of trade policy by imposing 'regimes of "special protection" to insulate important manufacturing and agricultural sectors from foreign competition' (Hufbauer *et al.* 1986:1).

Although interest groups were an important part of the policy process, they were dealt with in a manner which prevented groups that demanded protection upsetting the overall direction of trade policy. Trade policy was developed largely as the result of the interests of certain state actors in developing US economic and political dominance in the West. It did not derive as a response to group actions but from historical events – the depression; ideology – the strong belief in liberalism and free trade; external events – the need to rebuild the economies of Europe within the capitalist, rather than the communist, camp; the desire of state actors for a liberal world economy and, increasingly, because of external institutions like GATT and Bretton Woods which constrained the options for trade policy.

Central to the development of this policy was the domestic policy community. The community enabled state actors to have control over policy-making and to ensure that the policy and options were manageable. It largely contained policy-making within the executive sphere, although with controlled congressional input, and it successfully controlled, through the strength of liberal ideology and various safety mechanisms, demands for protection.

The trade policy community

Although the 1934 Act provided the necessary precondition for the policy community, executive dominance, it did not really come into existence until after the Second World War when US hegemony could not be doubted and the benefits of liberal trade were finally accepted by a large number of interested groups and members of Congress. The trade policy community had two important components; one was the widely accepted liberal trade ideology and the other was the leadership of the Department of State.

The spectre of the inter-war depression, the rise of communism, and its closed trading bloc, and the domestic tradition of liberalism in the United States made a belief in free trade widely accepted, if not by the general public and particular industries, then by the governing elite. As Goldstein (1988: 182) emphasises:

In the U.S., liberal beliefs about trade policy have dominated the debate and thinking of those involved in making policy. In the post-depression period, liberalism gave decision-makers both a design for economic reconstruction and organising principles that directed what was seen as a problematic relationship between society and government. . . . In its early years, liberalism can be explained in that it served the interests of the U.S. and its central decision-makers. However, the existence of unprecedented postwar affluence and power of the U.S., which came to be associated with a particular international economic policy, elevated liberalism into a realm untouchable by interest group politics.

This had the important affect of depoliticising trade policy. The ideology removed the option of protection from the political agenda and so free trade was not a partisan issue (Destler 1986). As in Luke's third dimension of power, protection was at this time an option that was not conceivable. 'What really mattered, however, was that trade was not high on the list of public concerns. So governmental leaders had the leeway to press the policies they felt were needed' (Destler 1986: 5). This ideology made it difficult for the issues of protection to be discussed and therefore groups which wanted protection had little access to the policy process. Rather than the network having to deal with a range of groups calling for different policies, the strength of the ideology restricted policy to consideration of how liberal trade should be achieved.

This is not to say that groups which wanted some protection were excluded completely nor that protection was not discussed or demanded by particular issues. Opposition to trade liberalisation remained in the 1940s and 1950s with a range of industries testifying against giving the President power to cut import duties (Baldwin 1984).

The policy community coped with this pressure by establishing a number of special cases, for example, textiles, steel and agricultural. However, by making these special cases, the policy community managed to depoliticise even the areas where controversy was almost endemic. Safeguards were built into the legislation such as escape clauses and anti-dumping regulations in order to protect constituents who could not compete on the world market.

More importantly, Congress protected itself from interest group demands for concessions by creating legislation whereby 'interest groups could go to bureaucratic agencies whose legal task was to placate potential congressional clients' (Goldstein 1988: 188). By making steel, textiles and agriculture special cases and allowing some degree of protection through quotas or voluntary restraint agreements, the policy community was ensuring that these sectors were dealt with and so did not become subject to widespread debate. The policy community had its own 'pressure diverting management system' (Destler 1986: 36). Particularly important within this system was the International Trade Commission (ITC).

The ITC can, at the request of firms, Congress or under its own initiative, investigate cases of unfair trade and grant relief from foreign competition (Hansen 1990). This is important because it allows the administration to say that in its mission to achieve free trade it is not opening the US to unfair trade practices. There are safeguards, and, although the President does have a veto, the process abrogates the executive from the difficult position of having to decide whether particular industries need protection. It also allows the government to assure other countries that these measures are not arbitrary and political but the result of administrative, independent investigation.

This ideology and the institutional safeguards convinced Congress that it could play a limited role in trade policy. The majority of Congress accepted the liberal consensus and recognised that the only way to increase free trade was to allow the executive to act with a high degree of freedom in trade negotiations. As Baldwin (1985: 105) highlights, over the past fifty years, 'Congress has shown remarkable restraint in making trade policy.' It has not introduced protectionist legislation and it has supported the President in dismantling trade barriers.

This is not to say that Congress was completely absent from the policy process. Congress continued to constrain presidential action and the President's negotiating authority was granted by Congress, and only for limited periods of time (Pastor 1983). The President could not take measures that would jeopardise his future autonomy and greater presidential freedom was only achieved very slowly with each grant of authority gradually increasing the President's room for manoeuvre. For example, in 1958 Congress believed that the President was not using escape clauses sufficiently and so introduced an override to the presidential veto with a two-thirds majority (Pastor 1983). Congress continued to set the framework and limits of the free trade policy.

Perhaps most importantly, congressional input into trade policy was dominated by the Senate Finance and the House Ways and Means Committees. It was rare for trade policy to be discussed by other committees. Ways and Means was dominated by the Chairman Wilbur Mills who strongly accepted the liberal ideology. These committees supported the liberalisation policies of the executive and were prepared to quash attempts to introduce protection. The congressional input into the policy community was within the ideological consensus and so did not threaten the general direction of trade policy.

At the executive level there were a large number of actors involved in the policy community. The central actor was the State Department and within that the Bureau of Economic and Business Affairs. An important role was also played by the Treasury, and within the Treasury, the Office of the Assistant Secretary for International Affairs. 'With a staff of over 200 professional economists and access to economists in other Treasury Bureaus, OASIA has the resources to weigh in on any governmental exercises involving international economics' (Cohen 1977: 45). Increasingly important was the Special Representative for Trade Negotiation who was largely responsible for conducting GATT negotiations. Other organisations like USDA, the Department of Commerce, the OMB and even bodies like the CIA and National Security Council (NSC) played a role on a more *ad hoc* basis (Cohen 1977).

This raises an interesting point. Most closed policy communities involve a very limited number of actors but the trade policy community included a large number of powerful actors with diverse interests. Therefore, it is necessary to explain how this policy community managed to maintain such a clear policy line. The degree of consensus on a liberal trade policy was such that none of the groups involved were actually trying to pursue a different policy. Throughout the 1950s and the 1960s all those involved in the community were prepared to accept the leadership of the State Department. Schaetzel (1986: 234–5) claims that State became, 'the chosen instrument for America's assault on a world constricted by trade barriers', and so 'the State Department's preeminence in this field instilled an unusual degree of order over how trade policy was handled in the executive branch'. There were conflicts over territory, in particular with the United States Trade Representative (USTR) and sometimes with Commerce (Destler 1992). Nevertheless, on most occasions, the role of other departments and agencies was to support the State Department rather than attempt to undermine the community.

This was helped by strong presidential support for the free trade policy and State's leadership role. Through the President, State had an important resource for securing its dominance and for ensuring that the free trade policy was widely accepted.

In addition to State's strength, the Department likely to support industries wanting protection, Commerce, was relatively weak. It did not have the resources or capabilities to make an effective impact on trade policy (Cohen 1977). Finally, the unity of the community was maintained by the limited role of interest groups. Industry had little institutional access to the policy community and was generally committed to the liberal trade policy. As we have seen, the industries with special demands were provided with safety valves. Hence, there were few interest groups pressurising agencies within the community to pursue a different policy.

The trade policy community was dominated by a consensus that a liberal world order was necessary for the United States' economic prosperity. This community involved a number of actors but there was a core or primary policy community made up of State, the Treasury and, unusually, the President which was committed to free trade and was successful at excluding dissenting voices. Pressure groups had a limited role within this policy community. They neither had institutional access nor much impact on the direction of policy. Indeed, the existence of the policy community was the result of the necessity to depoliticise trade policy in order to pursue state goals of creating a liberal market. This was seen as essential for political and economic reasons, and the policy community was successful in allowing various Presidents to negotiate substantial reductions in trade barriers. The trade policy community was strongly state-centred. It was established in order to isolate state actors from pressure groups which then allowed state goals to be pursued in trade policy. Infrastructural power was created by developing administrative structures within the state to deal with trade policy issues.

Yet, during the 1960s, this policy community was already demonstrating signs of stress and by the 1970s it had more or less disintegrated. The consensus on policy no longer existed, groups were not prepared to be excluded, Congress increased its role in trade policy and there was no longer a single institution providing policy leadership. It is now necessary to examine how this policy community collapsed so quickly.

The decline of the trade policy community

The hegemonic thesis suggests that the collapse of the liberally dominated trade policy community is the result of the end of US hegemony. With the loss of hegemony, the United States no longer has the desire or the ability to police the world's economic order (Keohane 1984). This explanation seems overly deterministic. It does not explain why the state, at the executive level, has continued to support a liberal trade policy, nor does it pay attention to the political factors that have led to the collapse of the community. Undoubtedly, the changing position of the United States in the world economy has affected the making of trade policy but it is only one of a numerous range of factors. As Ikenberry *et al.* (1988: 5) confirm 'the theory of hegemonic stability identifies only with the international constraints placed on nation states. Without a theory of domestic political process, it is limited to explaining recurrent patterns of behaviour within the international arena.' Indeed Keohane (1984: 213) concludes:

> Many major forces affecting trade regimes have little to do with the decline of US power. For any adequate explanation of changes in patterns of cooperation and discord in trade, other factors – rapid structural change, domestic economic and political factors and the strategies of domestic political actors – have to be taken into account.

The trade policy community had the seeds of its destruction embedded in its very make-up. It contained a number of powerful political actors who were able to work together whilst there was agreement during a period of growth in US trade. Once policy differences began to arise the potential for rapid politicisation of the policy area was very great as each actor fought for control of policy-making. The community was also reliant on both Congress and industry accepting that the Executive should control trade policy and protectionism should be limited. Again, whilst the fruits of liberal trade were apparent, industry and Congress could accept their sacrifices but as economic problems developed they were less willing to be so restrained.

There were always major difficulties within the community. 'From the mid-50s the politically powerful cotton textile, coal, and domestic petroleum industries . . . were asking for protection' (Baldwin 1984: 12–13). The pressure-diverting system managed to cope with these pressures during the 1950s and 1960s. However, the weaknesses in the policy community became increasingly evident as economic problems grew. Through the 1960s and 1970s the US economy became gradually affected by foreign competition with the oil shocks of the 1970s creating stagflation and an increasing awareness of US relative economic decline. As a consequence, there was a fall in the US's share of world trade. As economic pressure on the United State increased, Richard Nixon, imposed an additional temporary tax of 10 per cent on imports as early as 1971 (Destler 1992). Moreover, this increased competition particularly hit the traditional industries of steel and automobile production. This led to increasing calls from unions, members of Congress and the steel and automobile industries for protection. In 1979 Ford and General Motors made record losses and the Automobile workers petitioned the ITC for import relief (Destler 1986). This could be seen as a post-industrialist explanation of the policy change. As the world economy shifted to new industries the traditionally powerful sectors attempted to protect their position. Yet, this underplays the important political changes that occurred.

From the early 1970s, Congress became less willing to be excluded from the trade policy. As the impact of free trade began to affect constituencies, and particular industries, Congress introduced hundreds of bills trying to achieve special concessions (Pastor 1983). None of these bills passed but they signified a change of attitude within Congress. Importantly, the 1974 Trade Act revived some of Congress's powers. The Act required the President to consult with members of the Ways and Means Committee and the Finance Committee before signing trade agreements. It became statutory for at least ten members of Congress to be accredited members of the US trade delegation (Krasner 1978). Both houses also refused the President complete discretion in trade bills and the Act made it easier for industry to obtain import relief (Baldwin 1985). This led to an increased use of administered protection through the ITC in the 1970s and 1980s (Rugman and Anderson 1987).

More generally, changes within Congress have affected the policy community. Congress had institutional access to the policy community through the Ways and Means and Finance Committees. However, with the reforms of Congress in the 1970s, and the consequent dispersal of power, it became much more difficult to control which members of Congress were involved in trade policy (Pastor 1983). A number of caucuses developed within Congress calling for protection of particular industries and trade issues were no longer confined to the traditional committees. Cohen (1977: 60) maintains: 'On hot and complex issues . . . jurisdiction is fragmented *ad nauseam.*' Consequently, there have been increasing demands for protection from within Congress. It is no longer prepared to accept the free trade consensus. In the 1980s:

> Congress was hit with unprecedented trade-political pressures, generated mainly by unprecedented trade deficits. And the Reagan administration was slow to respond. So legislators of both political parties seized the initiative, demanding tougher executive action to enter resistant foreign markets, and passing the first congressionally initiated omnibus trade bill since Smoot-Hawley (Destler 1992: 66).

Congress did not become protectionist but was more grudging in the freedom that it gave to the executive (Destler 1992: 66).

Of even greater importance have been the changes within the executive level of the policy community. Power has gravitated away from State with the Treasury, USDA or the White House taking the lead on most trade issues (Cohen 1988: 58). As early as the late 1950s it was felt that State was too concerned with the interest of foreigners and so new centres of power have been created to protect domestic interests. The Trade Policy Committee was established which increased the power of Commerce over the operations of trade agreements. With economic performance becoming of increased concern, economic goals have replaced foreign policy goals as central to foreign economic policy and this has increased the power of the Treasury. This shift in power has been reinforced by the tendency of most Presidents to treat the Secretary of the Treasury as the top economic official; Congress increasing in Treasury power through new economic legislation, and concern with the balance of payments deficit (Cohen 1988: 60–1).

A further important factor is the rise of the 'White House supercoordinators and of the Office of the United States Trade Representative' (Cohen 1988: 64). An increased number of coordinating groups have been established within the White House. These institutions have removed leadership from State and given the President increased input into trade policy. The USTR is located within the White House and has become the ' "Chief representative" of the United States in all trade negotiations' (Cohen 1988: 66), thus removing a central function from State. In the 1970s and early 1980s the USTR became the lead department in trade policy. However, under Reagan its position was challenged. The Reagan administration established a network of coordinating committees on trade policy and the Commerce Secretary, Malcolm Baldrige was made chair of the committee. Baldrige used this position to try to establish 'government-wide trade dominance' for a new department of trade. However, the tradition and support of Congress for the USTR meant that neither Commerce nor the USTR was in position to dominate trade policy (Destler 1992).

Commerce has substantially increased its role and power in trade policy now being the 'chief administrator of import and export programs' (Cohen 1988: 69). There has also been a flourishing of trade policy coordinating groups. For trade policy there are three main groups with more than 50 subcommittees plus some inter-agency groups operating outside of the trade policy coordination committee. Increased numbers of state actors involved in trade policy have resulted in a proliferation of interest groups in the policy arena. In addition, with economic hardship biting, industries are no longer prepared to accept the logic of the free trade argument. With Congress increasing its role in trade policy, it has been much easier for groups to obtain access (Cohen 1988).

Hence, the relatively stable, consensual and free market-orientated policy community of the 1950s and early 1960s has disintegrated into a diverse and fluctuating issue network. No longer does the State Department provide the lead in pursuing a free market trade policy rather a whole range of actors have become involved in what is now a highly conflictual issue. Although the Executive generally supports a free trade policy, agreement on how to achieve it, what concessions and exceptions should be made, and who is in charge, is increasingly hard to define. Moreover, Congress is becoming increasingly protectionist with a whole range of protectionist legislation going – but not passing – through Congress.

Although, as yet, there has been no generic shift to a protectionist policy, there are an increasing number of protectionist exceptions being made with steel, automobiles and semiconductors all receiving some form of protection even if 'voluntary' (Cohen 1988; Tucker 1988). As the policy-making mechanism has changed from one of order to disorder, it has been increasingly difficult for state actors to control the direction of policy. Policy-makers have been forced to subsume the state's interest in free trade to the demands of Congress and sections of industry.

The Reagan administration increasingly accepted the argument that the US market was open to unfair trade practices and so was increasingly prepared to meet domestic demands for special protection (Pearson 1990). There was also a general shift in trade policy under Bush with the administration taking an increasingly tough line on GATT whilst being more prepared to make bilateral trade agreements with particular nations in order to establish free trade areas (Schott 1989).

The trade policy community collapsed because of external and internal pressures. The external pressures were the changing economic circumstances of the United States and the threats from the EC. Internally, pressures resulted from conflicts within government over who should control trade policy, and from outside as Congress and industry became more concerned with the level of imports. As new groups and issues developed, the relative power of various government agencies changed and it became increasingly difficult for the State Department to control the agenda and the community. Moreover, although the policy community was strong and effective at its peak, it was inherently weak because of the number of important actors within the community. Once interests diverged the potential for rapid politicisation and internal conflict was very high.

This policy area demonstrates how the power of business fluctuates and varies according to time, the organisation of the state and the focus of analysis. In the 1950s, because of fear of its protectionist demands, industry was excluded from trade policy in general whilst having influence in particular areas. In the 1970s and 1980s, as an issue network formed, industry was to some degree in a better position to influence policy but it was not in a particularly privileged position and pressure was through overt lobbying. However, as Wright (1988) reminds us, it is necessary to look at the subsectoral level of policy-making because within specific subsectors different types of networks can develop. The chapter will now briefly focus on coffee and steel trade to demonstrate how policy networks vary within particular sectors.

Trade policy communities at the subsectoral level

In the 1950s, and early 1960s, a fairly well integrated policy network existed at the macro-level of trade policy. This policy community generally excluded groups and was made up of various state actors. Its main concern was with the general direction of trade policy within the framework of GATT and the commitment of the United States to a free trade world order. In addition, there were a range of issues that arose at the meso- and micro-levels which were concerned with the detail of trade policy for particular sectors. At these levels, the policy networks took on different forms. Two areas which have been researched are coffee and steel trade.

Coffee policy in the 1960s provides a very good example of how closed policy communities can exist within a subsectoral level of policy. In this sector an integrated relationship evolved between government and groups even within an apparently adversarial and pluralistic state such as the United States. Coffee was in a subsector of the overall trade policy community and was, in fact, the responsibility of the Department of State. State supervised the Office of International Commodities and, within this agency, the Tropical Products (TRP) division was responsible for coffee and cocoa (Short 1985).

> TRP is charged to 'maintain liaison' with private *industry* groups, but not with any number of groups that might have a continuing interest in commodity trade, for example, foreign affairs, consumer or union groups. The explicit mandate concerning industry groups, at the very least, reflects the fact that business groups have insisted on the right of consultation which other groups have not done . . . and furthermore, the business view and expertise are valued and respected in a specific way (Short 1985:86).

The interests of coffee producers were represented both by a limited number of individual coffee firms and by the National Coffee Association (NCA). The NCA's institutionalised relationship with State was indicated with the department's preparation of its ' "positions" in the evolving negotiations' on an International Coffee Agreement (ICA) and assisting in the department's involvement in the UN Coffee Conference (Short 1985: 161). According to Short, the NCA was able to establish such a relationship because: other interests failed to demand a hearing; coffee producers were prepared to channel their views through the NCA, hence creating a strong peak organisation; the NCA could provide State with information necessary for the ICA negotiations; NCA endorsement of a coffee agreement would be advantageous in getting Senate consent and finally there was a high degree of compatibility and value consensus between the NCA and State.

In developing an International Coffee Agreement, State and the NCA worked closely and had a shared view on the nature of the final agreement. In doing so they managed to achieve the support of Congress in the development of policy.

Congress was prepared to leave policy to the community because it did not want to take the lead on an issue of foreign policy; it was concerned about the growth of communism in Latin America and it was influenced by the endorsement of the ICA by the Coffee producers (Short 1985: 195).

Coffee trade policy provides an example of an almost ideal-typical closed policy community. There was a limited and stable number of actors. Policy making was dominated by the NCA, a few large coffee producers and a particular section of the Department of State. There was a high degree of consensus between the members of the community. For example, during the negotiations for the International Coffee Agreement, the department and producers had an agreed negotiating position and shared views on what the agreement should include. Groups which were liable to upset the consensus, such as consumers, were excluded. Although Congress was involved through ratification, it did not dissent from the prevailing direction of policy.

Short (1985: 314–15) concludes that the coffee industry developed a 'quasi-institutional advisory relationship with the state department for coffee and cocoa issues, and a wider network of informal and formal relationships in conjunction with these'. This was not, however, completely state-centred. The relationship was one very much based on dependence. The coffee industry wanted access to government and the negotiations on coffee agreements, and the State Department wanted a manageable policy area, political support for its negotiation position, and the information that the producers could provide. Policy 'evolved out of close and continual bargaining between group leaders and officials, with the support of both groups largely essential to the consensus for each of the policies' (Short 1985: 312).

In the steel policy area where the degree of conflict and the external pressures have been much greater, the network has operated in a different way. Steel again demonstrates that groups can be important in influencing policy. The steel industry always had good contacts with government due to its economic importance and its relations with Congress. From the late 1960s, the steel industry had become concerned with the dumping of European steel. By 1977 the steel producers had filed a number of anti-dumping complaints to the ITC, and as a response, President Carter introduced a trigger price mechanism (TPM) whereby if steel fell below a certain price the government would initiate anti-dumping procedures (Levine 1985: 12). However, the steel companies did not believe that the TPM was working well enough and so in 1982 filed another 132 cases to the ITC of which 96 were against the European Community (Levine 1985).

The United States did not want to act unilaterally against the EC, preferring a negotiated settlement. Again, it can be seen that state interests were an important influence in policy outcomes. EC/US relations were an important factor in steel policy. The US was generally supportive of the EC and was wary of taking measures which undermined the organisation. The US was stationing additional missiles in Europe which was testing EC/US relations, and there were already disagreements over agriculture and the Soviet gas pipeline. The US saw steel as an area where compromise could be reached (Levine 1985).

As a result, the Commerce Secretary Malcolm Baldrige and the USTR Brook met with the Vice-President of the EC and discussed an agreement on EC steel imports. Baldrige had kept in touch with the Chief Executive Officers (CEOs) of the major steel companies periodically during the negotiations but he met them the day after the agreement to outline the proposals. The steel producers said that they did not like the flexibility of the agreement. A new set of proposals were discussed which were again unacceptable. As the day, June 10, approached when countervailing duties would automatically be applied, Commerce had a further round of discussions with the industry before redrafting the proposals. However, the date passed and US industry would not agree to proposals that were acceptable to the EC. Discussions continued and on August 5 the EC and Baldrige reached agreement but again the industry rejected it. Eventually the EC sought a view on what would be acceptable to US industry and following this the EC made a number of concessions. Similarly, this proposal was rejected. The industry sent new demands to the EC and Baldrige asked the EC to make a few concessions so that he could say that industry demands were unreasonable but the EC has been prepared to move some of the way. This eventually led the way to agreement (Levine 1985).

This is a very interesting example. There was a fairly well integrated network with the steel industry having access to Commerce on a personal basis and being closely involved in steel import policy negotiations. However, the interests of the steel industry and state actors diverged because the President wanted to maintain good relations with the EC. Commerce was prepared to negotiate an agreement which took account of the EC's concerns whereas the industry wanted the best agreement possible. The executive was not in a position to impose an agreement on steel because without the support of steel, the industry would use the ITC to impose countervailing duties on government:

> the US Steel industry was able to use the leverage provided by a judicialised system of trade dispute to force its government to accept a political system of import protection that it would otherwise have refused. The Reagan administration in 1982 would not have acceded to steel import quotas of any sort merely because of domestic industry pressure, but when EC pressure for protection from US laws was added, it could not refuse (Levine 1985: 111).

The irony of the situation was that the US state's interests combined with the system of import relief to give US steel a veto over the policy. If the US government had not cared about the EC, or the steel industry relied on usual pressure group resources, the government could have ignored the steel industry. The steel industry had access to the negotiations through a well-established policy network and it then had a resource it could use to influence the final agreement.

These two studies demonstrate that when it comes to particular subsectors, the role of groups is important in making trade policy within the context of external constraints and state interests. In order to achieve their goals, state actors are dependent on particular groups: in the case of coffee to formulate policy and in the case of steel to prevent a vetoing of the policy. Groups can be ignored but then the costs to state actors in achieving their goals may be high. In the case of steel, it was almost impossible for the goals of state actors to be achieved without the cooperation of the steel producers. This demonstrates the dangers of focusing too much on either state or societal actors. In both cases state goals were partially a response to societal pressures and, in the example of coffee, developed in cooperation. It is necessary to avoid exaggerating the state/society dichotomy and to see that state goals are developed in the context of societal demands. These case studies also highlight how policy networks can have various levels. The trade policy network had a macro-level which set the general framework of trade policy and made international agreements and developed national legislation. Meso-level networks dealt with particular industries and sectors. Within each of these sectors the type of relationships can fluctuate greatly.

The case of trade policy demonstrates that policy communities can develop at both the macro- and meso-level in the United States, and with business groups. Nevertheless, to develop such relationships, particular circumstances have to prevail. Either state actors have to have very clear goals, or it has to be a specialised area of policy-making. Even in these situations, the maintenance of communities can be difficult. The difficulty of developing integrated networks with economic actors is forcibly highlighted by the example of British industrial policy.

British industrial policy and policy networks

In British agricultural policy, a highly integrated policy community developed and this resulted in farmers achieving substantial influence over agricultural policy and receiving a high level of support. The result can be seen as a highly successful, in terms of productivity, agricultural policy (see Chapter 5). Despite the fact that Britain is primarily an industrial nation, and has been dependent on manufacturing industry for economic success, such a close relationship has not developed between industry and government. In industry close relations have been difficult to achieve, and so government has not established a coherent industrial policy with the ability to reverse Britain's relative economic decline. It is an interesting paradox that an industrial nation has apparently lacked the ability to develop integrated networks in industrial policy.

Marquand (1988) and Gamble (1990) suggest that the reason for Britain's industrial policy failure and subsequent economic decline lies in the liberal nature of the British state. Whilst this is undoubtedly the case, it is necessary to examine the relationships that were developed and failed to develop in the industrial sector. This section will look at the failure of Britain to evolve a coherent long-term industrial policy. It will suggest that the failure to advance such a policy was the result of the absence of an integrated industrial policy community and look at some of the reasons why such a community failed to materialise.

At the end of the Second World War the British economy was to a large extent state-controlled, and in 1945 a Labour government was elected with a commitment to nationalisation and planning. It therefore seemed an unrepeatable opportunity to create an interventionist industrial policy based on planning similar to the industrial policies of France and Japan. However, rather than the Labour government developing these wartime mechanisms of intervention, they were gradually abandoned (Gamble 1982: 120) and a bonfire of controls was announced. Although the Labour Party proposed a planned economy, 'Labour still had no clear and coherent policy on planning. The Party's programme seemed to treat planning as of secondary importance . . .' (Leruez 1975: 37). The government did create the central economic planning staff (CEPS), development councils to assess how to make industry more efficient, and economic planning boards. Yet, these bodies did not result in a comprehensive system of planning. The CEPS lacked any power, economic crisis made growth rather than planning a priority, the unions were more concerned with income than planning, and industry was distrustful of development councils seeing them as an attempt at backdoor nationalisation (Leruez 1975). Consequently less and less was heard of planning, and by the end of Labour's period in office only 20 per cent of the economy was nationalised (Sked and Cooke 1979).

Already the problems with establishing an industrial policy community were apparent. There was a lack of consensus between industry, unions and government with both industry and unions wary of too much state intervention. More significantly, there was a lack of commitment from government. The economic crisis of 1947 forced the government to think of the immediate problems of dollar saving, exports and economic growth, rather than long-term strategic plans. Hence, there was a failure to develop the institutional mechanisms necessary for intervention.

The abandonment of wartime planning accelerated under the Conservative governments of the 1950s which were committed to a *laissez-faire* approach in their relations with industry (Shanks 1977). Nevertheless, towards the end of the 1950s, as Britain's relative economic decline and the success of the French economy became apparent, several leading Conservatives and members of the Federation of British Industry (FBI) became increasingly attracted to economic planning. A growing consensus appeared to be developing with the FBI acknowledging that a plan similar to that used in France, 'might be relevant in Britain, not centrally to allocate resources . . . but to "establish the kind of economic climate in which a higher growth rate will occur by the normal processes of free enterprise and competition"' (Middlemas 1983). Macmillan was also greatly impressed by the French system and Selwyn Lloyd, the

Chancellor of the Exchequer 'found the idea of consensus planning, with its built in commitments from both parties increasingly attractive' (Middlemas 1983: 12).

After looking in detail at the French system the government set up the National Economic Development Committee (NEDC) which could have provided the institutional basis of a policy community and the mechanism for intervention. It involved representatives from government, industry and unions in setting targets for growth, demand, investment and balance of payments. None of the targets were achieved and the NEDC seems to be a further example of half-hearted attempts at intervention. The government did not give the NEDC the resources or the powers of the French planning commissariat. The NEDC had no powers of compulsion, or even any mechanism for forcing the government to adopt particular policies. Moreover, the government did not allow the NEDC to affect any other aspect of economic policy and so, for example, the value of sterling was seen as a completely separate issue (Leruez 1975; Middlemas 1983). The NEDC created a series of targets but lacked the means for ensuring that either the government or industry adopted measures to try to meet these goals. In substance, it provided neither a system of planning, a coherent industrial policy, nor the basis of an effective policy community.

Labour had also been influenced by the debate on planning in the late 1950s and 1960s, and when it came to power in 1964 it made the most substantial attempt at planning in the post-war period. The government acknowledged that part of the problem of economic policy was institutional, and so created the Department of Economic Affairs (DEA) which was responsible for long-term planning (Rodgers 1985). The DEA was charged with developing an industrial policy and a five-year plan through which to implement this policy (Leruez 1975). The subsequent National Plan aimed at a 25 per cent increase in national output between 1964 and 1970 (Cmnd 2764 1965).

Despite these good intentions it soon became apparent that the National Plan would fail. On publication, the targets were immediately seen as unrealistic but a balance of payment crisis forced the government to deflate the economy and this made the plan's targets completely unobtainable (Leruez 1975). The Labour government's concern with not devaluing the pound left it with little choice but to deflate the economy and effectively scupper the plan, although it has been pointed out that even had the pound been devalued, deflation would still have been necessary (Stones 1988).

The plan failed for a number of reasons. First, the Treasury was far from happy over its loss of a monopoly on economic policy. It therefore tried to maintain as much control as possible over economic policy. It was not prepared to abandon its traditional commitment to maintaining the value of the pound and containing inflation. The DEA failed to overcome Treasury resistance to the National Plan and a high degree of state intervention (Hall 1986; Shanks 1977). Treasury dominance meant that the most likely reaction of the British state to crisis was a return to the market, and with the international orientation of the British economy a desire to protect sterling (Gamble 1982).

Second, the DEA did not have the resources to ensure that the targets it set were met. Unlike agriculture, where the government used price as an incentive to meet planning targets, the government was not prepared to provide direct investment into specific sectors in order to encourage growth. Third, industry was unprepared to allow the state any control over its investment plans, prices or production. Consequently, as in the 1940s, industry was wary of government, especially a Labour Government's, involvement in the economy – on terms other than those laid down by industry.

In 1970, after the failure of planning and intervention, the Heath government came to power with the intention of returning to the market. Consequently, a 50 per cent reduction in spending on industry was proposed (Cmnd 4578 1971: 6). With rising unemployment the government abandoned its free market policy and adopted policies 'which were more interventionist than any implemented by previous governments' (Denton 1976: 121). Under the 1972 Industry Act financial assistance was given to a large number of firms. However, much of this assistance went on regional aid and on bail outs. There was little attempt to create new institutions or a coherent industrial policy (Walkland 1984). This intervention was an *ad hoc* response to crisis rather than a coherent strategy.

In 1974 Labour came to power with the intention to build on Heath's interventions in order to create a comprehensive system of planning with price controls, extensive public ownership, planning agreements with industry, and a system of industrial democracy. Through Sector Working Parties (SWP) concerned with developing policy in particular sectors, the Labour government did create a system of institutionalised access for industry. There were thirty-nine SWPs which covered 40 per cent of manufacturing output and they undertook detailed discussion of industry's problems on a regular basis and within a consensual atmosphere (Grant 1982; Hall 1986).

Again, however, Labour's attempt at planning failed. As Grant (1982: 51) explains, Labour's 1975 Industry Act 'did contain some radical provisions . . . but they were never used'. Only one planning agreement was ever established and that was broken, and the National Enterprise Board, rather than investing in promising sectors, reverted to bailing out lame ducks (Coates 1980). From 1977, after severe economic crisis and an IMF loan, the government was forced into retrenchment and started to disengage from industry.

Within this context, the Conservatives' commitment after 1979 to reducing state intervention in industry might not seem as radical as at first supposed. Whilst the Conservatives did disengage to some extent at the macro level and, at least in the first year, adopt a strongly *laissez-faire* approach to industrial policy (Wilks 1984), they still undertook a substantial amount of *ad hoc* intervention. Large sums of money have gone into public enterprises, and through selective intervention in new technology, money has gone into the private sector. Between 1981 and 1984, for example, a range of discretionary grants were provided for companies such as Ford, Metal Box, ICI, Phillips and more (Hall 1986). The Government also provided large grants and tax breaks for overseas industries to relocate in Britain. In addition the government retained a limited regional policy through regional selective assistance and regional development grants. There was also some regional aid provided by the EC. Nevertheless, the Thatcher government did greatly reduce the role and expenditure of the Department of Trade and Industry, and particularly cut regional aid, and attempted to loosen the institutional connections between business and government.

Thus, the history of post-war industrial policy in Britain demonstrates a continual failure of the state to intervene successfully in industry, and a tendency to return to non-interventionist approaches at times of crisis. The failure of state intervention is due to the lack of capability to intervene. The state has not managed to build the institutions which would allow the necessary cooperation to develop between industry and government for intervention to work. Whilst there have been a range of different networks, and tripartite and bilateral organisations, these have not been well integrated, they have been unstable and they have lacked the capability to direct policy. The British state did not develop the necessary infrastructural power for a successful industrial policy.

The networks that were established usually lacked consensus. Industry was generally hostile to government intervention (Hall 1986) and there were major differences between government, industry and the unions over the form and degree of intervention that was acceptable. Even the unions opposed any planning which would limit their rights to free collective bargaining, and they preferred a voluntaristic framework to legalistic industrial relations (Coates 1989). In addition, union power tended to be negative, concentrating on preventing the rationalisation of industry rather than being involved in a state-led programme of modernisation. Consequently, these networks were very unstable with membership changing according to particular political circumstances – i.e. which party was in government and the policy being introduced. There was little consensus between the parties and so no long-term consistency to policy followed or groups favoured.

Amongst state actors there was little agreement on industrial policy and no single organisation could either lead or organise industrial policy. The strongest potential leader of a policy community was the Treasury but it generally preferred macro-level intervention in the economy, and was not prepared to support detailed industrial policy. Therefore, within and outside government, industrial policy remained political and a set of shared values failed to develop.

There are a number of factors which account for the failure to develop an industrial policy. First, the international orientation of the British economy has made policy-makers concerned about the value of sterling. A fall in the value of the pound could have resulted in the widespread selling of sterling which would have presented Britain with liabilities that it could not meet (Stones 1988). Because of these liabilities when Britain was faced with a balance of payments deficit, the government has been forced to deflate, rather than devalue, and so the demands of the City have had priority over those of industry. Zysman (1983) makes the point that the financial system 'proved an obstacle to government efforts in the 1960s to establish an interventionist approach'. The Bank of England saw its role as protecting the banking and financial system rather than industry, and so it could not become an instrument of state intervention. Policy-makers have often prioritised City interests which has made a policy of industrial intervention seem undesirable. This, according to Hall (1986: 78), is not the result of 'a pluralist mechanism' but, 'Once again the structural features of Britain's international position'. The structural advantages of the City made an interventionist policy undesirable and created conflict between financial and industrial interests.

Second, economic policy has been dominated by the Treasury. Within the inner core of the economic bureaucracy, 'there were no spokesmen for industry' (Zysman 1983: 201). Indeed, Britain did not even have a ministry for industry until the 1960s. The Treasury has had very close ties with the City through the Bank of England and has been concerned with sterling, public expenditure and inflation rather than manufacturing industry. It has not been prepared to act as the central actor in an industrial policy community nor to act as an advocate for industry (Hall 1986). As a consequence, 'industrial policy decisions and the administration of industrially orientated programmes are unusually fragmented' (Grant and Wilks 1983: 22).

Third, the civil service has little experience of industry and little knowledge of how it works and so 'Interventionist policies run against the training and traditions of the bureaucracy' (Zysman 1983: 202). Officials, especially within the Treasury have been poor at establishing links with industry.

Fourth, the dominant ideology within the British state, despite increased intervention and collectivism, is one of liberalism and the free market. 'Britain industrialised under a *laissez-faire* regime and prospered in circumstances which confirmed for capital and the state that the business of government was to keep well clear of business.' As a result, 'The *laissez-faire* compulsion has proved astonishingly powerful . . .' (Grant and Wilks 1983: 25–6). The dominant belief of policy-makers has been that the role of the state in the economy should be limited. Although Keynesianism was adopted after the Second World War, it was only at the level of aggregate demand, and not as a policy of detailed intervention (Eatwell 1982). As a result, 'Britain has had one of the most unconstrained market systems in the world' (Hall 1986: 48). Therefore there has been a great reluctance amongst policy-makers to intervene in the economy. No government in the post-war period came close to creating the degree of intervention that exists in France or many other capitalist nations. Both Labour and Conservative politicians have seen the role of tripartite organisations as consultative, rather than policy-making, institutions. Hence, the NEDC was separated from Whitehall and produced a 'debating society and an internal lobbyist' (Zysman 1983: 211). Industrial policy lacked an essential feature of a policy community, an ideology that could hold the community together by setting the agenda, defining the consensus and determining the potential actors and policy problems.

Finally, the nature of groups has made it difficult to establish an integrated network. On one hand economic actors – both capital and labour – are very strong, especially at the plant level, and have been able to resist government attempts to coopt them into reorganisation policies (Hall 1986). On the other they have substantial weakness in that they lack strong peak organisations, they are often very divided, and whilst being economically strong in a negative way they are weak politically. This has created difficulties in establishing constructive relationships within government. They have often been concerned with short-term economic goals rather than being involved in long-term policy goals, and this has made any possibility of depoliticisation extremely remote.

Hall has outlined how the organisation of the state, capital and labour has affected the way the economic policy is made and the nature of the policy. In Britain, these factors have led to the failure to develop a closed policy community in industrial policy or a coherent interventionist industrial policy. As Zysman (1983: 225) makes clear:

> In Britain, the efforts to expand the interventionist capacity of the state simply drove the parties and producer groups apart, for each policy introduced to promote industry was also viewed as a challenge to the position of business and finance. Each political cycle has exacerbated the free-market-versus-nationalisation dichotomy, leaving no intellectual or political space in which to build a strategy by which the state could nurture private enterprise.

The ideology of the state, capital and labour, and the political parties has made it very difficult to establish the consensus necessary to build a policy community. In addition, the City and finance has been privileged and the central economic policy-making organisation has paid little attention to the demands of industry. Consequently, the state has failed consistently to develop the capabilities to intervene in industrial policy.

This policy area raises some interesting questions about state/group influence. It is not exactly clear who had power or to what degree the state had autonomy. In one sense the City and the Treasury were influential in preventing the development of a policy community. One part of the state formed a relationship with a societal group and it constrained other state actors. On the other hand, it is not clear that industry wanted an industrial policy or a close relationship with government, and it seems to have been successful in preventing state intervention. Therefore state autonomy has been limited. Various governments have been unable to implement their industrial policies successfully because of a lack of infrastructural power. However, the consequence of the lack of a policy community is that business has had little impact on the direction of industrial policy. It has not been involved in detailed policy-making and often found itself facing policies which it viewed with distaste. This demonstrates the problems of defining power in zero-sum terms. The absence of a policy community reduced the state's capability to make and implement industrial policy whilst reducing the influence of industry on the industrial policy that was made.

However, as with US trade policy, it is important not to make generalisations at the macro-level which might not apply at the subsectoral level. If we look at two examples of the chemical industry and consumer electronics, it appears that whilst an industrial policy community did not exist, at the sectoral or subsectoral level, policy communities have developed.

Policy communities at the subsectoral level

Recent research within the ESRC's government–industry initiative has demonstrated that despite the difficulties of establishing a policy community at the macro-level of industrial policy, they can exist in particular industries or sectors. Grant *et al.* (1988) discovered that for the chemical industry there was a 'core policy community' plus a number of 'more specialised policy communities in terms of particular subsectors of the industry or particular policy areas' (1988: 55). The core chemical industry deals with the issues which affect the industry as a whole and it includes: the chief executives and government relations staff of the main chemical firms; the Council of the Chemical Industries Association and the chemical and textile sector of the DTI. It also has a European level which includes the European Chemical Industries Association; the government relations staff of the leading firms and Commission officials at DG III and DG XI. The industry has very good and stable relations with government through established procedures and there is 'mutually beneficial exchange'. There is a substantial degree of shared values within the community and it provides the industry with support within government and in the EC. Consequently, until the rise of environmentalism in the 1980s 'the industry has not had to face a countervailing force' (Grant *et al.* 1988).

An alternative example is the consumer electronics industry. Cawson *et al.* (1990) demonstrate that this industry had important links to government through the DTI and its sponsorship section, the NEDO and its Sector Working Party (SWP). However, to a large extent government has always left consumer electronics to the market and this became even more so after 1979. Yet, even here the government provided a high level of support for the development of teletext:

> In November 1980 the D.o.I constituted the Teletext and Viewdata Steering Group comprising civil servants and industry representatives. The Group's objectives were to examine the issues facing teletext and viewdata, and to develop a concerted marketing strategy for the promotion of these technologies which would be acceptable to the industry and form the basis of specific commitments. ... the policies were to be framed as part of a consensus-forming process involving industry representatives, and they were to be implemented by industry actors and not by government itself (Cawson *et al.* 1990: 252).

The department then assisted in the training of salesmen and the 'Treasury approved the halving of rental downpayments and HP deposits for those acquiring teletext' (Cawson *et al.* 1990: 253). Here was a clear example of a group developing an institutionalised relationship with government where goals were shared and policy-making was cooperative. Yet, generally the consumer electronics industry was left to the market and to developing relationships between companies. The government did not even prevent the disappearance of the British television production. Cawson *et al.* conclude that there have been major changes in the consumer electronics industry and its relationship with government because of changes in government policy, the disappearance of a national industry, increased transnationalism and the greater role of the EC. The role of the government in these changes has been limited and the most important networks have existed between firms rather than between government and the industry (Cawson *et al.* 1990).

These examples raise the question of why policy communities have managed to exist in these areas and not wider industrial policy? There are a number of important reasons. Often the issues involved in these areas are technical and specialised, and so rarely become political. The specialised nature of many of the issues makes it very difficult for those without knowledge to become involved. There are, as a consequence, significantly fewer actors and this makes it less difficult to develop a consensus. Often trade unions are excluded and so the relationships are almost bilateral. The government is also highly dependent on the respective industries for information and for the ability to make policy. As a result, the industry is often highly privileged with regular access to government on a formal and informal basis, and it is in a position to be very influential on policy, but even this is not guaranteed. The Conservative government's desire to disengage combined with economic change weakened substantially the power of the British consumer electronics industry to the point where it has almost disappeared.

Conclusion

Despite the economic strength of business, it often has great difficulty in establishing stable and well-integrated relations with government which often limits its political impact. The instability of business policy communities derives from the unwillingness of business to encourage state intervention, the large number of actors involved, the conflicts of interests between actors, the political nature of many of the areas where business is involved and the organisation of the state.

Yet, it is possible for policy communities to develop at certain times and in particular policy sectors as we have seen with US trade policy, coffee, and chemicals. Nevertheless, there is also a high level of instability in these policy communities as in trade and consumer electronics, and even greater difficulties in establishing policy communities as in British industrial policy.

Why should policy communities exist in some sectors and not in others? What did US trade policy have that British industrial policy did not? First, state actors and, in particular, the executive, was clear on the direction of trade policy in the United States whilst in Britain there was a high level of disagreement both within and between governments over the degree and type of intervention desirable in an industrial policy. In the United States there was also great awareness of how a liberal trade policy tied in to the wider interests of the state. In Britain an interventionist industrial policy was seen as harming Britain's overseas interests and its concern with the value of sterling. In the US, state interests were pursued within trade policy whereas in Britain there were conflicting views of the state's interests. Importantly, in the US the dominant ideology was supportive of liberal trade policy whereas in Britain it was opposed to an interventionist policy and therefore it was very difficult to exclude those who questioned the policy. Trade policy had an ideology which supported the policy community and helped to exclude certain groups and issues. In Britain the dominant ideology hindered an interventionist industrial policy.

It was also the case in the United States that the main political actors concerned with trade policy agreed with a liberal policy whereas in industrial policy there was a high level of conflict over the direction of policy. In Britain powerful actors – the City and the Treasury – opposed an interventionist policy. Trade policy for a time had a single executive body, in the Department of State, that could provide the centre and leadership of the policy community. In British industrial policy there were several powerful conflicting bodies. No single institution had the degree of control to become the centre of the industrial policy community. Finally, in US trade policy, through the policy community, GATT, State Department, and White House, the capabilities to make and implement policy existed. In Britain without the cooperation of business or the City, the state was incapable of implementing its policy. The main economic institutions, the Treasury, the Bank of England and the Board of Trade had neither the desire, nor the ability, in terms of links with industry and planning mechanisms, to intervene. All these factors resulted in US trade policy being consensual whilst British industrial policy remained highly political. This made it almost impossible to establish the exclusion and stability necessary for a policy community.

This raises some important points about the nature of power in state/business relations. It is clear that state organisation and interests are important in determining the nature of policy. The state might not have autonomy in relation to business, but that lack of autonomy or capabilities affects the outcome of policy. The fact that the British state found it difficult to intervene in industry, affected the outcome of industrial policy. At the same time, it is the case that the power of business varies greatly and that economic power is not necessarily linked to political power. Moreover, power is not zero-sum. The absence of state autonomy might not be due to business power but state organisation, and this lack of autonomy, or more correctly capability, may reduce the impact that industry or a sector industry has on policy. It is also true that the power of business is highly sectoral both in terms of policy, industries, and even firms. Some businesses may have influence on some policies. It is apparent that the existence of a policy community does not necessarily increase business influence. The trade policy community effectively excluded business which threatened the dominant agenda.

Therefore, pluralism is wrong to see policy outcomes in terms of the resources and activities of the groups involved. The impact of groups will depend on the organisational terrain on which they operate (Ikenberry 1988b). The capabilities of the state, the way certain beliefs and options are institutionalised into the policy process and goals of state actors all influence the impact and even the nature of the groups. However, marxist approaches also fall short because the impact of these variables on policy means that the policy process is not always going to suit the interests of capital even in the long term. Capital, like other groups is constrained by the organisational framework, and this framework often favours the interests of the state rather than the interests of capital.

Chapter 7

PROFESSIONAL POWER:
The Doctors and Health Policy

Of all the pressure groups studied in this book, doctors' organisations are most frequently cited as being influential and powerful in both Britain and the United States (Mohan 1990). Doctors' pressure groups are well resourced in terms of finance, leadership, organisation and status. They also have, through their professional knowledge, a resource that is unavailable to the majority of groups. In most cases, they have relatively easy access to the centres of government. Hence, doctors' groups are seen as having a substantial impact on government policy, and of establishing particularly close contacts with government (Eckstein 1960).

Yet, as this book has pointed out, there are problems with this approach. Eckstein attributes the success of the doctors in health policy to certain characteristics of their organisation (Marmor and Thomas 1972: 423) and, therefore, pays little attention to the context within which policy-making occurs. However, if we examine health policy in Britain and the United States it is clear that the success or failure of the doctors in influencing health policy has not depended on their pressure group activity, but is actually the result of the interests of state actors, the forms of policy networks in health policy and the wider forces within the policy process. In other words, the relationships between doctors' organisations and government are not a priori close, and so the influence of doctors on health policy is not preordained. An examination of health policy in Britain and the United States will demonstrate that the nature of the relationships is highly variable and can often be conflictual.

In British and US health policy we have an interesting contrast. The British system of health care is almost wholly public whilst the provision of health care in the US is almost exclusively private (although there is significant state support in a number of areas). This contrast will demonstrate that variations in the goals of public policy affect both the nature of doctor/government relations and the influence of the doctors. This chapter will begin with a discussion of the nature of professional power. It will then examine the development of health policy in Britain and the United States. The chapter will demonstrate that in Britain, where the government developed a public health care system, a closed policy community developed as a means of implementing this policy. The chapter will demonstrate how this policy community developed, how it operated and the threats it has faced in the 1980s particularly from a government less enamoured with the public provision of welfare.

Policy-making in Britain will be contrasted with the process in the United States where state intervention has been more limited and *ad hoc*. As a consequence, an adversarial relationship has developed between the doctors and government. This adversarial relationship, combined with a multiplicity of agencies involved in the provision and scrutiny of health care, has produced a health policy network which is closer to an issue network.

Professional power

In terms of pressure group influence, professional groups are seen to be in a stronger position than the majority of groups because they have, through their professional status, a resource that is unavailable to most groups. According to Johnson (1972: 41), in differentiated society specialised occupational skills 'create relationships of social and economic dependence' and therefore establish social distance. The professions control a body of knowledge which is important for other actors in society but which is technical and specialised, and therefore not easily available. If society desires some specific services it is dependent on the profession to provide these services. In addition, professions have their own regulatory authority that specifies the knowledge necessary to become a professional, who can join the profession, and the number entitled to practice. Through limiting entrants, professionals have a strong market position which enables them to dictate terms to their clients. The professional is the expert whilst the client lacks relevant knowledge. This allows the supplier to dictate the terms on which services are provided and the standards of services (Turner 1987).

The medical profession is seen as the archetypal profession:

> in many ways the profession of medicine has exemplified autonomous control of its knowledge base, of its clinical practices, and of allied and subordinate occupations. It has also developed a very substantial degree of control over clients of all kinds, and through all these features has escaped the managerial and bureaucratic constraints integral to most forms of work (Larkin 1988: 117).

The consequence of this professional power in the health field is 'medical dominance'. In determining health policy, government is dependent on the medical profession for their expertise and their assistance in the implementation of health policy. This places doctors in a very strong position. The government is reliant on the doctors for both the information they can provide and their cooperation in ensuring that decisions are implemented. Doctors' clinical autonomy means that not only are they dominant at the macro-policy level but they also dominate in the delivery of health care. Hence, Rhodes (1988: 78) defines a specific type of network to account for the power of the professions.

> Professionalised networks are characterised by the preeminence of one class of participant in policy making: the profession. The most cited example of a professionalised network is the National Health Service, wherein the power of the medical profession is substantial.

According to the perspective of professional dominance, doctors have power over policy-makers through their essential role in health policy; over other occupations in the health sector through their dominance of the supply of health care; and over the consumer through the asymmetry of the doctor/patient relationship.

Nevertheless, it is important to ask whether the power of the doctors in the making of health policy is preordained? Undoubtedly, doctors through their professional knowledge have an important resource. But, as within other policy areas, the usefulness of that resource depends to some extent on government policy. If doctors are to have an impact on health policy, government has to perceive professional knowledge as an important resource and the doctors have to be able to build a positive relationship with government. So the nature of government/doctor relationships, and their impact on health policy, are not pregiven, and are not solely the result of professional power. An examination of health policy in Britain and the United States demonstrates that the reality is complex and the nature of doctor/government relationships is highly variable.

Health policy in Britain: the development of the health policy community

In Britain, for most of the post-war period, the relationship between the government and the doctors can be characterised as a closed policy community. This policy community developed partly as a result of government policy, and it was this policy, rather than the intrinsic power of the medical profession, which accounts for the power of the doctors. This is demonstrated both by the way the policy community developed and by the threats to its existence during the Thatcher years.

The hypothesis is that state actors, both politicians and civil servants, have been as important, if not more so, as the doctors in the development of post-war health policy. Once the state decided to become involved in health policy, it needed the doctors in order to establish the necessary infrastructural power. However, the exceptional nature of professional power means that the government was highly dependent on the doctors in the development of health policy. Therefore, British health policy developed out of a combination of state interests and medical power. This hypothesis is strongly demonstrated by examining the way the National Health Service (NHS), and the supporting policy community, developed.

The first steps towards the health service and the institutionalisation of relations between the doctors and the state began in 1911 with the establishment of health insurance. Day and Klein (1992) indicate that, when initially establishing national insurance, Lloyd George did not want to consult the doctors. He was, however, forced to change this position in response to the doctors' reaction. As a consequence, the BMA 'successfully edged its way in to the "private conferences" with Ministers and their officials, and in so doing asserted its right to be involved in the policy-making process' (Day and Klein 1992: 265). Subsequently, it was the doctors, rather than the insurance companies, that controlled the administration of the scheme. Immediately the state became substantially involved in health provision, it had to involve the doctors in order to develop the capabilities for intervention. This intervention ascribed power to the doctors because it created a dependency, to use Rhodes' (1985) term, on the doctors. The doctors' power derived from state policy rather than the organisation of the British Medical Association (BMA).

The policies which led directly to the establishment of the NHS first evolved in the 1930s. Again, this development was due not to the pressure of the main doctors' organisation, the BMA. It was the result of politicians and civil servants realising that the problems of health provision in Britain required a change in policy. Civil servants recognised that if radical change was to occur with the minimum of disruption, the doctors would have to be involved in the process and it was this realisation that led to the development of the policy community.

During the 1930s it became apparent to politicians, civil servants and doctors that there were severe problems with the provision of health care. First, many people were not adequately covered. The 1911 Health Insurance Act ensured provision for the employed working class but not the unemployed. Provision for the destitute was provided by municipal and voluntary hospitals but here the coverage was patchy and the standard of care highly variable. Moreover, with the depression of the 1930s, the number of people covered by insurance, and the standard of coverage, fell (Honigsbaum 1989). Second, voluntary hospitals (basically charity hospitals run on donations and voluntary payments by patients) were becoming increasingly unviable and were beginning to look for some type of public support (Klein 1989). Third, medical specialists gravitated to areas where the public could afford to pay. There was little relationship between the number of patients and the number of doctors, and so the standard of care was highly variable across regions (Klein 1989). Fourth, doctors were becoming increasingly concerned with their lack of control over the delivery of health services. Although doctors were well represented on the panel which administered national insurance, in other areas doctors faced a number of influential interests. For instance, the voluntary hospitals and insurance companies had substantial control in their respective domains. In the administration of policies by friendly societies, doctors had 'no voice in administration' (Honigsbaum 1990: 696). In addition, local authorities were becoming more involved in the provision of health care through maternity and welfare clinics and doctors were concerned with their increasing influence (Honigsbaum 1990).

Pressure for changes in health policy did not derive from the strength of the doctors' lobby. If anything, it was their weak position in the face of insurance companies, friendly societies and local authorities which made them more favourable to state intervention. Rather, the pressure for change came from the muddle of the existing system (Klein 1989: 5).

Hence, the health policy network started to develop in the pre-Second World War period from two interdependent strands. One was the relationship established between the doctors and the state as a result of health insurance. The second was that the problems of health provision demanded greater state intervention. As the BMA had already established relations with government, and were central to the creation of a more interventionist health policy, it was they the government turned to when extending health policy capabilities further.

In 1936, as a response to the obvious deficiencies and inefficiencies of health provision and public pressure, the Ministry of Health began to plan the extension of national health insurance services through a merger with municipal services. Sir Kingsley Wood, the Minister of Health, asked the Chief Medical Officer to prepare a report on the feasibility of a national health service. According to Honigsbaum (1989: 13): 'even outside the department it was believed that the government intended to start a comprehensive system before its term of office expired.'

The intervention of the war rapidly developed the health service issue. The government established the Emergency Hospital Service which resulted in comprehensive links between the Ministry of Health and the voluntary hospitals. Simultaneously, there was an almost complete acceptance of the need to provide a comprehensive health service. In 1940 a committee was formed within the Ministry of Health (MoH) which developed the concept of a comprehensive health service through national health insurance. The BMA called for a hospital and specialist service to be added to the provision of a GP service, and as early as 1941 Beveridge called for a 'free universal health service' (Honigsbaum 1989).

These developments were extremely significant. The recognition of the need to create a comprehensive health service provided a degree of consensus which allowed negotiations to develop between the government and various interests involved in health provision. The government's increased involvement in health policy as a result of the war, and the likelihood of increased involvement after the war, meant that institutional relationships rapidly formed between the MoH and doctors. In other words, although there were many conflicts over the nature of future health policy and many interests involved in the policy process, and as such the health policy network at this time was not very well integrated, the structures of the future policy community were being formed.

By 1943 the Ministry of Health had completed work on the GP service and started discussion with the profession. Negotiations were largely conducted with the BMA but the Ministry also created a medical advisory committee which included representatives from other branches of medicine (Honigsbaum 1989). Nevertheless, the doctors were greatly opposed to many of the proposals from the Ministry. They objected to the degree of central control in general, and the role of local authorities in particular, and they were also opposed to the notion of a salaried service (Grey-Turner and Sutherland 1982; Jones 1981). The doctors were highly suspicious of the Ministry, seeing many developments in health policy as an attempt to gain control of the profession (Fox 1986a) and negotiations over the form of the new health system were highly conflictual. Throughout the negotiations John Maude, the Permanent Secretary, tried to reassure the doctors by giving the doctors representation on the management boards (Honigsbaum 1989).

Consequently, after many hours of negotiations between doctors, hospitals, local authorities and civil servants, the 1944 White Paper was produced. The White Paper reflected the institutional relationship between the various groups involved in negotiations. Although there was a consensus on the need for a comprehensive health service, there was a lack of agreement on how this should be provided. No single group was dominant in the policy process and this relatively loose network of doctors, hospitals, local authorities and civil servants produced a White Paper which was a compromise and lacked the strong support of any group (Godber 1988; Klein 1989). In order to appease the local authorities, they were given day-to-day control of the health service and the Ministry was charged with strategic planning. Yet, in order to allay doctors' fears over local authority control, the doctors were to be represented on Health Service Councils which would advise on policy at national and local level. In addition, GPs were also to remain independent with a recommendation to form health centres where income would come through capitation fees. Voluntary hospitals were to continue but government funding would depend on them joining planning exercises (Klein 1989: 10–15).

It is important to note that in the development of this White Paper, it was the civil servants who played the key role. As Klein (1989: 10) confirms: 'Only occasionally and exceptionally do the politicians play a central role in the drama.' Yet, the Ministry of Health did not have the administrative ability, the information nor the authority to develop a health policy on its own. It was highly dependent on the interest groups involved in health policy. This resulted in a relatively loose policy network forming the policy framework for the new health service. There were several well-resourced interest groups involved and a government department which itself was torn by the differing demands of the coalition partners in government. The department was responding to the demands for a national health service, and indeed saw this as an important policy, but in developing and implementing the policy, the department had little autonomy. It was highly dependent on other actors in the network and hence the highly compromised solution which pleased no one.

Compromise and conflict did not end with the publication of the White Paper but continued during the discussions over the Bill that was to be introduced. The doctors were very unhappy with significant parts of the White Paper and the proposed Bill. Many doctors were opposed to the idea of health centres and the centralisation they saw as resulting from the Central Medical Board whose role was to direct doctors into certain areas. It was perceived as leading to a government-controlled salaried service. The doctors then broke off negotiations until January 1945. When talks resumed, the doctors wanted a slow expansion of national health insurance and a strengthened role for doctor representation in policy-making (Honigsbaum 1989: 76–89). 'bit by bit Willink [the Minister] was driven back to the point from which Maude had started. Medical pressure forced him to retain essential features of the panel system' (Honigsbaum 1989: 89). The Central Medical Board was dropped, insurance committees were re-established, health centres were to be experimental and not salaried, and local authorities were to retain responsibility for the hospitals (Klein 1989: 16).

The strength of the doctors, and the Ministry's lack of a clear direction, led to deadlock and many of the original plans for the national health system being substantially watered down. The doctors were concerned with remaining free to practise how and where they wished with no interference in clinical autonomy. The role of the state was to provide and coordinate resources. The notion of a salaried service and local authority control was unacceptable (Fox 1986a). Civil servants had for the most part been responsible for the negotiations over health policy during the war. According to Honigsbaum (1989: 216), the 'Ministers, Elliot, Macdonald and Brown all slavishly followed their lead'. However, the civil servants were concerned with compromise rather than conflict. They lacked the political authority and the resources to impose solutions on the doctors. Consequently, the doctors 'all but imposed their will on the department. It took a strong Minister like Bevan to hold the line and prevent the structure being whittled away' (Honigsbaum 1989: 217).

The role of the civil service demonstrates the importance of state actors in health policy. However, they were state actors who lacked autonomy due to an absence of political authority and the inability to implement policy without the cooperation of the doctors. They therefore adopted an approach which was technocratic, and they were prepared to compromise and back down.

As civil servants took the lead and operated in a non-political technocratic way, the doctors could easily establish an institutionalised relationship with government. They were guaranteed access to the policy process and the development of policy was a process of negotiation between the doctors and the civil servants. However, this network had not developed into a policy community. It lacked the degree of consensus necessary for a closed community to exist. A number of powerful actors were involved in the policy network – local authorities, voluntary hospitals, insurance companies and doctors – and each had a different view of what a national health policy should look like and how it should be achieved and this made it very difficult for the state to implement the policy it desired. It therefore took Aneurin Bevan, the new Labour Minister of Health, to break the deadlock and establish the compromise which could provide the basis of the policy community.

Bevan and the establishment of the policy community

The election of the Labour government in 1945, and the appointment of Aneurin Bevan as health secretary, changed the political balance of power within the policy network. The Labour government had a clearer idea of the type of health service it wanted, and through its landslide electoral victory had a high degree of political authority for achieving this goal. More importantly, Bevan was prepared to use political authority to challenge the doctors. At the same time he was also prepared to make important compromises which could break the deadlock and allow for the establishment of a health policy consensus. Bevan was prepared to use his despotic power in order to create infrastructural power. The public support for Labour, and its welfare policies, provided Bevan with a high degree of political authority that he could use with limited political costs.

Bevan's first act of major significance was the nationalisation of the hospitals. In undertaking this measure he solved a number of problems. First, he created a unified structure for the development of health policy by putting ultimate responsibilities for the hospitals in the hands of the government. Second, he removed important actors from the health policy network – the municipal and voluntary-run hospitals – and thus simplified the process of achieving agreement on the direction of policy.

Yet Bevan still faced a high degree of opposition from the doctors to Labour's proposals for the National Health Service. In 1947, after the passing of the NHS Act, a BMA plebiscite opposed entering negotiations with the government by 55 per cent to 37 per cent. (However, despite the vote, the BMA Council actually decided to negotiate (Grey-Turner and Sutherland 1982).) This placed Bevan in a difficult position. He realised that the doctors were essential for the successful establishment of the NHS. He knew that he had little choice but to negotiate with the doctors and to gain their cooperation (Jones 1981). This demonstrates the importance of the doctors to the government. Once the government was committed to a national health service, it was essential to have their cooperation. Health delivery could not be delivered by administrative machinery or force. The doctors had to be involved.

Therefore, Bevan made a number of important concessions. In order to appease GPs, Bevan announced that doctors would still be allowed to carry out private practice; that doctors would not be state employees; that pay would be related to the number of patients and GPs would be free to practice where they wanted (Pater 1981). Bevan also split the profession by offering further concessions to the consultants. Consultants were to be protected from local authority control; they were to be given influence in the administrative structure of hospitals; they were promised a certain number of private beds in NHS hospitals; and special arrangements were made for the running of the London teaching hospitals (Honigsbaum 1989). Following these concessions, the consultants decided to cooperate with the Minister and negotiate independently of the BMA.

Despite Bevan's concessions, the BMA remained opposed to the Health Service Act claiming it allowed too much state domination, and was a step towards a salaried service. Even though a majority of BMA members voted not to participate in the new National Health Service, the BMA recommended acceptance of the new system and doctors quickly signed up to the NHS. It appeared that the government had beaten the doctors. However, Bevan and preceding Ministers had made important concessions to GPs and consultants. Health centres became marginalised; the idea of a salaried service was dropped completely; the original plans for local authority control were modified remarkably and private practice was built into the system. Yet, the Labour government achieved a comprehensive national health service which was free at the point of delivery.

The state's decision to develop a national health policy greatly increased the power of the doctors. The doctors were absolutely necessary if there was to be a national health service. A state health policy could not be built without their support and so they had substantial bargaining power. Thus it took a Minister with a high level of political authority and political determination to force the doctors to accept a policy which provided the minimum for a fair and just health policy.

In establishing this compromise, Bevan created the basis of a closed policy community. Bevan clearly presented the government's goals, and he unified the forces within government in order to create a single dominant government interest. Bevan reduced the importance of local authorities and was strong enough within Cabinet to limit the influence of other Cabinet Ministers. He also reduced the number of non-state actors who could influence health policy. Bevan realised that the only important actors of any significance were the doctors and therefore he concentrated on winning their cooperation. This was helped by the fact that the key doctors' pressure groups were the BMA and the Royal Colleges. Once the NHS had the approval of the Royal Colleges, the BMA had little choice but to accept the new system.

The central compromises were built into the running of the NHS. Doctors would provide a free health service funded by the state and in return the doctors were granted clinical autonomy to enable them to control the day-to-day operation of the health service (Klein 1989). The government got their health policy but doctors were given substantial medical representation throughout the administrative structure (Parry and Parry 1976). Consequently, the medical profession 'achieved the ability to veto policy change by defining the limits of the acceptable and by determining the policy agenda' (Day and Klein 1992: 468). It was on this basis that the doctors were prepared to accept the NHS and membership of the policy community. The doctors, through the BMA and the Royal Colleges were given representation in health policy-making. It was a bargain whereby doctors cooperated in the development and implementation of policy as long as action which prejudiced the interests of the profession was not taken without consultation (Jones 1981).

The health service was established as a result of government decisions concerning the need to overcome the deficiencies of health provision. In order to do so, the support of the doctors was essential and this gave them substantial political power. Nevertheless, state actors were crucial in the formation of health policy. The framework of the health service was essentially established by civil servants in the early years of the war. Its implementation was the result of Bevan's political authority which he used to override some of the wishes of the doctors. Ultimately, as Klein (1989) points out, the establishment of the health service was a compromise. This compromise enabled the establishment of a core or primary policy community which was centred around the Ministry of Health, the BMA and the Royal Colleges. Other actors such as the nurses and semi-professional occupations, were involved in a wider policy network and allowed access on specific issues which affected them in particular. It was the core policy community which was responsible for overall health policy whilst other actors, such as other health workers, doctors in other organisations and the patients were excluded.

The government could not establish a health policy through despotic power. If it wanted a comprehensive health policy it needed to develop the mechanisms for implementing such a policy. This infrastructural power could only be developed through negotiation with the doctors. In this case the government could not establish an alternative administrative mechanism, and a health service based on coercion was not viable in a liberal democracy. Therefore, the government was highly dependent on the doctors and hence established the health policy community. The next section will now examine how this policy community worked.

The policy community in operation

As result of the bargain outlined above, doctors became dependent on the state for their income whilst the state was reliant on the doctors for the running of health policy. 'The subsequent history of the NHS can, in institutional and political terms, be seen largely as a series of attempts to manage this mutual dependency' (Klein 1990: 700). The 'mutual dependency' was institutionalised and organised through a policy community based on a single Ministry (the Ministry of Health up to 1968, the Department of Health and Social Security (DHSS) from 1968 to 1988 and the Department of Health (DoH) from 1988) which had an almost complete monopoly over health policy (Eckstein 1960). The other key member of the community was the BMA which represented the majority of doctors. Although there were other important organisations like the Royal Colleges, it was the BMA which has remained pre-eminent (Eckstein 1960; Jones 1981).

The unity of this policy community was maintained by a very strong ideology based on: the central importance of a free health service; a belief in doctors' clinical autonomy, with only doctors referring and admitting patients; a high degree of self-regulation by professional associations; GPs being self-employed; and guaranteeing doctors a central role in the making and administration of health policy (Harrison, Hunter, and Pollitt 1990). This ideology was of crucial importance to the policy community. The free health service was seen as generally desirable. The role of the Ministry and the doctors was to ensure that this worked as effectively as possible. In a sense the policy community was technocratic rather than political, and so there was little need for the involvement of other groups in the policy process. Hence the ideology largely justified the exclusion of other health occupations, Parliament and the public. The health policy community was extremely close with agreement between the key actors on the outline of policy, and very closed with a strong belief that there was no need for other participants.

This ideology was the basis of a very strong consensus within the policy community. The consensus was based on the clinical autonomy of the doctors; the belief that doctors were experts and therefore had to be allowed to make rational decisions without political interference (Klein 1984, 1990). It was accepted that, 'Whatever the organisation, the doctors taking part must remain free to direct their clinical knowledge and personal skill for the benefit of the patient in the way they feel to be best' (Ministry of Health quoted in Wistow 1992a: 59). Whilst the state provided the money, doctors determined which patients needed what treatment. Therefore:

> Doctors were given support services, placed under a few tight financial and administrative constraints, then left to get on with the services each practitioner thought fit. Doctors had no boss and their individual performances went unmonitored. (Strong and Robinson 1990: x)

The role of managers was to smooth out internal conflicts rather than to lead. They serviced rather than controlled the doctors (Wistow 1992a). Managers did not have influence equal to the doctors and were largely producer-orientated (Harrison *et al.* 1990).

With clinical autonomy all developments in health policy had to be negotiated with the doctors because it was the doctors who would implement any policy changes. The whole process of health policy-making was predicated on the notion of having to discuss changes with the doctors. Eckstein (1960) described how negotiations between doctors, health officials and Ministers took place throughout the Ministry. Usually these negotiations were highly private and took place 'out of the public limelight and insulated against both interdepartmental relations and pressure for the grassroots of the profession' (Eckstein 1960: 88). Subsequently, disagreement was rare and when it did occur it was usually when one of the sides was subject to external pressure, the Treasury or BMA membership, and so they lost 'their normal freedom of accommodation' (Eckstein 1960: 89). Hence, the policy community played the role of routinising decision-making, eliminating unexpected problems, reducing the number of demands and increasing the autonomy of the key actors.

In order to facilitate this consensus, relations between the doctors and the Ministry were highly institutionalised. It was this policy community that was responsible for the running of health policy in the post-war period. The policy community thus institutionalised the medical profession into all stages of the policy process, 'An important feature of the DHSS is the strong professional input into decision-making. Parallel to the administrative hierarchy are a number of professional hierarchies' (Ham 1985: 102). So for instance, the Chief Medical Officer who is a doctor has direct access to the Minister, and health professionals advise civil servants throughout the administrative hierarchy (Ham 1985). Doctors, in particular the BMA leaders, had constant and formalised contact with the Ministry:

> Consultation may take place through a variety of channels through standing advisory committees or groups, through ad hoc enquiries or working groups set up to advise on particular issues; and through the more or less regular pattern of negotiation and discussion in which the DHSS engages with pressure groups of various kinds (Ham 1985: 106).

As Eckstein pointed out, 'Medical politics consists chiefly of relations between the Ministry of Health and the BMA's leaders and officials.' This he maintained was a closed network, where the input of other interests was highly limited. This relationship was institutionalised through a whole range of routine and non-routine meetings between the Ministry and the doctors largely to the exclusion of other actors.

Moreover, doctors were highly institutionalised into the decision-making process at regional, district and hospital level. Management in the process of health delivery was not through a single boss but by a group of equals (Strong and Robinson 1990). However, it was a group of equals where some were more equal than others, and where there could be no interference in what the doctors defined as clinical decisions. Management had to be through consensus with the doctors effectively having a veto. The NHS was 'controlled simultaneously both by Whitehall and thirty thousand doctors' (Strong and Robinson 1990: 18). The medical profession had formal and institutionalised links with the organisations making policy and those implementing policy. In doing so they excluded other actors such as Parliament, other health workers, other organisations representing doctors, and the consumer.

Hence, health policy in Britain provides a classic example of a policy community. The network contained a small number of well-integrated policy actors who were stable over time and had a shared outlook on policy problems and the nature of the policy. They excluded other actors who did not share their perceptions of health policy. This exclusion occurred through institutional arrangements – when making policy the ministry gave formal recognition to the doctors – and through ideology – the notion of clinical autonomy meant that it was the doctors alone who had responsibility for health policy in the last instance. This raises the question of how much power the doctors had in health policy and what room it left for the autonomy of the state or the DHSS.

It is clear that the relationship between the power of the doctors and the power or autonomy of the Health Ministry is very complex. With their professional power and the Ministry's dependence on the doctors for implementation, the doctors were in an exceptional position. In some ways, it might be more correct to speak of the privileged position of the professions rather as Lindblom does of the privileged position of business. The doctors have resources unavailable to all other groups in health policy, and this has provided privileged access to all levels of the policy process. It is clinicians who decide 'who gets what health care when . . . and the use of funds remains determined by tradition and the political clout of practitioners' (Maynard, A. 1988: 10). Ham (1981: 198) suggests that at the level of implementation, 'the distribution of power was weighed heavily in favour of the professional monopolisers' (i.e. the doctors). Eckstein (1960: 154) concludes that 'British medical policy has simply been BMA policy.'

However, such a conclusion is simplistic. It is equally clear that the doctors' influence has depended on the health policy of government. It was ministers and civil servants who set up the NHS and, to a large degree, they did so against the wishes of the doctors. In establishing such a policy they actually increased the power of the doctors. Klein (1989) points out that at the turn of the century the doctors were a poorly paid proletariat. It was the decision of government to establish a public health service which transformed the power of the doctors by creating mutual dependence. The doctors then became important. They did not have intrinsic power either because of their political organisation or their professional power. Once the government became involved in policy-making, the relationships between the government and the doctors became institutionalised. The basis of the community was a consensus on the need for a public health service and the maintenance of clinical autonomy. Although there were conflicts on particular issues, a consensus existed over the basic structure (Klein 1979: 464).

The doctors were dependent on the government for their power. In return they had to agree to the implementation of a national health service free at the point of delivery. As, Eckstein (1960: 92) somewhat contradictorily points out, 'the BMA has lost all the crucial public disputes over medical policy in which it has engaged during this century.' The government did impose the basic framework of health policy on the doctors. In doing so the government realised that it needed the doctors' support and so built the doctors into the health policy community almost to the total exclusion of all other groups. This had the advantage of coopting the most important group and, through the consensus, ensuring that conflicts over the basic direction of health policy were eliminated. Although the policy community provided the doctors with substantial power, it was established by the government as a means to implement health policy. It increased the infrastructural power of the Ministry by creating the mechanism to make policy. Power was not a zero-sum. The doctors and state actors depended on each other for power. The dependence of the doctors on government is demonstrated by the changes in the policy community which occurred after 1979. First, we will examine how threats to both the community and the consensus arose in the 1970s.

Challenges to the health policy community

Despite the strength of the health policy community, it always contained its own stresses and contradictions. In particular, there were strains over professional autonomy and the desire of government to control costs. There was a continual potential for conflict between the insider groups and other groups which were excluded from the core policy community but involved in the wider health policy networks. Moreover, there were problems resulting from the disparity between what the health service promised and what the consumer felt it actually delivered. During the 1970s these stresses became increasingly apparent and began to threaten the policy community.

The problem with the compromise was that it divorced 'political decisions about the NHS's total budget from professional decisions about the allocation of resources to individual patients' (Klein 1984: 86). Consequently, it was very difficult to contain costs. The NHS, despite facing the problem of continually rising costs, was unable to provide every citizen with complete health care when it was required. The result was rationing through certain people not being treated, a lack of capital expenditure, or waiting lists (*The Economist* 6 July 1991). The economic shortages became even greater in the 1970s when a combination of Britain's low economic growth and world recession made it increasingly difficult for governments to maintain high expenditure on the welfare state. This has led Gough (1979) to suggest that there was a crisis of the welfare state with the state unable to maintain both the required level of capital accumulation and the existing expenditures on the welfare services like the NHS.

This crisis manifested itself in a number of ways. First, relationships within the policy community became more conflictual. One example was the conflict between doctors and the 1974–9 Labour government over the issue of the treatment of private patients in NHS beds. The Labour Party's manifesto was committed to phasing out pay beds in the NHS and, once elected, they proceeded to carry out this policy. In response the BMA threatened a work-to-rule. The conclusion to the conflict was a compromise whereby only a thousand beds would be phased out immediately with the remainder being phased out according to decisions by an independent board (Klein 1979). The significance of this event was that the government attempted to break out of the consensus and as a consequence the doctors rejected the traditional rules of the game. Moreover, as Klein (1979: 475) points out, the reason for Labour's policy was partly in response to economic circumstances preventing Labour from giving priorities to increased expenditure and higher salaries. In addition, there was a growing militancy on the part of the doctors. In the 1970s doctors took industrial action over pay and, in particular, junior doctors managed to achieve a contract for overtime (Klein 1989: 113).

Second, there were threats to the policy community from groups in the secondary network and from attempts to impose greater managerial control. With increasing costs and the difficulties of controlling expenditure, health authorities attempted to introduce planning and the 'purpose of planning in the . . . service was to introduce an element of challenge by corporate rationalisers as represented by the Ministers and the Department into the policy system' (Wistow 1992a: 60). In other words, there was an attempt to impose managerial criteria on the doctors. Pressures also came from the unions of other health workers. Until 1973 union membership in the health service was low and industrial relations were largely non-conflictual (Harrison *et al.* 1990: 95). However, in the 1970s union membership grew and the unions became more militant. Initially unions were concerned with increasing pay but increasingly they demanded an input into wider issues of health policy such as the general level of expenditure (Klein 1989).

Third, the efficiency and effectiveness of the National Health Service was being called into question. Whilst costs were continually rising, the problems of the health service were also increasing. Most acute patients could still get immediate attention but this was not the case for people with minor and chronic illness, and those in the areas of mental illness and the elderly (Social Services Select Committee 1988: ix). There were also increasing questions over the equity of the service and the quality of health care being provided (Black 1988). Therefore, there has been increased consumer dissatisfaction with the health service and as a result consumers have also attempted to gain access to the policy community through organisations such as the Community Health Councils, MIND and other organisations representing particular groups of patients (Klein 1989).

Despite these threats and pressures, the health policy community managed to stay largely intact during the 1970s. Both the Labour government and the doctors were committed to the maintenance of the consensus and the National Health Service. Despite increased conflicts, the process of institutionalised negotiation continued as before. The real threat to the community came in 1979 with the election of the Conservative government which had a new perspective on health policy and was prepared to challenged the established interests, thus demonstrating that changes in policy communities require not just structural change but the existence of both an alternative vision and political will.

The Thatcher governments and the health policy community

The Thatcher governments were only too aware of the problems facing the health service. Elected on the basis of cutting public expenditure and reducing the role of the state, the government was greatly committed to the need to control health expenditure. The perception of the new right which greatly influenced, especially later on, the government's approach to health policy, was that the problems in health were not the result of underfunding. Instead they blamed the inefficient use of resources and the integration of special interests into government which were able to demand increased resources (Powell 1976; Goldsmith and Willets 1988). Initially it was suggested that the government's goal was the transformation of the NHS into a safety net for the very poor (*The Times* 4 October 1982). However, the public reaction to a Cabinet think-tank paper on cuts in the NHS was so adverse that the paper was withdrawn. The government quickly moved away from any attempt to radically change or dismantle the NHS (Klein 1984).

Instead the government 'redefined the problems of the NHS as the need to find ways to control costs in the face of limitless demands for health care' (Plamping 1991: 737). Government policy was concerned with increasing efficiency and breaking the power of the policy community (Wistow 1992b). Initially, policy concentrated on the imposition of rigorous cash ceilings to control expenditure and to increase efficiency (Social Services Select Committee 1988: x) and changing the structure of the NHS through abolishing one of the administrative tiers (Klein 1984). More recently, the government has gone even further:

> To secure improvements in efficiency, the government's recent policy has comprised a battery of centre-driven top down initiatives and controls, including a regional review system, performance indicators, policy initiatives, cost improvement programmes, competitive tendering, and changes in management structure and processes (Harrison *et al.* 1990: 86).

To achieve these goals the government has proposed a number of measures, an increased role for the market, greater use of the private sector, stronger management direction, consumer power and changes in the structure of the NHS.

In addition, the government has been prepared to challenge professional power. Groups and individuals which have influenced government policy have suggested that 'clinical freedom is not sacrosanct' (Goldsmith and Willets 1988: 7). The government is no longer prepared to allow the doctors to have a veto over changes in health policy. For example, the government was increasingly concerned about the lack of budgetary control over the expenditures of GPs and therefore decided to introduce a system of cash limits and contracts in order to control expenditure. After many hours of negotiation with the BMA there was no sign of agreement and so the Health Secretary Kenneth Clarke wrote to individual GPs explaining the new contract and saying it would be imposed without agreement (*Sunday Times* 7 May 1989). For the government, the doctors were no longer an essential partner in the development of health policy but a vested interest that had to be challenged. This can be seen as an example of political actors both within and outside the policy community attempting to exercise their autonomy by overriding and breaking up the policy community.

Two events were central to the governments attempt to undermine the policy community and to increase the efficiency of the NHS. The first was the Griffiths report and its affect on the management of the NHS, and the second was the NHS review and the subsequent policy developments. One of the central problems facing the NHS and the government was what the Public Accounts Committee saw as an absence of 'proper control' over the NHS. The committee concluded that the DHSS lacked the information necessary to monitor its performance effectively (Wistow 1992b: 103). As a response to these problems Sir Roy Griffiths, the Chief Executive of J. Sainsbury, undertook a review of the management structure of the National Health Service in 1982. Not surprisingly the subsequent Griffiths report found that the NHS lacked a 'clearly defined management structure' (Ham 1985: 33). Therefore, Griffiths recommended a policy which was a challenge to the traditional approach of the NHS and an attack on the policy community.

Griffiths placed a single general manager at every level of the health service. Management for the NHS as a whole was devolved to the NHS management executive chaired by the chief executive. Above the management executive is the NHS Policy Board chaired by the Secretary of State for Health (Cm 555 1989). More importantly, 'it was general managers, not the clinical trades who were now to decide on the division of labour, on the training, on the structure and the measures that were needed, on appropriate individual performance' (Strong and Robinson 1990: 23). This directly challenged the system of consensus management that had existed in the health policy sector (Social Services Select Committee 1984: xxi). However, it is clear that the system that has been established is a compromise with managers making concessions to traditional forms of organisation (Strong and Robinson 1990: 149). Consequently, it has been questioned whether management has penetrated beyond the high levels of management. It seems that there is little sign of change in the manager and clinician relationship (Wistow 1992b).

To date the Griffiths recommendations have not solved the problems of the

NHS. Criticism of the government's handling of the NHS continued throughout the second term and it was one of the few areas where Labour led the Conservatives in the 1987 election. After the 1987 election, the issue of health appeared to reach crisis point. Conflicts arose between the government and the consultants over the level of financing and the implementation of health service reforms. As a consequence of the government's policy of awarding pay rises larger than the increase in budgets, and forcing hospitals into making efficiency savings, a severe financial crisis hit the hospitals in late 1987 (*Sunday Times* 24 January 1981). According to one report, the President of the Royal College of Surgeons met the deputy Chief Medical Officer and 'blew his top' because he believed that the financial situation was ridiculous. He maintained that there was insufficient money to carry out operations (*Sunday Times* 31 January 1988). At the same time, the government accused the consultants of not implementing the new management system (*Sunday Times* 13 December 1987). The crisis was such that the government admitted the need to provide the NHS with an extra £1.1 billion.

The Prime Minister and Minister of Health recognised that this was just a short-term solution. The government was in a dilemma. It realised that something had to be done but did not want to raise the profile of the NHS issue. Nevertheless, the Prime Minister acknowledged that the government had little choice but to examine the options. Towards the end of January 1988, the Prime Minister announced that she was involved in a thorough review of the health service with the aim of increasing value for money in order to find alternative sources of finance (*The Times* 26 January 1988). It was intended that the review would put all options on the table and so ideas, such as hotel charges and tax relief on private insurance, that had previously been ruled out, were back on the agenda (*The Times* 27 January 1988).

The way that the review was conducted had significant implications for the health policy community:

> It was a high speed exercise, lasting only a year; it was secretive, carried out by a small group of politicians, civil servants and their advisers, these last being drawn from 'new right' think tanks and strongly associated with radical reform proposals emanating from these bodies, or NHS personnel identified as sympathetic to the government's point of view (Griggs 1991: 422).

The review was directed by the Prime Minister and so an actor from outside the policy community had become deeply involved in health policy-making. The Prime Minister was prepared to use her political authority to cut across the traditional community and therefore challenge the policy consensus. More importantly, the review was conducted largely without consultation with the key medical pressure groups. There were no representatives of either the BMA or the Royal Colleges on the review working groups, and even the role of the DoH was peripheral (Day and Klein 1992: 471). Instead of using the traditional network, the Prime Minister tended to consult her own personal advisers and right-wing think-tanks such as the Centre for Policy Studies; the Adam Smith Institute and the Institute for Economic Affairs. The Prime Minister believed that if the doctors were involved they would merely hinder the review by raising objections and pointing out the problems of radical change. Kenneth Clarke said that, 'Private formal consultation . . . was no way to run a system of parliamentary government' (quoted in Klein 1989: 224). Hence, with the policy review the doctors, 'lost their right of veto over policy' (Day and Klein 1992: 472). As Klein (1989: 237) points out:

> the Review was a private affair. It was designed to produce policy options for the Prime Minister, not a consensus about the NHS. It was in effect a three-ring circus revolving around the Prime Minister with ministerial, managerial and medical working groups competing to generate ideas for her.

Despite the closed nature of the policy process during the review, its conclusions were less radical than many had feared. Although the proposals contained some radical measures, they did not fundamentally undermine the NHS 'as we know it' (*British Medical Journal* 10 December 1988). It appears that the Prime Minister was constrained both by the support for the NHS and the lack of constituencies within the health service to implement such changes (*British Medical Journal* 8 October 1988; Klein 1989). The basis of the proposal was to:

> introduce competition in health care by separating responsibilities for the funding of health care from the provision. District Health Authorities as the main purchasing bodies will be able to offer contracts and buy blocks of services from competing hospitals. Hospitals . . . will compete for these contracts for services offered by DHA's and some budget-holding GPs (Social Services Select Committee 1989: 3).

In addition, the government proposed that some hospitals could become self-governing trusts whereby they should set their own conditions of service and employment, and be permitted to sell their services to other health authorities freely (Cm 555 1989). All GPs would be given prescribing budgets and certain larger practices allowed to have practice budgets which they could use to purchase treatment. In effect, the review and subsequent legislation has attempted to create a system of internal markets (to increase efficiency through competition) whilst maintaining a system of health care which is paid for out of general taxation and free at the point of delivery. However, what is most important in terms of this book is not the policy changes that occurred under Thatcher, but the impact that these changes have for the policy community and what they indicate about state autonomy.

A new policy network?

It is clear that in reforming health policy, and in changing the management structure, the Thatcher governments were prepared to challenge the existing policy community. Through the implementation of a system of general management and increased use of performance indicators, the government has challenged the notion of clinical autonomy. As the Social Services Select Committee (1988: xv) has pointed out:

> In the context of the NHS philosophy of offering diagnoses and treatment without reference to the patient's ability to pay and an inexorable rise in the scope and cost of diagnostic tools and treatment available, the time has come to question the doctor's right to commit resources without reference to the NHS's ability to meet the commitment.

There is an increasing attempt for managers to oversee the work of practitioners and for greater peer review of practitioners' work. For example, the distribution of merit awards to consultants, 'will be determined not just by doctors but also the managers who hold the contracts', and in opted-out hospitals management determination of pay and conditions will be even greater (Maynard, A. 1988: 23). The White Paper was concerned with making doctors accountable 'for the consequences of their decisions in terms of both costs and quality' and therefore each practitioner should be subject to a medical audit of regular and formalised peer review (Social Services Select Committee 1989: 25–6). Central to the reforms, was an attempt to change the distribution of power by separating managers and clinicians, and removing the right of doctors to veto certain decisions (Wistow 1992a). According to Wistow (1992b: 115), 'the changes of the mid-1980s and the 1989 White Paper do represent a significant expansion of management authority from the top down and contain significant challenges to medical autonomy . . . .'

The government also claimed that the reforms increased the power of consumers. The internal market will make hospitals more competitive and presumably more responsive to consumer demands. Through internal markets money will follow patients and so DHAs will have an incentive to attract patients. In addition, the government has removed obstacles to changing GPs and increased the proportion of GP income from capitation fees and so made it essential for them to attract patients. However, there are also dangers in the reforms with some DHA authorities not providing certain services, patients having to travel further for treatment and the potential for costs to rise for particular services (Social Services Select Committee 1989; Maynard, A. 1988). Moreover, there is no provision for increased consumer representation in either policy-making or administration. '. . . the White Paper intends a model of consumerism based on choice through the market-place rather than participation in decision-making' (Wistow 1992a: 68).

Changes in the policy community have also occurred at the policy-making level. As we saw, when examining the Thatcher reforms, policy-making has moved away from being consensual to being conflictual to the extent that the government has been prepared to exclude traditional members of the policy community and include new groups such as the new right think-tanks. None of the Royal Colleges were consulted either before or after the publication of the White Paper. As a consequence, relations between the doctors and the government have deteriorated. As the BMA, and to some extent the Royal Colleges, have been prevented from operating within the policy community they have had to adopt more overt, pluralistic, forms of lobbying. In 1989 the BMA launched a concerted campaign against the government's reforms using posters, direct lobbying, contacts with MPs, threats of mass resignation and use of the media. Through the poster campaign they were even reduced to directly insulting the Secretary of State for Health. In July 1989, the BMA voted not to cooperate with the implementation of the Government's reform proposals on internal markets, hospital contracts, self-governing trusts or GP practice budgets (*The Times* 5 July 1989). Yet, the result was that, 'In April 1990 the government, for the first time imposed a new general practitioner contract on the medical profession' (Day and Klein 1992: 469).

Nevertheless, the doctors have accepted the reforms but at the same time have continued to criticise the government's handling of the NHS, and consultants have continued to oppose the establishment of NHS trusts (*British Medical Journal* 15 December 1990). Moreover, in order for the government to ensure that the implementation of the reforms as a whole went ahead, the government did in the end consult with GPs and make a number of small concessions on payments for vaccinations, screening and minor operations (*The Times* 7 October 1989).

Undoubtedly, then, the government has changed the nature of the policy community. Wistow (1992a: 71) concludes that, 'Taken together, the package of proposals ... appears to represent a ministerial commitment to achieve a substantial transfer of power and influence from medicine to management.' In addition, there has been a fragmentation of power with decision-making being moved from the centre to district level and, in the case of trusts, to hospital level (Klein 1989).

The government has attacked the consensus and ideology of the policy community by questioning clinical autonomy and removing the doctors veto over both decisions of implementation and of wider policy. Consequently, conflict and new groups have entered the network and undermined the closed policy community that previously existed. Yet at the same time this has not become a loose issue network. Doctors are still important to the process of making and implementing policy, and the structures of institutionalised access still exist. In fact the Secretary of State for Health, Virginia Bottomley, admitted that if the government had consulted more during the policy review they might not have faced the same problems of convincing the doctors that the new policy has benefits. As Day and Klein (1992: 475) suggest, 'Following the confrontational crisis, it was in the self-interest of government to be conciliatory and to revert to administering policy through the medical profession.'

However, the Thatcher years are interesting in terms of the question of state autonomy. Mrs Thatcher was prepared to use her political authority – even her 'despotic power' – and capital to challenge an established policy community by making policy outside of it. She realised that if reform was left to the community it would be emasculated and therefore she demonstrated that political actors could take decisions without the support of the key interest groups. Nevertheless, this did have costs. Mrs Thatcher, if not constrained by the policy community, was constrained by public opinion, and thus the radicalism of the policy change was limited. In addition, the bypassing of the community created a high level of ill-feeling amongst doctors and so made the development of policy and, in particular, its implementation more difficult. As a result doctors could not be completely ignored, and although management's role has been increased, the doctors continue to have a major impact on policy and implementation.

Yet this case demonstrates that political leaders can challenge policy communities and force changes in policy that otherwise would not have occurred. Even in areas where there are groups with apparently high intrinsic resources such as doctors, they still rely to some extent on the interests of the state. When the interests of the state change, their power and relationship with the state change. Policy communities are not inevitable in health policy and this is confirmed if we briefly examine health policy in the United States and contrast it with the forms of political organisation that developed in Britain.

Networks and health policy in the United States

In the United States health policy has developed out of conflict rather than consensus and therefore the networks which have evolved in the health policy arena are very loose. This raises the question of how much power the state and the doctors have in the development of policy. In this section we will examine the conflicts over health policy in the United States and demonstrate how this has led to networks with little integration and as a consequence it has been very difficult for either the doctors or the state to control health policy.

Health insurance, Medicare and Medicaid: conflicts between doctors and state

A constant dilemma in US health policy is the role the state should play in the provision of health care. The degree of state intervention in health policy has been constrained by the dominance of liberal values, the belief that people are responsible for their own health, and the nature of the American state:

> Not until the beginning of the twentieth century . . . did the US federal, state and local governments make much headway in the bureaucratization and professionalization of their administrative function. With the greatest changes coming first at municipal and state levels, bureaucratic–professional transformations happened piecemeal through reform movements spearheaded by the new middle classes. As the various levels of government were thus partially reorganized, the fragmentation of political sovereignty built into US federalism and into the divisions of decision-making authority among executives, legislatures and courts continued throughout the twentieth century (Weir *et al.* 1989: 18–19).

This fragmentation reduced the demands for federal welfare policies and made it difficult for the federal state to develop and implement health policies. As a result, the majority of health care is provided privately. People, usually through their employers, contribute to a private health insurance system which is used to purchase private health care.

Nevertheless, there is substantial federal government involvement in health care with over 46 per cent of health care expenditures being spent by the government (*The Economist* 6 July 1991). Much of the health policy debate in the US has centred around how much and what sort of health policy provision there should be. There have been strong pressures from particular groups, for example the unions, members of Congress and certain Presidents for greater national provision. On the other hand, US doctors have been strong supporters of liberal ideology and have favoured a low level of state intervention in health care. Consequently, they were very keen to protect their autonomy and the private provision of health care. Therefore, attempts to expand state involvement in health care have resulted in conflict.

The degree of this conflict is apparent over the issue of national health insurance and the development of Medicaid and Medicare in the 1960s. The issue of a system of national health insurance whereby everyone could purchase health insurance through a state scheme was first discussed early in the twentieth century. Before 1916, the American Medical Association (AMA) supported the move to national health insurance (NHI) (Laumann and Knoke 1987: 78). However, the pro-insurance lobby made a number of tactical errors which turned the doctors against the scheme (Fox 1986a: 12–13). Consequently, national health insurance became a highly contentious issue with the doctors being implacably opposed to any scheme. Therefore, the inter-war years did not see any serious attempt to establish NHI to the extent that there was not even a new deal for health policy (Fox 1986a). The strength of the AMA's opposition to NHI was such that it managed to remove the issue from the agenda. Even President Roosevelt did not push national insurance and omitted any reference to it from the Social Security Act (Laumann and Knoke 1987).

With the Second World War, federal involvement in health care greatly expanded and, with increased numbers of doctors and greater specialisation, increased costs (Riska 1985). The greater costs and the wider acceptance of state involvement in health care led to increased public demand for national health insurance. In addition, there were international pressures with the Beveridge report receiving coverage in the United States and the International Labour Organisation creating an international agency to expand social security. In a 1942 opinion poll, 74 per cent favoured a system of national health insurance. By the end of the war FDR had privately told health reform leaders that they would have his support (Peon 1979: 29–31).

Following these developments, President Truman made national health insurance a central item on his domestic agenda. In 1945 Truman presented his health plan to congress which included health insurance, funds for research and hospital building (Peon 1979). The AMA's response was immediate. Seeing these proposals as an attack on the autonomy of doctors they organised a counteroffensive (Riska 1985: 55). In the inter-war period, the doctors could rely on structural power to keep the issue of health insurance off the agenda, and therefore had little need for overt political activity. Health insurance was ideologically unacceptable and so was not seriously considered as an option. As Campion (1984: 129) reports 'Up to this point, the AMA had won its battles without doing a great deal more than developing factual reports and putting its case before a respectful public.' However, with the growing support for health insurance, and especially because it had presidential backing, the AMA had to become activated. According to Laumann and Knoke (1987: 82), 'the AMA emerged as a potent political actor at the national level'. The AMA then organised a loose coalition which included the American Hospital Association, American Bar Foundation, and doctors and other groups opposed to increased government intervention.

The doctors launched a concerted lobbying campaign to prevent the passing of national health insurance legislation. The AMA employed professional lobbyists and spent $5 million in order to spread the message on health insurance. The strategy of the lobbyists was to contact thousands of groups to obtain their support for the AMA's position. 'The point was to convince lawmakers as quickly as possible that many groups and many political constituencies besides the AMA thought that the voluntary approach to health insurance was more desirable' (Campion 1984: 162). In addition, they used the strength of liberal ideology and the rapidly developing fear of communism to support their case. The hyperbole of the AMA President Elmer Henderson became common: 'American medicine has become the blazing focal point in a fundamental struggle which may determine whether America remains free or whether we are to become a socialist state' (quoted in Campion 1984: 161).

The AMA was not without opposition. There were a number of powerful groups which were strongly committed to national health insurance. Some doctors supported NHI through the Committee of Physicians for the

Improvement of Medical Care, and a number of unions organised in support of insurance through the Committee for the Nation's Health. However, most important was the strong support from federal government. In particular, the Federal Security Agency drafted the legislation and provided the supporters of insurance with much information and argument (Campion 1984).

Despite this rising support, legislation for national health insurance was unable to pass through Congress. Truman could not build sufficient support within Congress for national health legislation despite it being introduced annually. Initially legislation was blocked by a Republican/Southern Democrats coalition. In 1948 Truman was re-elected and again promised national health insurance but he was again unable to win sufficient support within Congress. The Republican House and Senate steering committees said that health insurance legislation was not even on the list of legislative actions. In 1949 several important lobbies declared against the national health insurance and this, according to Peon (1979), was due to the AMA's lobbying campaign. The supporters of health insurance lost momentum and the unions started to use collective bargaining as a means of achieving employer-financed insurance (Peon 1979). In 1952 Eisenhower was elected and his philosophy was close to that of organised medicine. As a result, 'the AMA now enjoyed entree to the White House' (Peon 1979: 210). Consequently, health insurance was no longer an issue which threatened the interests of the doctors.

Realising that there was no possibility of a system of national health insurance in the foreseeable future, the proponents of insurance adopted an incremental approach. They channelled their efforts into achieving health insurance for the aged, realising that this was much more difficult for the opposition to dismiss. In 1957 the Forand Bill, which proposed up to 120 days of hospital and nursing care for the elderly, was introduced (Laumann and Knoke 1987). However, at no time during the Eisenhower administration did a system of health insurance for the aged 'have a chance of congressional enactment' (Marmor 1970: 31).

President Kennedy, on the other hand, was prepared to give a high degree of support to health insurance for the elderly and he made a number of highly publicised speeches supporting its introduction. In 1961 the King–Anderson Bill was introduced which proposed for retirees on social security pensions ninety days' free hospital care, some nursing care but almost no physician's service. The AMA opposed this bill because they saw it as a first step to the socialisation of medicine and they demanded a system where health provision was related to ability to pay (Campion 1984: 256–61). The AMA again launched a large publicity campaign and the bill was defeated in Senate (Marmor 1970).

With the assassination of Kennedy, and the subsequent democratic landslide, President Lyndon Johnson used the swell of public opinion to ensure that Medicare legislation was passed. In fact, the chairman of the Ways and Means Committee, Wilbur Mills, was faced by two alternatives, the King–Anderson Bill and two bills proposing the purchase of private health insurance. Mills integrated the bills to produce both Medicare and Medicaid. Medicare covered hospital care for the retired with supplementary voluntary insurance for physician services. This was to be provided on uniform premiums with matching funds from general revenues. Medicaid widened cover to indigent people under 65 and was to be funded with matching federal and state funds (Campion 1984; Laumann and Knoke 1987; Marmor 1970). Although national insurance was never implemented, a system of health insurance for the poorest sectors was established against the opposition of the AMA.

The major features of US health policy developed almost totally out of an atmosphere of conflict rather than cooperation. Throughout the period from 1920 to 1965, there was almost no agreement between federal government and the doctors, or within Congress, over the nature of health policy. Although there was some agreement on the need for some type of Medicare policy, it was a consensus that excluded the AMA (Fox 1986b). This conflict meant that during the post-war period, doctors failed to establish well-institutionalised relations with government. As a result health policy was a highly pluralistic arena where the key actors were often in conflict. The doctors used the techniques of lobbying and publicity to challenge government policy. It is frequently argued that the AMA was very successful in using these methods because of their resources and they were a very successful pressure group, the 'supreme legislative stringpuller' (Marmor 1970). Its influence was demonstrated by the AMA's success in preventing the passage of health insurance legislation.

However, as Marmor (1970: 57) indicates:

> Neglected in this stereotyped portrait is the distinction between the results the AMA approves (or disapproves) and those they produce. The AMA has few resources for coercing individual congressmen to change their votes, especially senior autonomous figures in committees like ways and means. National health insurance failed to become law because of the opposition of Congress, not the doctors. Congress was dominated by a majority who believed that the role of federal government in social policy should be limited. They did not want to see a socialised system of medicine or increased taxation. The legislation was already doomed because of the strength of the conservative coalition in Congress, and the inability of the Truman administration to marshal liberal constituencies to support its program (Fox 1986b: 85).

To a large extent, the development of health policy did depend on the autonomy of political actors, especially the President and the key congressional committees. It was Truman who chose to make national health insurance an important issue whereas FDR had ignored it. Likewise, Eisenhower effectively ensured that the issue was removed from the agenda. The support of Kennedy and Johnson was crucial to the passing of Medicare and Medicaid. To a large extent the implementation of Medicare and Medicaid was the result of outside events (Fox 1986b). The role of Johnson was to harness these events so that they could be used to pursue major developments in social policy. Johnson made health policy central to his great society programme and so played a central role in raising it onto the political agenda (McKay 1989: 33). He also used his political skills to ensure that the assassination of Kennedy and the election of a large number of liberal congressmen could be directed into achieving social reform (Fox 1986b).

Another key actor was the Chairman of the Ways and Means Committee. Before 1964 Mills used his political skills to block health legislation (Falcone and Hartwig 1984). Once he realised that political circumstances had changed and legislation was inevitable, he used his position to ensure that he shaped legislation (Marmor 1970). Therefore, to a large extent, the development, or lack of it, of health policy was not the result of the power of the AMA, but the result of the balance of forces within Congress, the attitudes of Presidents and the external environment. The absence of a policy community meant that the doctors had limited impact on health policy because they lacked any real input into the process at the federal level. The policy did not change because their power increased but because the views and power of other political actors changed.

Nevertheless, it would be wrong to say that the doctors had no effect on policy. The AMA, in their resistance to national health insurance were in fact strongly assisted by the structure of health policy-making. There was a structural bias in their favour. First, federal institutions often lacked the ability to intervene in a number of policy areas. Second, the dominance of liberal ideology opposed government intervention. There was an absence of a social democratic tradition either to develop or to push a coherent and fundamental reform of health policy. Third, the process of policy-making was highly fragmented within both the executive and Congress and therefore it was relatively easy to block proposals for reform. Fourth, the federal system fragmented health policy even further making it difficult to plan any national system of health provision (Paton 1990: 3–27). Hence there was a mobilisation of bias within the health policy arena against any increased government intervention (Paton 1990: 28) and the AMA played to, and reinforced, this bias.

The AMA concentrated on using the structural constraints to block reform measures, and reinforcing the ideological bias by referring to measures as 'socialist'. Therefore, the AMA's power was negative. In a more positive sense they were successful in limiting the range of options available. By calling national health insurance socialist, reformers were forced onto the defensive and so, 'The pattern of medicare proposals over time illustrated the capacity of the AMA to influence the agenda of discussion and limit the alternatives policy-makers would suggest' (Marmor 1970: 114).

The failure to develop national health insurance cannot be attributed to the power of the doctors but was the result of the structure of the decision-making process and the opposition of Congress. The subsequent development of Medicare and Medicaid resulted from changes in the membership of Congress and from presidential initiatives. In addition, reformers realised that any proposals for health policy had to take place within the framework of the organisation and ideological nature of the US state. Consequently, health policy developed in the United States not on the basis of consensus, but out of conflict. It also involved a large number of political actors. Hence although state intervention did substantially increase with Medicare and other policies, the networks which developed as a result of this intervention were not very well integrated.

Intervention and issue networks

Although there were limits on the extent to which the government could become involved in insurance, the degree of government intervention in other areas of health policy increased substantially in the post-war period. Whilst Congress was continually opposed to national health insurance, it did pass, with the support of the AMA, legislation to provide federal support for hospital building, medical education and research (Fox 1986a). In addition, the government provided a number of health programmes for specific groups of the population. The federal government established: Community Health Centre Programs for those in deprived areas; home health programmes for the elderly, programmes for children, native Americans and migrants. The state also directly provides medical services for members of the armed services and veterans (Thompson 1981). The federal government spends a vast sum in absolute terms on health policy. At least $60 billion is spent on the uninsured alone (Havighurst *et al.* 1988). In the 1982 budget there were sixteen government agencies with health-related budgets (Finegold and Greenberg 1984: 101).

In addition to direct involvement in the public provision of health care, government has played an increasing role in the planning of all health care. Mechanic believes that medicine in the United States is highly regulated and increasingly bureaucratic. The government is involved in regulating standards, planning the provision of services, and through efforts to restore the deficiencies of the system (Mechanic 1981: 7–8), 'Government involvement comes, however, not through a few broad strokes but rather through hundreds of programs and thousands of guidelines.'

The American system of health care is one of largely private provision but with government intervention in a whole range of areas. The lack of consensus and broad vision of health policy means that many agencies are involved at all levels of government. There is a lack of a single overseeing authority that can coordinate programmes and impose an order on the policy arena. Health policy is made within loosely integrated networks.

Finegold and Greenberg (1984: 99) suggest that 'the federal health policymaking structure in the United States is fragmented, with a large number of health programs in many different agencies.' In addition, there is also a lack of consensus over who should run health policy and the level of state intervention. Rather than doctors becoming integrated into the policy process, as they have in

Britain, the relationship between government and the medical profession has been one of confrontation. The government has attempted to impose some order and policy direction on the health care system, and the doctors try to prevent any policy which they see as threatening their autonomy.

Despite the complexity of this network, Laumann and Knoke (1987: 245) suggest that it does have a core. The central actor is the Department of Health and Human Services (DHHS) (previously the Department of Health, Education and Welfare) which accounts for 77 per cent of expenditures (Finegold and Greenberg 1984). However it is joined at the core of the network by the 'White House Office, the OMB, the Health Resources Administration, the HCFA, the FDA Commissioner, one senate subcommittee, and four private sector groups' (Laumann and Knoke 1987: 245). Close to the core are specialist organisations like the AMA, AHA and the main insurance organisations plus most of the federal agencies. Although there is a core at the centre of the network, it contains many more actors, with more disparate interests, than the British policy arena. Unlike Britain, where policy is dominated by the DoH and the doctors, there are a number of powerful actors on both the state side and the interest groups side. Many of the core actors, such as the OMB and the Food and Drug Administration (FDA), have the resources and authority to develop their own health policies. There is no single state organisation defining the nature and limits of health policy and so the potential for conflict is very great. In addition, through the OMB and White House Office, the President has access to the arena which makes it difficult for a policy community to act autonomously from the executive.

Even these core organisations are highly fractured when it comes to making health policy. The DHHS contains a large number of relatively independent agencies. The Health Care Financing Administration supervises Medicare and Medicaid, the Veterans Administration is a federally funded agency to provide care for veterans, the US Public Health Service is an umbrella within the DHHS for a range of services but it is often in conflict with its parent body (Thompson 1981). Each of these agencies has its own priorities in health policy, and so there are numerous conflicting goals. In order to support their position within the executive, to lobby Congress to increase congressional and public support and sponsor legislation, these agencies attract interest groups into the health arena as a political resource (Campion 1984). This increases even further the number of groups in the policy network.

This disaggregation is exacerbated by the role of Congress in health policy. With health policy becoming increasingly controversial and health care costs rising, Congress has attempted to regulate health policy through establishing Professional Standards Review Organisations and a national health planning system (Falcone and Hartwig 1984). Health policy is overseen by three committees in each house and 'several dozen other subcommittees, each with its own narrow focus of interests, have jurisdiction over health and health related programs' (Finegold and Greenberg 1984: 103). In addition there are *ad hoc* committees and committees taking an irregular interest in health. Consequently, the health policy arena is fissured by conflicts over territory (Falcone and Hartwig 1984).

Further divisions are created by the role of state governments which often play a significant role in health policy. 'Within certain limits ... states have the authority to determine the services to be covered by medicaid' (Thompson 1981: 17). Local administrators also have a substantial impact on the implementation of policy, and the intergovernmental lobby has become another important organisation within the national health policy network trying to influence federal policy (Thompson 1981).

Health policy in the United States contains a large number of groups – both interest groups and government agencies – and no single group or set of groups is dominant. Although Laumann and Knoke (1987) indicate that a (large) core does exist, the network also contains a whole range of groups connected to these core actors who are likely to enter the policy arena depending on the issue. For example, in their quantitative analysis of health policy network, Laumann and Knoke discovered 151 organisations involved in the health policy domain. Within this domain they found fourteen distinct issue publics – i.e. groups with interests in a particular subsector of policy. Although there were some connections and overlaps between the issue publics, Laumann and Knoke suggest that there is often a high degree of disagreement between groups, and so groups did not cluster tightly around issues. In other words, there were many groups involved in health policy and relationships between them are not very close. Although there is a core, it is a core that is divided on policy goals and often in conflict. Attached to this core are groups whose influence and interests vary, and this creates a high level of conflict over health policy goals.

The result of the complexity of this policy network means that it is very difficult to specify who has power in the US health policy arena. It is clear that the doctors have had some power but this has been largely negative. They have been able to reinforce the tendency of the American system to oppose greater intervention in welfare. The number of actors and interests involved in health policy has made the blocking of reform relatively easy.

At the same time doctors have had a high degree of power over the delivery of health policy. Because the health system has remained private, and doctors have protected their professional autonomy, they have a monopoly within the health system over the development and allocation of resources (Alford 1975). Havighurst (1987: 132) suggests that, 'the medical profession long exercised one-party control that effectively pre-empted consumer choice on virtually all important questions affecting the delivery of medical care.' The medical profession controlled who could do the treating, how many doctors were trained and medical standards. The profession was also successful in controlling patient access to hospitals and insurance, and so prevented greater competition in the provision of health care (Havighurst 1987). Hence, the medical profession's power was not in influencing policy but in creating an extremely strong market position which gave it a great deal of control over the delivery of health care. Consequently, doctors were not dependent on the state and the state was not dependent on the doctors. In that sense, the doctors have tried to maintain their power by depoliticising medicine. They have attempted to ensure that health policy decisions are medical and market decisions, and not issues that should involve government (Riska 1985: 129).

This approach has certainly given the American doctors significant influence. However, their opposition to government intervention, and their subsequent confrontational attitude, has limited the impact the doctors have had on federal health policy. As their position has been one of opposition, they have tended to exclude themselves from government. In some ways they have maintained a hostility to government, and policy has developed through conflict rather than consensus. Therefore, doctors have failed to establish well-integrated relationships with government and so lacked a substantial influence on national policy.

Subsequently, much national policy is the result of initiatives from the President and, to an extent, from Congress. The degree of conflict has resulted in political actors attempting to act autonomously as a means of reforming health policy. The key developments in US health policy have relied on substantial presidential support. However, Presidents have also been limited in the degree of freedom they could exercise over health policy. The number of actors in the network, the ideological opposition to state intervention, and the fragmentation of the health delivery system have made reform very difficult and major reform rare. No President has been able to develop a comprehensive national health policy (Peon 1979).

From the 1940s to the 1960s Presidents were unable to expand health provision without substantial compromise. Since the 1970s, Presidents have faced great difficulty in attempting to contain the cost of health care and impose some order on the system. For example, with the rising cost of health care in the 1970s, President Nixon became increasingly concerned with the cost and so the OMB took a much more active role in health policy (Finegold and Greenberg 1984). Nixon introduced a number of measures such as professional standards review, Health Maintenance Organizations (HMO) and local certificate of needs programmes in an attempt to limit costs. Both Ford and Carter attempted to bring in greater federal mechanisms in order to control the professionals and limit the rising costs of health care (Brown 1987). However, the lack of consensus and the high number of actors in the policy network have made changing the system extremely difficult to achieve. The result has been a crisis in the health care system. Havighurst (1987: 141) points out that 'even when government tried to impose specific checks on the industry's spending impulses, it found that it was politically impossible to make much difference. Professional advocacy for patient interests was too effective to resist in most close cases.'

The US health care system is frequently said to be in crisis. In 1962 health care cost 5.2 per cent of GNP, by 1986 it was 11 per cent and by 1990 12 per cent (Feldstein 1988: 1; Marmor *et al.* 1990). Health care takes 15 per cent of the federal budget compared to 10 per cent in 1975 and in real prices spending per head increased from $950 in 1970 to $2,350 in 1989 (*The Economist* 16 November 1991). With the ever increasing cost of health services, large numbers of people can no longer afford health care. It is estimated that between 30 and 50 million people have no, or inadequate, insurance (Marmor *et al.* 1990). The cost of health insurance is now so high that many middle-class people can no longer afford health care (Peters 1986: 185). The reasons for the inability to control costs are related to the organisation of health delivery: there is duplication of high cost services in regions because hospitals compete against each other; health insurance plans mean that there is little incentive for efficiency and keeping costs down; there is a maldistribution of resources; there is little incentive to use paramedics; and the delivery of many public programmes is fragmented (Braverman 1980).

Moreover, as we have seen, the nature of the health policy network has made it increasingly difficult for Presidents and the executive to deal with the problems. In the 1970s both Nixon and Ford attempted to revive national health insurance as a way of controlling costs but both were thwarted (Laumann and Knoke 1987). There were also attempts during the 1970s to introduce greater planning and cost control mechanisms. In 1974 Health Systems Agencies were established to prevent unnecessary capital expansion but they lacked any financial carrot. A system of certificate of need was established for hospital building. In order to receive federal aid, a hospital project had to be deemed necessary. A Professional Standards Review Organisation was established to monitor the quality of care and the Health Care Financing Agency was created to try to control costs of Medicare and Medicaid (Marmor *et al.* 1990). There were also price freezes on health care prices and wages from 1971 to 1974 but prices rapidly increased once they were removed (Feldstein 1988). In 1979 Carter proposed a Hospital Costs and Containment Bill but there was vigorous opposition from doctors and hospitals (Braverman 1980).

Despite these measures, federal government failed to contain costs. Therefore the Reagan administration made a further attempt to reform health care in order to contain costs. Mohan (1990) suggests that Reagan attempted to challenge the traditionally powerful doctors by increasing competition within the delivery of health care. The initial approach of the Reagan administration was to introduce competition, rather than federal regulation, as a mechanism for controlling costs. In order to achieve greater competition the administration proposed:

> reducing or eliminating tax deductions for health insurance premiums by employers and the excludability of health benefits from employees' taxable income; providing multiple health plans for employees, Medicare and Medicaid beneficiaries; requiring an equal contribution of the employer or government toward the purchase of these plans ... (Oliver 1991: 458)

Reagan's procompetition measures failed to get through Congress because of the opposition of many of the interested parties and so the administration retreated to a 'strictly fiscal policy' (Oliver 1991: 473).

Thus, the most effective mechanism during the 1980s remained regulatory rather than market mechanisms. Under Reagan, Diagnosis Related Groups (DRGs) were introduced whereby doctors receive a fixed price for treating Medicare and Medicaid patients, and it has been claimed that this has reduced the rate of increase in costs from 16 to 20 per cent to 10 per cent per year (Havighurst *et al.* 1988). There has also been the encouragement of Health Maintenance Organisations, which were set up in the 1970s, whereby people pay a fixed price each year to cover all their health care treatment rather than pay for what they receive. In addition, the power of doctors has been weakened by increasing numbers of both doctors and hospitals, and it is believed (or hoped) that this will contribute to a reduction in costs. The Reagan administration also substantially cut budgets for federally funded health programmes.

Nevertheless, the problems of rising costs continue. Neither Reagan nor Bush managed to introduce significant reform, and so the health care crisis remains an issue (*British Medical Journal* 22 June 1991). There is increasing dissatisfaction with both the provision and cost of health care. Through the 1990s over twenty Bills have been submitted to Congress in an attempt to reform health care. President Bush also made health care reform central to his first 'state of the union' speech (*The Economist* 16 November 1991). As yet there has been no fundamental reform. The nature of the policy network makes it extremely difficult for the President to reform health policy or control costs. It is much easier to prevent, than initiate, change.

Conclusion

It is undoubtedly the case that doctors in both Britain and the United States have a number of resources which can be used to influence health policy. In both countries doctors did have a substantial impact on certain aspects of health policy. In Britain, in particular, the development of the National Health Service occurred with a great deal of consultation and consideration over what was acceptable to the doctors. In the United States, the impact of the doctors on health policy was more negative. To some extent the doctors reinforced the already liberal framework of policy options and were able to use this, along with other bodies like Congress, to stop certain policies.

However, it is also the case that the relationships that the doctors' organisations had with government varied greatly in Britain and the United States. In Britain, from the late 1940s until the end of the 1970s, the doctors were involved in a closed policy community. This policy community had a shared consensus on the nature of health policy and provided doctors with a privileged position in the health policy arena. In the United States, the adversarial relationship between the federal government, and the doctors and the large number of federal agencies involved in health policy, meant that policy was made in a loose network and consequently the impact of the doctors on health policy was limited.

These different networks also had important implications for state autonomy. In the United States the disparity of the network made it very difficult for the executive to control the development of health policy. At particular times, presidential initiative could galvanise certain parts of the network in order to achieve particular goals as in the case of Johnson and Medicare. However, the President's autonomy was clearly limited. To an extent the President was responding to public and congressional pressure and at the same time the range of policy options were still limited by the *laissez-faire* policy agenda.

In Britain, state actors have again been important in galvanising and changing the direction of the policy community. In the 1940s, Bevan was prepared to cut across the policy network in order to force through the health service without waiting for the slow process of negotiation between the doctors and the civil servants. Again in the 1980s, Mrs Thatcher was prepared to challenge and change the policy community in order to reduce the power of the doctors and introduce reforms. This suggests that despite the resources of the doctors, they have no inherent powers and still, to varying degrees, depend on the state if they are to influence policy.

It is clear from looking at US and British health policy that the types of networks that have developed have partly been a result of policy goals and partly been a cause of policy goals. In the United States, the belief in a private health care system has meant that the integration of doctors into state networks has been unnecessary, and therefore loose networks have developed. However, the development of these loose networks has subsequently created difficulties for the state. Without integrated networks, the state has lacked infrastructural power. In Britain, the development of a public health care system created the need for a policy community in order to ensure intervention in health policy. However, this also made health policy difficult to change because the policy came to be dominated by the policy community.

The different networks have also affected policy change in Britain and the United States. In both countries rising costs have created pressures on the networks and the policy. In Britain, the Conservative government has attempted to change health policy by challenging the policy community and by creating new structures of power. In the United States, attempts have been made to control the private sector and to make it more market-orientated. In a sense both have failed. Change has been limited and costs have not, as yet, been brought under control. In Britain, it could be argued that the failure to effectively reform health policy is a result of ignoring the policy community (Marsh and Rhodes 1992d) and in the United States it is due to the absence of a policy community limiting the means of implementation. In Britain the policy community would not implement policies it opposed and in the United States, Presidents have not established the consensus to radically change policy.

Chapter 8

PUBLIC INTEREST GROUPS AND POLICY NETWORKS:
The Case of Consumer Policy

The policy networks that have been examined hitherto, involved groups with either economic or professional power and, therefore, with resources to exchange with government. Consumer policy provides an interesting contrast. Consumer groups generally lack a high level of resources. They are frequently poorly organised, underfunded and have a low density of membership. Although in principle consumer groups do have economic power in terms of purchasing power, action such as consumer boycotts are extremely difficult to organise and usually ineffective. This apparent weakness raises the question of whether consumer groups can establish policy networks with government and, if so, what form do these networks take?

Post-industrial theory suggests that consumers are becoming increasingly important as a social group and should be in a position to influence government. According to post-industrialists, as societies move into their post-industrial phase, individuals increasingly see themselves as consumers rather than producers because consumption replaces production as the focal point of political activity (Bell 1974; Gorz 1989). With work and class being less important, consumption becomes a key factor in explaining voting behaviour (Dunleavy and Husbands 1985). Even the left has abandoned its traditional anti-materialism and now views consumerism as central to the socialist case (Labour Party 1989; Smith 1986).

However, in Britain and the United States, which some claim to be in the post-industrial phase, it is doubtful that consumers have become central in the political battle or even that they have become politically more important. Dunleavy and Husbands' belief that consumption cleavages have become the main determinant in voting behaviour has been widely challenged (Marshall *et al.* 1988; Saunders 1990). It is clear, that in both Britain and the United States, consumer groups have developed from organisations concerned with production testing to groups with institutionalised access to government. This chapter will assess the development of consumer networks in Britain and the United States. It will demonstrate, contrary to the post-industrial theorists, that the growth in consumer activism is not the result of social change but of political factors. The chapter will begin by looking at the development of consumer groups from those concerned with product liability to those with institutionalisation. It will examine why they were more successful and more advanced in the US. It will then look at how consumer power waned in the late 1970s and 1980s with the rise of the new right and how, in recent years, new forms of consumer political action have developed.

From product testing to institutionalisation: the rise of consumer power

Consumers face a number of difficulties in organising compared with farmers, business or doctors. Initially there is a problem of defining a consumer. As the National Consumer Council (NCC) recognises, consumers are 'everybody in society at one point of their life: that is as a purchaser and user of goods or services, whether publicly or privately provided' (NCC 1979: 6). Offe (1984: 228) similarly argues ' "consumers" do not constitute a clearly delimitable and organisable complex of individuals.' As many people do not primarily see themselves as consumers, it is very difficult to organise mass consumer groups. Consumers lack a shared definition, they do not have common interests, they rarely meet collectively, and they do not have the resources to build strong political organisations. Olson's (1965) collective action problem is very great for consumers. As the benefits of consumer policy are jointly supplied, consumers receive them whether they join consumer groups or not, and so it is not worthwhile paying the costs of joining a consumer group. Hence, when consumer groups have formed it is usually on the basis of selective benefits rather than collective goals. Groups like the Consumers Association (CA) in Britain, and the Consumers Union (CU) in the United States, have made the selective benefits of consumer magazines (*Which* and *Consumer Reports*) their main priority.

Despite these constraints, consumer groups have been established in Britain and the United States. Their development has gone through three stages. They began as organisations concerned with product testing. They then developed into political movements which, finally, established institutionalised relations – policy networks – with government in consumer affairs departments. The United States always led Britain in this process and developed each stage to a much higher level.

Before consumer groups could even become product testing organisations there has to be some acknowledgement of consumers and consumer problems. According to Silber (1983: 1), between the end of the nineteenth century and the 1920s 'a national culture of consumption emerged' in the United States. This was clearly a prerequisite of any consumer movement. Simultaneously, there was the growth of the Progressive Movement (Barbrook and Bolt 1980) which, although largely concerned with corruption of government, raised the issue of the dominance of producers. People like Upton Sinclair in the United States highlighted issues of adulteration of food and this led to increased food regulation (Forbes 1987: 4). Likewise, abuses of the monopoly position of the railways led to the formation of the Interstate Commerce Commission as the first regulatory authority for protecting consumers (Nadel 1971: 22). In Britain, similar questions were raised about food adulteration (Burnett 1989) and the co-operative movement started in order to organise and strengthen the market position of consumers (Tivey 1974). However, at this time there were no consumer groups as such and any consumer regulation was to protect the consumer from direct physical or economic harm (Nadel 1971: 7).

Yet, this was an important stage in the growth of the consumer movement, particularly in the United States. Once a category called 'consumers' came into existence, and consumer problems were identified, consumer groups developed largely as product testing organisations. This product testing role clearly had a political aspect. It provided the consumer with information on which to base his or her choice of purchase and, in that sense, was an attempt to organise in order to challenge the market dominance of business. The information was also used to pressurise government to introduce regulations which protected consumers. If these groups gained a reputation for serious and scientific research they could then provide the government with technical information and so in some sense become insider groups.

As if to confirm the arguments of the post-industrialists, these groups developed first in the United States. The Consumer Research Bulletin was formed in the US in the 1930s. It was a response to the increasing consumption of consumer durables, concern about the consistency of standards, and the depression which emphasised the importance of value for money and the need to organise the economic power of consumers. By 1935 it had 50 staff and 200 outside consultants (Silber 1983: 19–21). In 1936 a strike caused a split in the organisation and the Consumers' Union (CU) was formed which by 1939 had 85,000 members (Silber 1983: 28). It has since gone on to become 'easily the largest and perhaps the most influential consumers' organisation in the world today' (Thorelli and Thorelli 1974: 420).

In Britain, it was not until 1957 that the Consumers' Association (CA) became the first national product testing organisation. The Consumers' Association was established as a response to consumerism in the United States and the failure of the government to create a consumer advisory service (*The Times* 5 October 1978). It also reflected the growing concern with consumer issues in Britain. The Consumers' Association was launched with a loan from the Consumers' Union and with a few volunteers in the East End of London (*The Times* 7 October 1978). By 1980 this had grown to 685,000 members and had 'acquired pre-eminence as a spokesman for the consumers' (Smith 1982: 284). However, despite the respect and importance of these organisations in both Britain and the US, they largely failed to acquire a wider political role in the sense of providing a consumer input into wider political questions. Barbrook and Bolt (1980: 237) point out that: 'for most of its existence Consumers' Union has hardly been a pressure group in the strict sense of the term', and it was only in 1969 that the Union established a Washington office (Thorelli and Thorelli 1974: 437).

Both the CU and the CA have had problems widening their appeal.

Although in terms of numbers their membership is high, it is drawn from a very select group – the middle class – who join it solely as a means of gaining information, not to partake in any political activity. This has made it difficult for these organisations to establish themselves as the political representatives of consumers. Smith (1982: 290) claims that much of the energy of the CU and the CA has been absorbed in maintaining the finance and membership of the organisations, rather than political activity. Consequently, product testing organisations were able to establish very loose networks with government on the basis of the information they obtained through product testing. They were insider groups in the sense that governments accepted that they were legitimate groups, and there was an exchange of information between the groups and government. However, consumer groups did not have a policy role. They were consulted on specific issues but did not have access to the policy process on any substantive issues of policy. Governments, in Britain and the US, were unwilling to accept their views on wider political questions. Consequently, these organisations were very limited in their political activities (Silber 1983: 127; Smith 1982: 288).

Despite the limitations of these consumer groups, consumer issues did become more politicised in the 1960s and 1970s, especially in the United States. It changed from a movement being concerned with the value, efficiency and safety of products, to one which saw consumers as having specific interests which needed to be represented in all areas of government and to challenge corporate power. The growth and strength of product testing organisations made politicians realise that consumers were becoming increasingly important as a political group. Consequently, in 1962 President Kennedy outlined a consumer Bill of Rights which for the first time established a consumer policy in embryo.

President Johnson went even further and adopted a set of consumer legislative proposals as central to his policy package (Nadel 1971: 31). This presidential leadership, combined with increased technology, a wider range of products, more sophisticated marketing and the growth of multi-outlet retailers, began to change the relationship between retailers and consumption (OECD 1983: 10). In the US, political entrepreneurs exploited this greater complexity and concern in order to make consumer issues political.

In 1965 Ralph Nader published *Unsafe at Any Speed* which detailed how General Motors was cutting back on safety measures to reduce costs (Barbrook and Bolt 1980: 231). Nader used the controversy created by this issue to establish a network of groups and individuals to pressurise government on consumer issues. Nader and his supporters politicised consumerism by outlining a wide range of demands from product liability laws to the establishment of a consumer protection agency. They also inspired the creation of grassroots consumer groups to lobby on the consumers' behalf at state and local level (Thorelli and Thorelli 1974: 461). In addition, the media was very willing to take up consumer issues and gave a high level of publicity both to the failings of business and the actions of consumer groups.

This increased politicisation provoked important changes within government and Congress by creating a new political climate in the area of consumer affairs. The Federal Trade Commission (FTC), which had traditionally been seen as part of a pro-business iron triangle, was reorganised and reinvigorated (see Pertschuk 1982). Under Miles Kirkpatrick consumer protection became a major responsibility of the FTC, and the Food and Drug Administration adopted a less trusting approach to the drug industry. In Congress a number of liberal democrats became active in consumer protection, and the Democratic Study Group developed a package of consumer proposals (Nadel 1971: 64 and 101).

Consumer issues moved from being questions about the quality of goods which were translated into technical issues at the governmental level, to being questions at the centre of political debate which were highly controversial. Consumer politics was no longer about products. It became concerned with the means of creating consumer representation at all levels of government and challenging the power of business. As a result, a wide range of consumer legislation was introduced in the US between 1966 and 1969. In 1966 Congress enacted four pieces of consumer legislation and, according to Vogel (1989: 35), 'These laws invoked the beginning of an upsurge in Federal legislation regulating corporate social conduct that would continue uninterrupted for more than a decade.' Between 1960 and 1980 twelve pieces of legislation were passed in the US. Some of this legislation broke new ground by moving away from health and safety issues and addressing the issue of consumer information (Flickinger 1987). Consequently, consumer affairs received a high level of attention for the first time, and provoked substantial business opposition. This conflict made the policy area highly political. A similar process of politicisation also occurred in Britain but it was much slower and much less thorough.

In Britain, the government has been much more rapid in institutionalising the consumer movement and thus preventing it becoming a wider political movement. Even so, consumer groups did become increasingly political in the late 1960s and 1970s. Local consumer groups were formed and the Consumers' Association widened its role to include the lobbying of central government. Both the present system of food labelling and the Unsolicited Goods and Services Act 1971 were the result of campaigns by consumer groups (Smith 1982: 233; *The Times* 18 March 1987). If anything British governments passed more legislation than the US. Yet, consumer groups in Britain never managed to develop the wider political movements or the high degree of controversy that existed in the United States.

With increased lobbying, organisation and political activity, the consumer movement was successful in building closer relations with government. To some degree these relationships became institutionalised and so integrated networks were established between groups and government agencies. In Britain, incorporation was more a means of controlling the consumer whilst in the US it was seen by consumer groups as a means for ensuring the representation of consumer interests.

In the United States the consumer movement tried throughout the mid-1970s to establish a Consumer Protection Agency which could then put the consumer case to various government agencies (Vogel and Nadel 1976: 9). This would have provided the basis for a consumer policy community. Although consumers were unsuccessful in this goal, they did manage to institutionalise interaction through other means. First, consumer groups had access to the President through the President's Committee on Consumer Interests, established in 1964, which was replaced in 1971 with an Office on Consumer Affairs (Thorelli and Thorelli 1974: 462). Under Nixon, the consumer office was downgraded and his consumer adviser met resistance throughout the administration but the office continued to have direct access to the President (Nadel 1971: 56). All Presidents from Johnson had a consumer adviser in the White House:

> President Kennedy established a Consumer Advisory Council (CAC) in 1962. In 1964 President Johnson added a Presidential Committee on Consumer Interests composed of the CAC and designated consumer liaisons in departments and agencies as well as a special assistant to the president for consumer affairs (SAPCA) (Lucco 1992: 243).

Every President, up to and including George Bush, has appointed a SAPCA and so maintained the consumer link with the White House. However, it is not clear that this gave consumer groups great advantages. As Lucco (1992: 250) points out, 'In all administrations but one, aids close to the president, not the consumer adviser, made the important decisions on consumer affairs.' Moreover, consumer advisers rarely reported directly to the President and usually met presidential advisers who passed on advice to the President. Sometimes, these advisers were not particularly sympathetic to consumers. For instance, under Nixon, consumer policy was coordinated by Peter Flanigan who was 'known to business as "our man in the White House"' (Lucco 1992: 254).

Second, support for consumer issues grew within Congress as the consumer vote was seen as increasingly important. This led to the Senate Commerce Committee changing the focus of the FTC, and so consumers were given institutionalised access to the bureaucracy. The FTC had traditionally been seen as a bastion of business power (Rothman Hasin 1987: 6). With increased interest in consumer issues in Congress, the Senate Commerce Committee started to investigate means to strengthen the FTC (Pertschuk 1982: 43). The Magnuson–Moss Act 1975 gave the FTC power to make industry-wide rulings, and this power was used to investigate issues which harmed consumer interests (Rothman Hasin 1987: 11). In addition, Carter had pledged his support to consumerism during the presidential campaign and so appointed Michael Pertschuk, a consumer advocate as Chairman of the FTC. Pertschuk's appointment placed a consumer group representative deep inside the FTC and he could ensure that the agency's role was one of actively supporting the consumer. Pertschuk further institutionalised the role of consumers in government by creating a Bureau of Consumer Protection and new consumer protection specialists. According to Rothman Hasin (1987: 61), it was 'possible to discern the beginning of the "iron triangle" of influence being forged to connect the Federal Trade Commission, the Senate Commerce Committee, and consumerists . . . .'

In addition, President Jimmy Carter attempted to improve access of consumers to all areas of government. In response to Congress's failure to establish a consumer protection agency, he established consumer representatives in thirty-five federal agencies. The role of these representatives was to report to the agency heads on how the policies would affect consumers and to ensure consumers participated in decision-making. It seems that Carter was explicitly attempting to create integrated networks because he claimed the these advisers would 'lock the consumer perspective into the very structure of government' (*New York Times* 10 October 1980).

During the 1970s consumers established institutional access to government, and shared values developed between consumers and the administration. However, this network was different to others in this book. It did not exist around a distinct policy domain but in large part consisted of an attachment to a range of policy areas. Although the FTC did provide a degree of institutional focus, consumer groups were attempting to influence a range of policy areas. Hence, they were not in a position to dominate a specific network in the way doctors or farmers could.

In Britain, institutionalisation occurred earlier than in the United States but did not result in consumers achieving the same degree of political influence. Institutionalisation was indicative of the different forms of political representation that are dominant in Britain. Rather than allowing the development of consumer groups and then giving them access to government, various governments have institutionalised consumer interests in a way that has prevented the development of a political consumers' movement. Hence, consumer groups in Britain have been underdeveloped politically but overdeveloped in terms of their degree of institutionalisation.

The Macmillan government established the Molony Committee in 1959 as a response to 'the new style consumerism' and this 'led directly to the creation of a new publicly-funded body called the consumer council' (Smith 1986: 8). Although this was abolished in 1970, the Heath government established the Office of Fair Trading which was given power to protect consumers in the market place (Smith 1986: 8).

The 1974 to 1979 Labour governments went even further. They created a Department of Prices and Consumer Protection (DPCP) which was supposed to admit consumers directly into decision-making (*The Times* 16 September 1978). The government also increased the powers of the Price Commission. Under the Price Commission Act 1977 all manufacturing and service firms had to give the Price Commission twenty-eight days' notice of price increases and the commission was given the power to investigate price increases and to freeze prices (HC Debs 930: c. 1255–6). In 1975 the government also established the

National Consumer Council (NCC) as an independent body whose role was to 'represent the consumer interest in dealings with the government, local authorities and the Director General of Fair Trading' (Smith 1986: 9; Harvey and Parry 1987: 44).

This high degree of integration of consumers disguises the true influence of the consumer movement. It is clear that the main purpose of the DPCP and the Price Commission was not to protect the interests of consumers but to administer the Labour government's pricing policy which was a major part of its anti-inflation policy. As Shirley Williams stated in the House of Commons (HC Debs 872: C.258):

> Unless steps are taken to control the projected rate of inflation, there will be no future for industry, any more than there will be for the consumer.
> It is for this reason that the government will give absolute priority in the short term to deal with inflation.

In addition, the government's attempts to control prices and to provide food subsidies were not a result of consumer pressure but trade union pressure. Price control was an important part of the Social Contract between the trade unions and the government. In return for wage restraint, the government promised price restraint.

The creation of the NCC and the Office of Fair Trading (OFT) was not a means of increasing consumer power but of limiting it. Unlike the consumer bodies in the United States, the NCC had no power. Its only role was to make reports to government. Usually these reports have been ignored or the government has commissioned reports when it knows the conclusions will support the government's position. The NCC does have access to consumer Ministers but this is for consultation rather than policy-making purposes. It is useful for government to have a consumer group which it funds, and whose leading members it appoints, to consult on issues that affect consumers. It makes policy-making more predictable and allows the government to claim that it has consulted without having to talk to more radical groups beyond its control. The NCC also provided a shield to government and protected it from more radical demands. This is not to say that the NCC has been without influence but generally the influence has been restricted to matters of detail on technical issues. Although the OFT does have real influence and several of the Director General's reports have been acted on, it is not a consumer body which represents consumer interests. It is a government body which exists to prevent restrictive practices.

The British attitude to consumer groups fits in with the general policy style of elitist policy-making in small and well-defined groups (Jordan and Richardson 1982). By creating the NCC, the government can claim it represents the consumer interest and refer all other consumer bodies to it. This prevents the consumer movement becoming a mass movement. At the same time, the government can justify its lack of concern in consumer interests by pointing to the fact that the NCC and CA are not mass movements and therefore lack legitimacy. As Robert McLennan, Under-Secretary at the DPCP said, if consumers were to carry weight in government they 'would have to face the need to acquire democratic legitimacy' (*The Times* 16 September 1978).

Consumer policy was highly institutionalised in Britain (Flickinger 1987). It was made almost solely by government-sponsored bodies. The network was organised around the DPCP and included other state-funded organisations like the OFT and the NCC. The consequence of this network was not necessarily a high degree of consumer influence but government domination of consumer policy.

In both Britain and the United States, the consumer movement has developed throughout the twentieth century from organisations that are concerned with product testing to establishing institutionalised relations with government. It is clear that in the US consumer groups have been much more successful. They have built broader movements, become more integrated within government and had a greater impact on policy. In the US, the FTC has been prepared to challenge producer power in favour of the consumer. Product liability laws are much stricter and Presidents have been more willing to listen to consumer demands. In Britain, although consumers achieved institutionalisation, they did so without becoming highly political and so did not really develop distinct consumer interests with a high level of interest group support. Does the progress of the consumer cause and its greater impact in the country that is claimed to be the most advanced in terms of post-industrialism, prove the post-industrial thesis? Has consumerism become central in politics? To demonstrate that this is the case it would be necessary to show that the rise of consumerism was the result of social causes and that consumer politics has continued to fare well in the 1980s. However, the greater success of consumers in the US is accounted for by political factors and, counter to the claims of post-industrialists, consumer movements have suffered in the 1980s.

Explaining the growth of consumerism

In looking at Britain and the United States, it is undoubtedly the case that political factors have played an important role in accounting for the differential success. As Vogel (1980: 623) illustrates, 'The public interest movement simply has no resources that can match the power of capital' and so 'its effectiveness [and] very existence has been fundamentally dependent on decisions made by the policy process'. The success of the consumer movement depended to a large degree on the interests of state actors and the extent to which they were prepared to provide political leadership. Consumer groups lack the resources of economic pressure groups, and so often depend on state actors perceiving consumer groups or issues as important.

In the United States, Kennedy first indicated interest with his consumer Bill of Rights and Johnson and Nixon followed with legislative proposals (Nadel 1971; Thorelli and Thorelli 1974). Carter went even further. He strongly supported the consumer cause, bringing consumer activists into government and backing the creation of the Consumer Protection Agency (CPA) (Vogel 1989: 128). There were a number of reasons why Presidents might have chosen to support consumer issues. Consumerism had a high level of support in the 1960s and 1970s. It was also a relatively cheap policy to introduce, needing little extra spending by government, and it was largely a consensus issue (Nadel 1971) with industry not being well enough organised politically to take on the consumer groups (Vogel 1989).

At the same time, members of Congress became involved in consumer issues and so were prepared to introduce consumer legislation. It suited their interests because at a time of growing concern with consumer interests, it helped career advancement to be involved with consumer legislation that would have wide publicity and a good chance of being passed. Senator Magnuson quickly became a supporter of consumer groups after 1962 when he came within 50,000 votes of losing his seat (Pertschuk 1982: 29). Without these political leads consumer groups would not have been able to have such an impact on policy.

In Britain, the weakness of the consumer movement meant that consumers were even more dependent on political leadership. Although this was forthcoming to some degree, its role was to try to limit rather than encourage the consumer movement. British governments created the DPCP and the NCC. However, they were not responding to consumer pressure but had economic reasons for wanting to intervene in price-setting, and it was useful to have a consumer body to legitimise these interventions.

The success of the US consumer movement was also highly dependent on the existence of political entrepreneurs like Nader and Senator Magnuson. Consequently, there were people within and outside Congress to galvanise the consumer movement. Entrepreneurs were a means of overcoming the collective action problem (Taylor 1987). Lacking resources and a collective meeting place, the consumer movement depended on entrepreneurs to raise consumer issues and to organise consumer protest (Pertschuk 1982: 23). Such political entrepreneurs did not exist in Britain, and to some extent, this accounts for the failure of the consumer movement to evolve. Often when such people looked liked making an impact – like Des Wilson – they were labelled outsider or even 'wildmen' and excluded from consultation.

Finally, the United States has a long tradition of 'public interest activism' and groups which are seen as taking on corporate and government power are accorded a degree of legitimacy that is not available to 'radical' groups in Britain (Vogel 1980). These factors made it easier for consumer groups to develop in the United States and then to gain access to government. In Britain, the elitist nature of policy-making meant that consumer groups were seen as illegitimate and only given access if they were government supported bodies or representation was on the basis of scientific evidence related to product testing. They took on a much less political role and institutionalisation was a limit on power rather than a source of influence. Although networks were established in Britain and the US, the types of networks were very different. In the US they were a means of consumer input into policy whilst in Britain they were a means of preventing real consumer influence.

The differences in the level of development of consumerism in Britain and the United States cannot be explained by the degree of post-industrialism in each country. The relative strength of the respective consumer movements is a result of different political factors – the degree of political leadership, the form of policy-making and political culture. The development of consumer policy was to a large extent dependent on the actions and interests of state actors. Flickinger (1987: 164) highlights that:

> While societal changes created a readiness for many people to respond to, and support, consumer policy initiatives, public opinion did not compel action. There was not a sustained period of agitation by groups and individuals outside government before consumer policy issues appeared on government agendas. This was particularly the case for the United States where government action on consumer policy, media attention to consumer concerns, and an active consumer movement arrived on the scene nearly simultaneously in the 1960s. Other factors, often linked to short-term political needs, play an essential role in explaining the emergence of consumer policy. .... [M]uch of the early action on consumer policy originated with individuals in Congress and the administration rather than with outside groups.

In addition, the fact that in the last ten years consumer movements on both sides of the Atlantic have suffered major set-backs suggests that the post-industrial teleology is too simplistic. The decline in consumer influence can also be explained by the changing interests of state actors.

Consumers in the 1980s: the right and retrenchment

In terms of pressure group theory, it is surprising that consumer groups were so successful in the 1970s. However, this power was short-lived, and the 1980s has seen a decline in the power of consumer groups and a change in the nature of consumer policy (Smith 1993). The weakening of the consumer movement was perhaps first apparent in 1978 when Congress defeated the proposals for a Consumer Protection Agency despite the support of consumer groups, President Carter and senior members of Congress (*New York Times* 14 January 1979). At the same time, the attitude of Congress towards the FTC changed remarkably.

Since the mid-1970s a belief had been growing that the consumer movement was becoming too influential (Vogel and Nadel 1976). By 1978 there was a strong anti-regulation tide within Congress. Increasingly members of Congress questioned the FTC's use of its extra power and opposition grew to its influence on consumer affairs. In 1979, the House Appropriations Subcommittee halted the Commission's consumer protection investigations and two of its major anti-trust investigations. The Committee wanted cuts in budgets and to end the FTC's power to make industry wide rulings (*New York Times* 15 September 1979).

This anti-regulatory feeling became policy with the election of President Reagan. Reagan entered office with an explicit programme of deregulation which saw consumer interests being protected through the extension of the market. To achieve this goal he created a task force on regulatory relief, he appointed deregulators to key regulatory agencies (Vogel 1989), and he increased the authority of the OMB over the regulatory agencies (Reagan 1987). The Reagan administration sharply reduced the budgets of both the Consumer Product Safety Commission (CPSC) and the FTC. In 1981 the CPSC faced the largest cut of all regulatory agencies, lost 160 staff and had eight regional offices closed (*New York Times* 4 October 1981). By 1986 its budget had been cut by 22 per cent and staff by 42 per cent (*New York Times* 12 April 1986).

Reagan also appointed J. Miller III as the chairman of the FTC. Miller had been in Reagan's transition team on deregulation and believed that the 'commission should no longer protect the consumer from defective products and unsubstantiated advertising claims'. He claimed that the FTC could cope with a 12 per cent budget cut, and that even a cut of 18 per cent might be appropriate. He did not see the role of the FTC to be keeping imperfect products from the market. In his view, 'Those who have a low aversion to risk – relative to money – will be most likely to purchase cheap, unreliable products' (*New York Times* 27 October 1981). Under Miller the FTC reduced its anti-trust activity and abandoned a number of consumer protection cases. The Reagan administration also reduced enforcement of consumer protection through staff and budget cuts and refocusing the work of agencies (*New York Times* 5 April 1982).

This anti-consumer ethos was strongly supported by Congress. The House Judiciary Committee has considered ways to reduce anti-trust obstacles (*Congressional Quarterly* 20 May 1989: 1194) and throughout the 1980s Congress failed to re-authorise the CPSC and, 'So while members have piled criticism on the agency as ineffectual, Congress has left the government's consumer protection policy unmoored for almost a decade' (*Congressional Quarterly* 3 March 1990). Congress also attacked the powers of the FTC. In 1979 the Senate Commerce Committee (the Committee that had reinvigorated the FTC in the early 1970s), unanimously approved a bill to restrict the powers of the FTC and to tighten legislative control of the Commission (*New York Times* 21 November 1979). The Congress then imposed a legislative veto on all FTC rule-making (*New York Times* 4 May 1980). Following this unprecedented move, Congress further restricted the role of the FTC. It was forced to drop its investigation into child advertising and 'state licensed professionals' were exempted from the FTC's jurisdiction. The power of the CPSC was reduced when Congress adopted a measure to prevent any agency rule taking effect until a joint resolution was passed and then signed by the President (*New York Times* 30 June 1983).

In Britain, a similar transformation of consumer policy has occurred. Policy has moved from a interventionist view of consumer policy through protection to a *laissez-faire* policy of improving the free market and consumer information in order to allow free choice. Like the Reagan administrations, the Conservative governments since 1979 have adopted a market-orientated approach. A deregulation unit was set up to investigate means of eliminating constraints on the market and cost compliance has been introduced whereby the benefits of any new regulations have to outweigh the cost to industry. If they do not, the new rule will not be introduced.

The Conservative government abolished the Department of Prices and Consumer Protection and shifted responsibility for consumer affairs to a Minister of State within the Department of Trade and Industry (DTI). Its importance was further reduced when responsibility went to a Parliamentary Under-Secretary. In July 1990, responsibility for consumer affairs was again given to a Minister of State, but this time in the House of Lords. The new government's view of consumer policy was outlined by the first Trade Secretary, John Nott: 'While giving the consumer proper protection, we must guard against the excessive demands of rampant consumerism.' In his view consumerism had grown in the last decade and had produced too much legislation which was a drain on the resources of trade and industry (*The Times* 16 October 1979). According to one consumer group official, the DTI became increasingly non-interventionist, very close to business and rarely listened to the demands of consumers.

However, the Conservative government has not completely abandoned consumer protection. In terms of safety regulation there has been a continual stream of new rules in the last ten years. Although the DTI has become less sympathetic to consumer groups, the fact that an ex-Conservative Minister, Sally Oppenheim-Barnes, was Chairman of the NCC between 1987 and 1989 made other departments more open to consumers and they were prepared to listen to well-argued and well-researched cases. The government also passed the Consumer Protection Act 1987, which was a major piece of consumer legislation making producers liable for defective goods whether or not the defect was the result of negligence (Gibb 1988). Yet, the government's poor view of positive consumer protection was demonstrated by the fact that this law was only as a result of an EC directive, and the government chose to implement the directive in a way which favoured business by allowing 'a state of the art defence'. This defence allows producers exemption from liability if they can show that the current state of knowledge meant they could not know that a product would be harmful. Consumer groups see this defence as undermining the law, and the EC has seen it as a failure to implement the directive by taking Britain to the European Court (*The Times* 8 December 1986).

The changes in policy that have occurred in the United States and Britain raise the question of why the policies have changed so radically considering the strength of consumer groups in the US and the fact that they managed to institutionalise their relationships through integrated networks. The case of consumer policy demonstrates that often pressure groups, even if they are well organised, are weak and dependent on the perceptions and choices of government in making policy. It is clear in the case of the consumer networks that although they were fairly well integrated, they were still relatively weak. There was no single site for the making of consumer policy – consumer interests needed to be taken account of in all areas but consumers could only establish close relations with specific parts of government, like the FTC or the DCPC. If more powerful sections of government chose to change the organisation of consumer policy, consumer groups lost their power base. Lacking resources, consumers were dependent on state actors seeing consumer policy as important. When government perceptions changed, the influence of consumer groups changed. Moreover, within consumer networks it was difficult to establish a consensus on consumer policy as the networks often included business interests which were directly opposed to consumers.

The weakness of consumers in terms of their lack of resources and the instability of their networks meant that once a new government was elected which had a different view of consumer policy, the policy would change. This occurred in both Britain and the United States. In the 1980s governments of the new right came to power and they were committed to the free market. This meant deregulation and enhancing competition and so according to De Witt (1981), 'A new emphasis on consumer education and information and a reduction in Federal activism appear to characterise the consumer policy evolving under President Reagan.' In Britain, the view of the Minister for Consumer Affairs, Michael Howard, was that, 'For the most part, the best protection that consumers can have is that provided by fair competition in the free market' (HC Debs 115, 27 April 1987: c. 51). The consumer movement was greatly affected by the changes in economic policy that occurred in Britain and America. Whilst the Keynesian paradigm was dominant, consumers benefited from the general increase in intervention and the belief that consumers should be involved; with the return to the market consumers suffered from the general belief in deregulation.

Clearly, then, the autonomy of state actors rather than the action of groups has been important in the development of consumer policy. Although this change has suited the interests of business, to a large extent it has not been the result of business pressure. As Dowding (1991) would claim, in this instance business has been lucky. The change of policy has to a large extent been the result of ideology and the fact that both the Reagan administration and Thatcher governments have seen freeing the market as the source of economic growth.

This is not to say that business has not been an important contributory factor in the change of policy. In the United States, in particular, business became much more active politically in response to the growth of consumer groups and legislation (Vogel 1989). Vogel points out that in the 1960s and early 1970s business was largely unorganised politically because of the lack of opposition and its privileged position in policy-making. In the mid-1970s business associations became much more active. Both the Chamber of Commerce and the National Association of Manufacturers improved their organisation, increased funding, started to lobby more actively and to some extent they copied the public interest groups by developing grassroots networks (Vogel 1989: 200–5). They realised the importance of publicity and major companies embarked on a national advertising campaign to highlight the cost of big government (*New York Times* 28 October 1979; Vogel 1989).

Business also used Political Action Committees (PACs) to provide funds to members of Congress who supported their causes against consumers. The interest group Congress Watch found a direct correlation between anti-consumer voting records and the amount of campaign contributions that members of Congress received from business PACs (*New York Times* 18 January 1982). The insurance industry launched a massive lobbying campaign to try to ensure the industry's exemption from anti-trust legislation. Four former Congress members contacted key members of the House and Senate, and 220,000 independent insurance agents vigorously lobbied Congress and business organisations (*Congressional Quarterly* 30 July 1988). A major change occurred in the US in the 1970s with the politicisation of business (Pertschuk 1982: 50). It is clear that business saw its interests threatened, and so organised in order to defend itself. The resources and privilege of business meant that it was in a position to have an impact on policy.

To a certain, but lesser extent this was true in Britain. Business had much better access to government, especially a Conservative government, and often the government was more sympathetic to its views. Clearly in the case of the Consumer Protection Act, the government took a great deal of notice of the views of business. It consulted with business as soon as the Commission announced its proposed directive, and tried to get a 'state of the art' defence inserted. Once the directive was passed business lobbied very strongly for a state of knowledge defence to be included in the British Act. The Confederation of British Industry (CBI) got individual company directors to write hundreds of letters to MPs and the CBI, and in particular, the drug industry had constant contact with the DTI. The Minister, Michael Howard, admitted that he had been persuaded by the forceful representations from a large number of industrial organisations that the absence of developmental risks could hold back development, increase insurance costs and limit profitability (*The Times* 2 July 1986).

Business lobbying and the role of PACs were important in changing the attitudes of Congress towards consumers but they were not the only factors. There was a growing feeling that the FTC was overstepping its powers. Measures to control children's advertising were seen as attacking the traditional American right to free speech. There was also concern that the FTC was becoming too bureaucratic and that it was operating independently from, and usurping the role of, Congress. Congress did not like the fact that its Frankenstein was out of control. Moreover, in the wake of economic crisis and Watergate there was increasing concern about big government. Members of Congress started to receive complaints from their constituents about the role of federal agencies (Pertschuk 1982: 92). 'Alleged and admitted excesses of some consumer advocates, and the failure of some consumer policy actions to work well also fed reaction. When consumer protection lost its political appeal, politicians moved on to other issues' (Flickinger 1987: 166). There was also a change in the members of Congress. The old New Deal liberals were being replaced by young right wingers who were more ideological and opposed to further regulation.

In both Britain and the United States, there was a change in consumer policy for a number of reasons. Interest groups and state actors played a role. However, in Britain where the consumer movement was much weaker and the networks largely underdeveloped, the change in policy was to a large extent the result of decisions by government. The consumer movement did not even have the resources of a mass movement to prevent retrenchment. In the United States, where the consumer movement had obtained real power through the FTC and presidential support, the change in policy was more complex and involved new pressures from interest groups, changes in public attitudes and changes within Congress. The move against regulation developed in the late 1970s but Carter's support for consumerism meant the integrity of the consumer agencies was retained. It was when this anti-regulatory thrust matched up with an anti-consumer President that 'the independent agencies could be seriously undermined' (*New York Times* 1 January 1980). In both countries, the consumer movement was greatly affected by the economic context and the rise of new economic thinking. This is not to say that consumers have had no influence in the 1980s. In recent years there has been a degree of backlash against anti-consumerism and the development of new forms of consumer political action.

Consumers in the 1980s: responses to defeat

Although the 1980s has clearly seen a decline in consumer power from its heights of the 1970s in both Britain and the United States, consumer influence has not disappeared. The policies of deregulation have produced various and sometimes unintended consequences. Perversely in Britain, privatisation has produced reregulation in the form of regulatory agencies to control the new private monopolies. Moreover, consumers have to some extent used the market as a political tool, and as consumption has become increasingly central in both

Britain and the United States, retail pressure has been used to support consumer interests. The United States has also seen a degree of backlash against the anti-consumerism of the early 1980s.

In Britain, one of the goals of deregulation and privatisation was to depoliticise certain issues and so reduce the problem of government overload. As a consequence certain consumer demands are intended to be satisfied through the market rather than through parties or pressure groups. Now complaints about telephones or gas prices are economic problems to be expressed through share prices or falls in demand (Smith 1990b). Yet, despite the government's free-market rhetoric, it was not prepared completely to leave the privatised industries to the invisible hand. Nationalisation was a means for government to have some control over the economy; when it disappeared the government had to find a way of controlling natural monopolies which are central to the economy as a whole.

Therefore, with privatisation, new regulatory bodies like Oftel and Ofgas were created. These bodies are intended to try to ensure increased competition and the representation of consumer interests where monopolies continue after privatisation. They have the powers to ensure consumer representation, that social obligations are met and that price increases are limited (Carsberg 1987; Gist 1990). Walker (1990: 150–2) claims that a lack of thought on the part of the government about the role of these bodies has led to the new regulatory offices being 'endowed with elastic powers' and so a great deal of potential exists for control over the newly privatised industry. Yet, so far, according to Walker (1990: 155), the government has ensured that these powers have not been used by appointing 'sound chaps'. Although Oftel has limited overall price increases this has not prevented British Telecom (BT) from increasing the cost of local calls by 35 per cent in 1984–6 (Gist 1990: 47). Oftel has contradictory aims, and to some extent the most important is to ensure competition and profitability within the telecommunications industry. This can undermine the commitment to the consumer.

Nevertheless Oftel does have some safeguards for consumers and mechanisms for consumer protection. With Oftel, regulation and ownership have been separated, and Oftel is prepared to use its substantial powers to protect consumer interests. Oftel has been fairly successful in dealing with consumer complaints and, because of BTs dependence on Oftel, it is often prepared to accept the regulatory body's recommendations. Consumers also have a number of means of access to Oftel. They can make complaints as individual consumers; there is a consumer advisory committee which is a committee of users appointed by the Secretary of State; there is a consumers' forum which provides for regular meetings between Oftel and various consumer groups such as the NCC and the CA. Oftel has introduced a consumer policy adviser to advise the Director-General on policy issues which is seen as a means of ensuring that the domestic user has some representation, and there are *ad hoc* meetings between consumer organisations and Oftel. Although these bodies have no formal power and Oftel's duties to competition remain, it seems that consumers have been successful in raising issues and Oftel has been prepared to force BT to take action which favours the consumer. In the view of Harvey and Parry (1987: 69) Oftel 'is generally regarded as having been successful in publicising grievances and securing a measure of reform to British Telecom's operator practices'. In 1992 the agency forced a large cut in BT prices to domestic users. The gas and electricity regulators have also forced price cuts on the industry and therefore do not seem to have been captured by their respective industries.

Oftel provides an example of the ways in which the new regulatory agencies can potentially protect the consumer. The regulatory agencies have a very wide range of powers and the use of these powers depends largely on the decisions of the Director-General. There are also means for ensuring that consumer interests are at least heard and to some extent the agencies do have a brief to take notice of these interests. What is most interesting is that the agencies' powers could become even more important in meeting consumer demands. The potential exists within the agencies to increase the extent to which they support consumer interests.

The new right brought a greater concern for consumer interests into the public sector during the 1980s. With the government's desire to shake up the public sector and threats of privatisation, the ideas of private sector management have started to permeate the public sector (Hambleton 1988). Thus, the government has attempted to introduce elements of choice and competition in order to increase the influence of consumers on the public provision of services. Elements of consumerism have emerged in a number of public sector areas. Certain local authorities are developing mechanisms for allowing consumers' interests to be better represented in local government (Potter 1988). The government has attempted to extend competition in the housing sector through the right-to-buy policy; the easing of the private rented sector, and by allowing public tenants to opt for private landlords (Flynn 1989). The government has also forced local authorities and other public services to contract out many of their services to private organisations.

Perhaps the greatest attempt at market reform and consumerism in the public sector is in health and education. Much of the government's stated aim behind health service reform is to make the NHS more responsive to the consumer and more subject to market discipline. Attempts to improve consumer responsiveness of the NHS have come in two major policy changes. First, the Griffiths report of 1983 said that the NHS Management Board and health authority chairmen should 'ascertain how the service is being delivered at local level' and 'respond directly to this information'. For Griffiths, 'Sufficient management impression must be created at all levels that the centre is passionately concerned with the quality of care and delivery of services at local level' (Griffiths 1988: 196).

Since the report, health authorities have attempted to improve public relations. 'The National Consumer Council [worked] with two district health authorities – Paddington and North Kensington, and East Dorset – to assess consumers' experience of the NHS' (Potter 1988: 160). Other local authorities appointed 'quality assurance managers' and have surveyed patient satisfaction (Hambleton 1988: 127).

More significant are the changes following the health service review (see Chapter 7). Again, the government claimed that one of the key intentions of the review was to make the NHS more responsive to the consumer. Indeed, the White Paper following the review was called *Working for Patients* (Cm 555 1989). The key feature of the White Paper is the establishment of internal markets so that patients can be treated by different health authorities. This provides competition between health authorities for the provision of services. In addition, certain hospitals have the ability to become self-governing trusts and thus act as extra suppliers independent of the health authorities (Social Services Select Committee 1988). Therefore health providers would have to be more attractive to the consumer in order to secure the necessary patients to remain viable. In addition GPs with over 11,000 patients can now become budget holders and will be able to purchase certain services from the cheapest providers (Maynard A. 1988). Thus the reforms divided the purchaser from the supplier and introduced an element of competition into the health sector.

The second area of important change is in education. The new right has long been concerned with increasing choice in the public education system. It has maintained that too much power is in the hands of bureaucrats, politicians and teachers, and there is a need to increase parental power (Green 1987). In the early 1980s there was some support for a voucher scheme which would allow parents to purchase education from whichever school they chose – public or private – providing the extra money where necessary (Green 1987). The idea of vouchers was abandoned in the early 1980s but the 1988 Education Act aimed at increasing market competition and parental choice by increasing the power of governors, allowing schools to opt out of education authority control and increasing parental choice of schools (Flynn 1989).

Through privatisation and marketisation, the government has clearly tried to make public services more responsive to consumer demands and to some extent it has been successful in this goal. However, there are difficulties in increasing the responsiveness of the public sector to the consumer. Often there is little real choice in public services (Hambleton 1988). Even if refuse collection is contracted out, the consumer still has no real choice. Time, convenience and location often make choices over schools limited. Parents can only have choice where room is available and so in reality choice is limited. It is also necessary to ask to what extent consumerism in the public sector is an important goal in government policy or whether it is one that can be easily attached to policies of privatisation and cost-cutting in the public sector (Potter 1988)?

The Thatcher government also emphasised the power of the consumer in the market, and maintained that it increased personal income and choice through its taxation and privatisation policies (Saunders and Harris 1990: 66). Some social theorists suggest that this has led to the development of a consumer culture. Consumption has become culturally and politically significant as it defines social position through lifestyle and citizenship in terms of the power to consume (Featherstone 1990). With deregulation and privatisation citizenship is no longer seen as a function of the welfare state, as Marshall (1973) had outlined, but of the ability to buy the various accoutrements of society. This change, of course, makes citizenship a particular rather than universal phenomena (see Therborn 1989).

Now, according to Mort (1989: 161) 'Consumption is at the centre stage in the political battle over the economy.' Or for Gardener and Sheppard (1989: 45):

> Consumption has ceased to be purely material or narrowly functional. . . . Today consumption is both *symbolic* and *material*. It expresses, in a real sense, a person's place in the world, his or her core identity.

This new politics and culture of consumption was partly the cause and partly the consequence of a revolution in retailing. A general move from manufacturing to services was exaggerated by an economic boom in the mid-1980s which led to the growth and change of the retail sector (Gardener and Sheppard 1989). Retailers have now replaced manufacturers as the economically dominant sector (Gardener and Sheppard 1989: 16–17). This economic importance has had political implications. Retailers have recognised the importance of consumer preferences and increased competition has resulted in some companies using their concern for the consumer as a means of attracting customers. These retailers have begun to use their economic power to defend consumer interests.

This has happened in two ways. Retailers' economic strength in relation to manufacturers has enabled them to impose regulations on the companies that produce for them. For example, Marks and Spencer demand very strict hygiene standards in the regulation of food handling. Sainsbury has removed food production from companies that have not met their standards. Safeway and Tesco have led the way in banning certain additives and providing a simple and comprehensive system of labelling. Food retailers have developed private policy which far exceeds government policy in the extent to which it protects consumer interests (Smith 1991) and this is to a large extent the result of consumers' market power.

This private policy has created a collective action problem for companies. If they impose tough regulations, this pushes up their costs. It is in their interest to get these regulations imposed on other companies and to have the force of law behind their own regulations. As a result, retailers have become more active in lobbying government in favour of consumer issues. The supermarkets have attacked the government over its secret testing of the milk hormone BST. At the European level a major British retailer has been lobbying hard for the Commission to impose tighter regulations on slaughterhouses (Mazey and Richardson 1990). So in the way that business was lucky in the early 1980s, consumers have been lucky in the late 1980s as their interests have coincided with those of the retailers. This has led to new alliances. In the case of misleading prices consumer groups and retailers agreed on policy proposals which they jointly presented to the DTI but which the DTI rejected.

Another important development for consumers in Britain has been the role of the European Community. The impact of the EC has to some extent been contradictory. On the one hand the Community has been very slow in developing consumer policy. The Directorate-General which deals with consumer affairs is very small. The Commission has not seen consumers as a priority group, and consumer policy has been accorded little importance (HL 192 1985/86). Consumer groups are often seen as lacking legitimacy, find it difficult to obtain access to Directorates-General or are consulted after decisions are made (Smith 1990a: 166–7). On the other hand the EC had been much more positive in its approach to consumer policy than the British government. One consequence of the single European market is that product liability laws need to be uniform. This resulted in the EC issuing the directive which forced the British government to introduce the Consumer Protection Act. The British government has often opposed EC consumer policy as it is much more regulatory than the government would like.

In Britain, the 1980s saw new forms of consumer power rather than the end of consumer power. This has been expressed through new institutions like Oftel and the EC and interested producer organisations such as retailers, rather than through consumer groups. Similar changes have also occurred in the United States, but have taken a slightly different path. To some extent there has been a consumer backlash since the first anti-consumer measures.

In the United States, consumers continued to see consumer protection as important (Bloom and Smith 1986: 11), and no longer believe that Congress is doing enough to protect their interests (*New York Times* 17 February 1983). Congress has taken some notice of these pressures. Although it was initially prepared to cut consumer agencies' budgets, and reduce their powers, it would not go as far as the OMB and the Reagan administration desired. Eads and Fix (1984: 1) claim that the Reagan deregulation programme was in turmoil by 1983. Congress was becoming less willing to deregulate further and so increased the FTC budget by $5 million dollars, feeling that the balance had swung too far in favour of business (Pertschuk 1983). It seems that the administration was more concerned with tax reform and failed to 'repeal or amend a single major regulatory statute' (Vogel 1989: 261). Since then Congress has repeatedly increased appropriations for the CPSC and FTC to a level higher than the administration wished. In 1990, Congress has appeared increasingly pro-consumer, introducing legislation to prevent price-fixing, to strengthen product liability and to increase the power and budget of the CPSC (*Congressional Quarterly* 13 January 1990; 3 February 1990; 23 June 1990).

In addition, while federal consumer activity declined it was increased at state and local level. Local groups remained active (Warland *et al.* 1986) and certain states were prepared to maintain strict consumer protection. In particular states, attorneys general started to work collectively to enforce consumer regulation.

The National Association of Attorneys General developed state-level consumer regulation which they could implement through court action in anti-trust and consumer protection cases. As a result, consumer groups often go to state level to plead their cases (*New York Times* 8 February 1988). This adoption of state-level laws has forced US companies to call for greater intervention at national level so that there is national uniformity and companies do not face differential costs. As Ralph Engel of the Chemical Specialties Manufacturers said, the states' product safety laws have 'caused us and other industries considerable discomfort and concern' (*Congressional Quarterly* 3 March 1990). Bloom and Greyser (1981: 136) see this as an indication of consumerism moving into a mature stage where 'consumerism is no longer the exclusive domain of the traditional movement' but it is now taking many different forms.

As in Britain, the growth of consumer culture has also led retail companies into taking a greater account of consumer interests. Increasingly companies are trying to improve product quality and customer service (*New York Times* 15 October 1988). Giant Foods initiated a consumer programme in 1970 which was built around Kennedy's consumer bill of rights. They introduced unit pricing, labelling, open dating and their own product safety policies. At one point they 'went so far as to explain the high price of beef and recommend that consumers buy something else' (Peterson 1982: 130). This policy has been followed by other companies who see consumerism as a way of increasing their market share. American Express has a consumer affairs department which assesses the impact of policies and products on consumers and Target Stores spends $500,000 a year to ensure that the toys it sells are safe (*New York Times* 15 October 1988). Although it is only a small proportion of companies that have such policies, they are still meeting consumer demands and this puts pressure on government and other companies to take consumer wishes seriously.

The 1980s has to some extent seen a decline in the national consumer movement and the networks that it established in the 1970s. Consumer policy has changed in both Britain and the United States, becoming a negative free-market policy with deregulation as the focus. Yet, this policy has had unintended consequences. It has resulted in shifts of power to consumers, as purchasers, and to retailers. Consequently, a new powerful economic interest has sided with the consumer. In Britain, deregulation has created new institutions which can be used to further consumer interests and, in the United States, Congress has not been prepared to allow total deregulation. Consumer power has changed but it has not disappeared and to a certain extent, in the case of Britain, it is perhaps more effective than before.

Conclusion

Although social change has had an impact on consumers and the organisation of consumer groups, a shift to post-industrialism cannot explain the impact of consumerism. The fluctuations in the consumer influence and the uneven development in Britain and the United States suggest that consumer power is dependent on political factors to a very great degree. However, these political factors are not solely the resources and tactics of consumer groups.

It is apparent from this study of consumers and consumer policy that the impact of consumer groups is only one factor in determining consumer policy and that the form of consumer intermediation changes from state to state and across time. In the United States, the dominant pattern of consumer representation was a 'deformed pluralism'. There were clearly elements of pluralism with consumer groups able to achieve access to various parts of the political system, influence policy, and to establish relatively open, but integrated networks, that gave institutionalised access to consumers. However, this pluralism was deformed because the privileged position of business constrained the impact of consumers. When consumer demands were seen to threaten the economic welfare of the US, the President and Congress tried to control the regulatory authorities, especially when faced with the resources and organisation of the business community.

In Britain, the relationship was one of 'elitism' where the British state institutionalised relations with consumers in order to prevent the development of a pluralistic consumer movement and to ensure that policy-making remained within an elite and reliable group. There was an attempt to make consumer policy predictable by creating a group of consumers which the government ultimately controlled but which could be used to demonstrate the government's commitment to the consumer cause. The government wanted to prevent the Nader-type politicisation of the British consumer movement and so it was institutionalised at an early stage. Consumers have been successful in Britain usually when they have tied their interest to another group or cause like the unions, the fight against inflation, the EC or retailers. Otherwise, any influence has been on matters of detail where the consumer lobby could provide the detailed information to demonstrate that there are major problems with the policy as it stands. Their sphere of influence has largely been confined to the technical aspects of Lindblom's (1977) 'secondary issues'. Consumer groups in Britain have never really been in a position where they could, on their own, influence central features of government policy.

There were consumer policy networks in Britain and the United States but the form of the networks was very different. In Britain, it was a highly institutionalised network consisting of government-sponsored or government-created bodies. In the United States, institutionalisation was a response to the level of politicisation and the strength of consumer groups. Consequently, the networks were much more effective in the United States than in Britain. Through the FTC, US consumer groups had access to an agency that could affect policy. In Britain, the NCC and the DPCP were often separated from arenas of consumer policy and their influence was limited.

Nevertheless, the form of networks that were established were inherently limited in their effectiveness. They never established a single decision-making centre and were often constrained by powerful economic interests. They were also unable to establish the shared value system necessary for a policy community. Consequently, when the perceptions and ideology of state actors changed, the power of the consumer networks was easily threatened. The lack of dependence of the governments on the consumer networks meant that the state could ignore the networks with very low costs.

In both Britain and the US, consumer policy has in varying degrees depended on the potential of state actors to take autonomous actions. In the US consumer policy only really achieved success when it was given leadership by Presidents and Congress. The downturn in consumer fortunes coincided with a change of President who had new policies and was able to ignore consumer demands. But in the case of the US the degree of autonomy was always limited. To some extent the political leadership was responding to various demands in civil society and it is impossible to completely separate the wishes of state actors from the social context within which they operate.

In Britain, the powerlessness of consumer groups has meant that state autonomy has been even more important. It was the Labour government which created the Department of Prices and Consumer Protection and the NCC. It was the Conservative government which chose to move from an interventionist to a free-market consumer policy. Consumer groups lacked the strength of institutional ties, or the resources in wider society, to prevent this change. It is interesting to note that in the case of consumer policy state autonomy was not related to infrastructural power. The importance of state interests was usually directly political. Interest in consumer policy was either related to wider economic goals or to immediate electoral interests.

The weakness of the policy networks meant that political actors could change the network and policy relatively easily with low political costs. The consumer networks changed rapidly in the 1980s because of changing economic circumstances, a new view of consumer policy and the reassertion of business power. The number of groups involved and the lack of consensus meant that consumer networks were unable to defend themselves from other actors within the network or from political leaders who wanted a change in policy.

However, the policies of the new right governments produced new forms of policy networks. In Britain, these networks bypassed central government. The new regulatory agencies enabled consumers to develop links with the recently privatised industries and so have some influence on their policy. With the growing economic power of the retail sector and increased market competition, retail companies are prepared to impose their own consumer regulation in the private sector without reference to government. In the United States, new networks developed at state level and again through retail companies but more importantly, towards the end of the 1980s Congress was prepared to protect the FTC and the CPSC from further cuts.

These changes suggest an important development in network theory.

Traditionally networks have been seen as forming around government and government agencies. In Britain, through regulatory agencies and retail companies, it appears that networks can develop without substantial government involvement. The decision-making centre of a policy network need not be a government actor but could be a body with sufficient autonomy and resources to affect policy independently. The local politics of the US and the 'private politics' of the British retailers mean that consumers can exercise power in the way Cohen (1982) and Keane (1988) suggest new social movements do, through interactions within civil society, independently of the state-centred policy networks.

The variation in fortunes and structures of consumer networks, and the fact that the consumer policy network has depended largely on political factors like organisation, ideology and political decisions means that the post-industrialist and post-Fordist views of the inevitable rise of consumerism are too wide of the mark. It is the case that consumer politics has become more important in recent years but there is no inevitability about this change nor does it appear that consumption is replacing production as the key source of political identity (Devine 1992).

Chapter 9

PRESSURE GROUPS, POLICY NETWORKS AND THE STATE

This book has demonstrated that the nature of the relationships between groups and the state varies greatly across policy sectors and time. More importantly, it is apparent that the nature of the networks formed between groups and government affects both policy outcomes and the degree of state autonomy. The goal of this chapter is to compare the various policy networks that have been examined in order to develop an understanding of why different networks develop in different policy areas, the effect they have on policy and state autonomy, and why change occurs in some policy sectors more readily than in others.

Policy networks in Britain and the United States

It is apparent from the Rhodes and Marsh typology (see Table 3.1) that the variety of policy networks is almost infinite because a network can diverge across a number of dimensions. In this book a range of networks have been identified. In British agricultural policy and US trade policy there were, for a period, highly integrated policy communities. The British agricultural policy community can be seen as the 'ideal typical' community. It was highly integrated, stable, had a limited number of participants, frequent interaction between participants and a high level of continuity. Trade policy in the US during the 1950s and 1960s was, likewise, highly integrated and close to the policy community end of the continuum. However, unlike the agricultural policy network it contained a large number of interests and a number of decision-making centres. There was, nevertheless, a high degree of consensus and the conscious exclusion of pressure groups. For a period, the trade policy community almost completely excluded interest groups that opposed the dominant agenda from the macro-level of trade policy. Yet, they were included at the sectoral level where there were a range of networks dealing with specific trade issues.

A further highly integrated community was British health policy. In the health policy community, there was a high degree of stability, frequent contact between members of the community, a limited number of groups and a strong consensus. It was also difficult for patients or health workers, other than doctors, to achieve access to the community.

The US agricultural policy network, from the 1940s to the 1960s, was relatively close to the policy community end of the continuum but less integrated than British health or agriculture. The network included more actors than British health policy, but the number was relatively limited and there was a degree of agreement on policy. Even so, the network remained highly political, and there was partisan conflict over the future of agricultural policy.

Less integrated communities existed in both US and British consumer policy. In both cases consumer groups developed institutional access to the policy process. Indeed, during the 1970s, consumer groups in the US established a distinct network around the FTC and made some significant gains in consumer policy. Yet, consumer networks were often a means of cooption rather than empowerment. Consumer groups, especially in Britain, were included in consumer networks as a means of excluding them from other policy arenas. Hence, consumers had very little input into health, agricultural or economic policy. Consumers only really had an impact on policy when they could build alliances with other interests be they retailers, trade unions, Congress members or Presidents. Consumers were integrated into networks but in these networks the asymmetry of power greatly favoured government and economic interests.

Finally, there were three issue networks in the case studies – British industrial policy, US health policy and US agricultural policy from the 1970s. Marsh and Rhodes (1992c: 254) emphasise that, 'issue networks remain networks, with the implication that relationships are ordered'. An issue network is a structure of relationships that is distinct from the pressure group universe. There are recognisable boundaries to the policy arena, there is mutual recognition of actors and there is still some exclusion. Interests need a minimum degree of knowledge or other resource to gain access and the 'rules of the game' still apply. However, access to an issue network is relatively easy and so new groups are constantly entering and leaving the policy arena. In addition, although there is mutual recognition of the policy arena, there is disagreement over the nature of the policy problems and, in particular, the available solutions.

Marsh and Rhodes (1992c: 254) claim that:

> An issue network, as opposed to a policy community, will exist only if there is no threat to the interests of either an economic/producer group or a professional group. Issue networks exist but they are the exception rather than the rule, at the periphery rather than the core of the policy agenda.

For Marsh and Rhodes, issue networks are likely to exist where the area is relatively unimportant in terms of macro-policy such as questions of abortion or leisure policy (Rhodes 1988). However, the cases in this book suggest that this is not always true. Issue networks do exist in areas of the core policy agenda and where the interests of economic groups and professionals are threatened. Perhaps the clearest example of an issue network was British industrial policy. In this network there were multiple decision-making centres, conflicts over policy, changes in the groups and interests involved in the policy process. Likewise, US health policy involved a large number of groups, several decision-makers and policy conflicts. In both these cases, issue networks have developed within core policy areas, and where professional and economic interests have been affected.

In British industrial policy, it appears that the interests of certain business groups have been very adversely affected by the nature of the network. Issue networks have developed in these areas because the issue areas are highly political. In both examples, the networks contain a number of conflicting interests between well-resourced groups. In industrial policy there has been conflict between different sectors of business, between the unions and business, between different unions, between the government and unions and business, and even within government. All of these actors had too many resources to be excluded and they all had different economic interests. Consequently, it was extremely difficult to build any consensus, and the policy area remained highly political.

In US health policy, there was similar conflict between a range of interests. Congress, various Presidents and the doctors all had disparate and changing views on the future of health policy. These disagreements were extended to hospitals, insurance companies and various interest groups such as organised labour and supporters of national health insurance. There was little agreement over the direction of health policy, even within government, and so the policy area remained highly political. Unlike British health policy, the state was unable to exclude many of the interests by developing a national health policy. Despite their professional power, the doctors were not able to develop a health policy community. Nevertheless, they continued to influence the delivery of health policy by preventing changes in health policy and through their market power in the private sector.

The final issue network was in US agricultural policy in the 1970s and 1980s. Again it existed despite the involvement of important economic interests. However, it was a different network to the two described above. Although it included a large number of actors and there was conflict over the direction of policy, there was quite a high degree of exclusion, and the network was primarily concerned with protecting the interests of the agricultural sectors. Unlike the other two issue networks, it does not include diametrically opposed interests. Moreover, access is restricted largely to agricultural and agricultural related groups. Access for consumers and environmentalists is still highly restricted. It is an issue network in that there are numerous actors and limited agreement on policy, but it is still highly exclusive and concerned with particular interests.

It is apparent from the above case studies that numerous relationships between groups and the state can develop. This raises two question: why do different policy networks develop in different arenas and what impact do they have on policy outcomes?

It is difficult to provide a general explanation of why particular types of networks develop. As we have seen, each network has its own pattern of development. Nevertheless, we can see some common features in particular forms of networks. Policy communities need a limited number of interest groups which have resources that they can exchange. It is easier to establish a policy community if there is a single decision-making centre and there is some consensus on the direction of policy. It is also important to have mechanisms for excluding particular interests. There are two problems with this explanation: it restates the definition of a policy community and it does not apply to one of the case studies, namely, US trade policy. A full account of a policy community does require analysis of the development of that particular network. Why a network develops depends on the long-term evolution of the policy area, the nature of the groups involved, and external factors.

However, one important variable in all networks is the interests and resources of state actors. Policy communities developed where state actors wanted to achieve particular goals, and needed to create the means to achieve their desired policy ends. In agriculture, the state wanted to increase agricultural production. In health, the state wanted to develop a system for the public provision of health, and in US trade policy, state actors wanted to ensure liberal trade as a means of maintaining US economic dominance. In the areas where issue networks developed there were conflicts within the state over the direction of policy; there was no clear state-led view of policy goals. In US health policy, Congress conflicted with the President over health policy and various Presidents had different goals for health policy. In British industrial policy, the Treasury disagreed with the Department of Economic Affairs, in the 1960s, and the Department of Industry in the 1970s, over the direction of industrial policy. There were also frequent changes of policy between, and even within, governments. For example, Edward Heath made a dramatic reversal in industrial policy in 1972 when it changed from a *laissez-faire* policy to an interventionist policy.

In an issue network, there are many interest groups and multiple decision-making centres which reflects, to some extent, the lack of a clear policy direction amongst state actors. Yet, a definite policy goal is necessary, but not sufficient, for establishing a policy community. It is also important that there are a limited number of groups, consensus between the groups involved, and mechanisms for exclusion. In both the health policy community in Britain and US trade policy, state actors ensured that they excluded actors who might upset the policy consensus. In Britain, Bevan had the resources to remove the hospitals, insurance companies and local authorities from the policy process. In the US, the President and Department of State removed Congress and protectionist-orientated interest groups from the centres of decision-making. Through the congressional subcommittees and 'let out' clauses in the legislation, they created safety mechanisms for interests that could upset the network. Thus, as will be discussed below, state interests are central to understanding the policy process.

The notion that policy communities develop in order to achieve state goals, suggests that networks should affect policy outcomes. As Marsh and Rhodes (1992c: 262) highlight: 'The existence of a policy network, or more particularly a policy community, constrains the policy agenda and shapes policy outcomes. Policy communities in particular are associated with policy continuity.' Policy networks affect policy outcomes in a number of ways. The structure of a policy community includes some groups and excludes others and therefore affects the policy options that are likely to be discussed. The agricultural policy community in Britain included farmers and excluded consumers. Consequently, the policy agenda was concerned with raising farm income rather than containing consumer prices. Policy options are further limited by the ideology of a policy community. The ideology also defines the policy options by defining the policy problem and the policy solution. In the US trade community, the problem was ensuring expansion for the US economy and the solution was liberal trade. Any other option was excluded. This is a clear example of Lukes' third dimension of power where issues are excluded from the policy agenda without the conscious decisions of individuals (Lukes 1974).

Policy networks also include particular forms of organisation that establish their own standard operating procedures (see Chapter 1). These procedures limit options and so produce particular policy outcomes. The Annual Review in British agricultural policy is probably the prime example. The Annual Review was established to assess the economic conditions in agriculture, and the economy generally, and to use this information to determine the level of prices that should be paid to farmers. Thus, the central policy-making institution was concerned with determining the level of agricultural subsidies, and not examining whether subsidies were a useful and efficient means of developing agricultural production (Smith 1989a). There was institutional bias towards providing farmers with high prices.

It is clear from the case studies that policy networks do affect policy outcomes. In the British health policy community, the network ensured that health policy was publicly provided and that doctors controlled the delivery of health care. In the US, the absence of an integrated network made it very difficult to develop any public provision of health care or national health insurance. The British industrial policy network resulted in the government frequently failing to achieve its industrial policy goals. Thus although, as Rhodes and Marsh claim, policy communities prevent policy change, it is also the case that issue networks make change very difficult to achieve. The existence of an issue network means that the state lacks control over the policy area. The conflict of interests reduces the infrastructural power of state actors. This indicates that there is an important link between state autonomy and policy networks. Policy networks have a major impact on policy outcomes because they are a source of infrastructural power.

Policy networks and state autonomy

The state-centred literature developed by Skocpol and Nordlinger was an important corrective to the society-centred approaches of pluralism and marxism.

Undoubtedly, it is the case that state actors have distinct interests, and they have the resources to impose these interests on society. However, Skocpol and Nordlinger oversimplify the relationship between the state and civil society. State interests and capabilities are variables that have to be included in a comprehensive analysis of the policy process. Yet, it is extremely rare in liberal democracies that state actors' interests develop in complete isolation from society and are then imposed against the will of societal groups. State actors are also members of civil society who have frequent contact with various groups, and to an extent depend on groups and individuals within civil society for their positions. The state's boundaries with civil society are vague and often changing, and so it is difficult to make a stark dichotomy.

Thus, state interests develop from contacts with groups, and often within networks. Moreover, there are layers of autonomy. The Prime Minister or President has a particular set of constraints on their autonomy; it may be electoral concerns, the need for Cabinet support or international obligations. However, the Prime Minister or President might be a constraint on other state actors. The chief executive does have a high level of authority and can force other politicians or groups to take particular actions. Yet, they have to be able to bear the costs of taking such actions. If state actors decide to impose decisions on groups they have to ensure that policy can still be developed if a particular network is undermined. They have to be careful that they do not lose the means of implementation (Rhodes and Marsh 1992b) or that the subsequent conflict does not damage their position.

It was also argued in Chapter 3, that policy networks are a means of increasing autonomy. They enable policy actors to close their arena off from other policy actors and their chief executives. In addition, they create the means for intervention in a policy area and increase state capabilities. Autonomy developed with one group or set of groups against other state actors and groups. So the agricultural policy community sealed off agricultural policy from the Treasury and the Board of Trade. The trade policy community squeezed out protectionist interests. More importantly, policy communities provided state actors with the mechanisms to intervene.

In British agricultural policy, health policy and trade policy, the policy communities increased the infrastructural power of state actors. In all these cases, state actors needed to develop policy communities in order to create the means to achieve policy goals. Agricultural production could not be increased without support from the farmers, a national health service could not have been established unless the state developed an integrated relationship with the doctors and allowed them a role in the policy process, and it would have been very difficult to develop a free trade policy without the exclusion of certain interests from the policy process. These goals were not forced on state actors by interest groups but developed with interest groups in policy communities. This demonstrates that power is based on dependence and not force.

Where state actors did not develop policy communities, it was much more difficult for state actors to achieve their goals. In US health policy, Presidents and Congress faced a number of problems in developing health policy. The lack of consensus between the doctors and politicians and the large number of decision-makers meant that it was very difficult to change health policy either to increase public provision, or in the 1980s and 1990s, to reduce costs. Similarly in Britain, attempts at interventionist industrial policy failed because the state had no mechanism for implementation. The failure to develop a policy community meant that business was not prepared to cooperate with government programmes as in the case of the national plan. The lack of consensus also meant that the Treasury attempted to undermine the policy.

This suggests that we need to reassess two of the traditional assumptions about group/government relations. The first is that a close relationship between groups and government results in pressure group capture. In most of these cases it seems that the relationship is the other way round. State actors have incorporated groups in order to achieve their own goals. Perhaps the one exception is the US agricultural network in the 1940s and 1950s which does seem to have been captured by the farmers. Yet, we have to be aware of the complexity of these relationships. Networks are relationships of mutual support and mutual dependence. Subsequently, interests and goals develop within the context of the network. The interests of a group or state actors are not metaphysical objective interests which derive from their structural position in society but are negotiated, changing interests which derive from the relationships between groups and the state. For example, British doctors were strongly opposed to Labour's plans for the National Health Service in 1945. By the 1980s doctors were amongst the strongest defenders of the NHS against what they saw as the onslaught of the new right.

The second assumption is that it is harder to change policy where there is a policy community rather than an issue network (Marsh and Rhodes 1992c). This depends on who is trying to change the policy. If a policy community exists, state actors have a mechanism for agreeing and implementing policy change. If an issue network exists it is difficult to build a coalition to support policy change, and then difficult to implement that change. This occurred frequently in both US health policy and British industrial policy. The issue network meant that coalitions could be relied upon to oppose changes in policy and, even if policy changes were agreed, there was great difficulty in implementing that policy. If, in a policy community, change is agreed then it is relatively easy to implement. The difficulty arises when change is forced on the community from outside and the community has the ability to prevent its implementation.

Policy networks raise interesting questions in relation to state autonomy. State autonomy is not a zero-sum. Increased autonomy for the Ministry of Agriculture can also increase the autonomy of the National Farmers Union. In doing so it reduces the autonomy of the Treasury. The Treasury and the Prime Minister have the resources and authority to challenge the agricultural community but if they do, they have to consider the costs in terms of implementing future policy, political disruption and increasing the complexity of the policy process. Policy communities have great advantages to government. They make the policy process predictable and stable and they enable governments to implement policy goals. Whilst they might reduce autonomy by making change more difficult, or forcing the government to make certain concessions, they also increase autonomy by developing infrastructural power and thus allowing state actors to achieve goals.

The role of groups

Recognising the importance of state interests and autonomy does not mean that groups are insignificant. The case studies in this book suggest that groups do not have the centrality that some of the traditional theories suggest. Even in the case of the most apparently influential groups like doctors and farmers, they only established institutional relations once state actors had decided, for a range of reasons, to adopt a particular policy. Frequently, they were used to achieve state goals. Nevertheless, once the state decided to adopt a particular policy which required group assistance a dependency was created between the groups and the state. The state needed the resources and assistance of groups for the development of policy.

In agricultural and health policy, the state saw the need to develop an interventionist policy and so began negotiating with the groups. Once negotiation started, the state had to make concessions to the groups. In both these cases the resources of the groups were important. It would have been very difficult for the state to use despotic power. In the case of agriculture, farmers could have been forced to produce certain types of food at certain prices but, as Stalin's collectivization policy demonstrated, such measures rarely produce increased output. In the case of the doctors it is almost impossible to develop a national health service using despotic power. The state could not have developed an alternative administrative structure that bypassed the doctors. Therefore once the state decided on a national health service, the doctors were in a very strong position.

Where issue networks existed, groups with a high level of resources could still influence policy but their impact tended to be negative. Business in Britain could stop the development and implementation of industrial policy but has had very little positive input into the industrial policy process. Likewise with the US doctors. Their professional power has ensured control over the delivery of health policy in the private sector but their input into health policy has been negative. They could, with the assistance of Congress, stop national insurance, delay Medicare and Medicaid and prevent measures to reduce costs, but they have had little direct positive input into policy.

The relationship between groups and the state is complex. Groups are important and their resources can affect policy. However, what is important is the perception of their resources and the sort of relationship that they have with state actors. In understanding the policy process, it is important to recognise that there are state actors and groups who both have resources and, in order to activate their resources with the minimum of costs, they need each other. The state could act without groups through legislation, force and nationalisation but this would produce conflictual and high cost policy-making. Groups could continually confront government but the cost of confrontation is high, and the cost of losing even greater. It suits groups and government to consult. In most cases, groups need the government more than government needs groups. The government does have alternative groups it could talk to, or alternative mechanisms for implementation, but groups only have one state and, usually, they cannot afford to become outsiders. Group/government interaction has to be seen as one of a relationship between analytically separate interests – state actors and groups – which are empirically defined through interaction. Both state interests and group interests derive from relationships within networks, making both state-centred and society-centred approaches too simplistic.

Policy networks and change

It was demonstrated in Chapter 4 that there are problems in explaining change when policy communities, in particular, are institutions which to varying degrees attempt to prevent policy change. It is clear that all the policy networks in this book have changed to some extent in either the nature of the network, the policy agenda or both. The British agricultural policy has seen a change in its policy agenda but the community, apart from its Europeanisation, has largely remained intact. US agricultural policy has changed dramatically from an integrated network to an issue network. The health policy community in Britain has seen some change in the network and in the policy agenda. The US health network has remained loose but there has been some change in the agenda with cost containment and marketisation becoming increasingly important. In British industrial policy, the agenda and the network have changed but not dramatically. The *laissez-faire* ideology of the community has become stronger and the network has become even looser with the trade unions being largely excluded. The US trade policy community has collapsed, although in principle the liberal trade policy agenda has remained. Consumer policy has seen the greatest change with networks breaking down and the agenda changing significantly.

Are the changes the result of the social and economic forces identified by the post-Fordists and post industrialists? Undoubtedly, the policy areas examined have been subject to new economic and social pressures. In addition, they have faced new challenges from the influence of new right ideology in Britain and America. Nevertheless, the impact of these changes has depended on the nature of the network. In agricultural policy and health policy, it is clear that the communities have faced new problems with which the established agenda could not cope. The agricultural and health communities in Britain were created to deal with specific problems, in the case of agriculture to increase food production, and in the case of health to provide a free health service. In the 1970s and 1980s both communities were faced with new problems. In agriculture, the problem was one of overproduction, rather than underproduction, and the policy community was unable to solve the problem. Thus, change was forced on it from outside. Other political leaders and international organisations have forced change in policy. However, actors within the community have managed to retain control over reform and have not allowed new groups into the network. There have been signs of a long-term 'war of position' as environmental groups attempt to change the concerns of agricultural policy but, as yet, their impact is limited.

In health, the problem was increasing costs and the apparent failure to meet the demand for health care. Again a solution was forced on the community in the form of general management and marketisation which both changed the policy agenda and the network. However, the government's reliance on the doctors has limited the degree to which the health policy community could be changed. The pressures for change on the health policy community were largely ideological and came from within government. There are almost no pressure groups that have challenged the position of the doctors or the nature of health policy.

In US trade and agricultural policy, the pressure for change came from changing economic circumstances. The decline in the US economy created problems for both industry and farmers. This broke down the consensus in both communities and led to calls for changes in policy. In trade policy, the demand for protection has become ever louder whilst consecutive Presidents have publicly retained their commitment to liberal trade. Nevertheless, continuing economic problems have resulted in the US taking a tougher stance in GATT talks because the overriding concern became the domestic economy rather than world trade.

Pressures for change have been internal and external. They have resulted from changes in the economy, tensions within the communities, and in the case of consumer policy the dominance of new right ideologies. This raises the question of why these pressures have produced a great deal of change in some networks like trade and consumer policy but little in British agriculture and health policy. The answer seems to lie in the nature of the networks. Although the trade policy community was closed and consensual, it contained a large number of political actors who were prepared to accept the liberal trade policy whilst it appeared successful. Once economic problems arose, conflict developed, and the policy community broke down as each political actor had an interest in drawing in interest groups to support its particular position. The agricultural and health communities were much more integrated, with fewer actors and a single decision-maker, and therefore, were in a stronger position to resist pressure for change.

The agricultural policy community was protected by the fact that policy was made in the EC rather than Britain and consequently it could resist pressure from the Prime Minister and the Treasury. The members of the community had, and have, a very high level of institutional support. They were also very adept at coopting reform pressures, and thus ensuring that they controlled the reform process. The health network was forced to change because of prime ministerial pressure, but the resources of the doctors and the public support for the health service meant change had to be incremental. The doctors have also been quite successful in winning the war of position. The government was not able to undermine the dominant ideology of the community.

It was in the consumer policy networks where change occurred most easily. These were networks that involved several decision-makers, the degree of consensus was limited, and the groups involved lacked resources. When new right governments came to power, they could change the policy community and the policy network with very few political costs and so in both networks there was substantial change in the 1980s. The consumer networks demonstrate that there is an important difference between networks containing economic or professional actors and those containing public interest groups. In a network with a public interest group, the degree of state dependence on the group is likely to be limited. This results in less integrated networks and makes it easy for state actors to ignore the networks. Therefore, it is again clear that groups do matter.

Do the changes in policy networks indicate a shift to issue networks as the result of an explosion of interest group activity? There is some evidence that this has occurred but the change does not seem to be as great as Heclo (1978) and Salisbury (1990) suggest. The two most integrated communities in Britain, health and agriculture, are still closed and elitist. Although the health policy community has changed, it has not been because of an explosion of groups but because new elite groups such as managers have joined the network. The agricultural community has faced increasing pressure from consumers and environmentalists but their input into the community is still limited. In the United States, where Heclo and Salisbury suggest such change has occurred, the networks do seem to have become more open. In both trade and agricultural policy there has been a substantial increase in the groups involved. However, it is necessary to be careful and ask what groups have joined the networks. In the case of agriculture many of the new entrants are commodity groups still concerned with maintaining the interests of farmers. There has been no general opening of the network to consumers or environmentalists. In trade policy, the new entrants are members of Congress and industries demanding protection. As a response there is increasing activity from importers and industries that use imported goods. They have certainly made the community more messy, but the community is not open to consumers who might have an interest in free trade. There are certainly more groups involved in networks now than twenty or thirty years ago but the nature of that involvement is not necessarily clear. To some extent they are consulted but are not necessarily influential. There is also a possibility that policy areas have gone through a period of transition in the 1980s as new ideas and groups entered the political arena and that over the next few years these groups will establish their own policy communities.

Networks have changed in other ways. They have become more international. In Britain, networks increasingly involve the EC. This is true in agricultural, industrial and consumer policy. More generally, it is the case that international bodies are involved in policy networks. GATT is involved in trade and agricultural policy and has had a significant impact on policy outcomes. The other way networks are changing is that they are beginning to bypass government. This is most advanced in consumer policy, where consumers are increasingly working directly with retail companies but it is also true in areas such as chemical policy (Grant *et al.* 1988). This suggests that the central actor need not be a state agency but it does need to be an organisation with sufficient resources to make authoritative decisions.

Policy networks and the state

Policy networks are a meso-level concept concerned with analysing relationships between groups and the state. As such the concept needs to be used within a broader macro-level context which is concerned with explaining the nature of the state. We saw in Chapter 3 that policy networks could be used by various theoretical positions that could focus on particular characteristics of networks. However, such an approach leads to an oversimplification of the state. Macro-theories make general statements about power within the state. It is a capitalist state, a corporatist state or a state that is open to the influence of groups. Such approaches ignore the subtleties of power within the state. As Jessop (1990) highlights, the state is a site of conflict and does not essentially favour any single interest. This suggests that it is important to take a multi-theoretic approach to the state (Dunleavy and O'Leary 1987; Marsh and Rhodes 1992c). This has two advantages. First, different macro-theories focus on alternative features within the policy process and so a multi-theoretic approach provides a more complete explanation of the policy process. Second, the approach allows for a sophisticated analysis of state/group relations by acknowledging that power can vary across policy sectors.

In this book the view of the state that has dominated is an elitist view, and in particular one variant of elitism, the state-centred approach. However, the book has demonstrated that it is not possible to take a one-dimensional view of the state. The state is a highly complex organisation and the policy network approach allows a very flexible view of the state. Although state interests are important, they do not always dominate and, as was argued, they have to be analysed within the context of state/group relations.

Moreover, the type of macro-theory that is used depends on the policy sector. US health policy is pluralistic whilst British health policy is highly elitist. US trade policy was elitist whilst British industrial policy was relatively pluralistic. Nevertheless, the general differences between the US and British political systems do seem to affect networks. Although policy communities have developed in the United States, they have rarely been as integrated as in Britain. It also appears, from the case studies in this book, that access to the US political system is easier than in Britain, and consequently, closed communities have opened up more rapidly. Although the British and US political systems have tendencies towards particular types of networks, it is still important to examine particular policy areas because there are many exceptions.

Relationships change because the state as a whole does not represent particular interests. The interests that a department represents result from a long process of negotiation, conflict and exclusion. There is no single state interest. There are conflicts between the state agencies and within state agencies. Some departments have a high degree of autonomy and some are very open to outside pressures. The state is not a capitalist state but an organisation which will serve various interests according to the arrangements that exist in particular sectors. Economic interests do have advantages because they have resources and are prepared to play by the rules of the game but neither trade policy nor industrial policy suggests that the interests of capital are consistently favoured. State actors have the potential to be the most favoured interest because they control such substantial resources but the deployment of the resources involves negotiation.

Hence, power is based on resource dependency. It is not a zero-sum but something that develops in a relationship which can increase the power of all actors involved. In addition, these relationships can become enstructured in policy networks. Policy networks are the result of past policy decisions, ideology and institutions. Consequently, they favour certain outcomes over others. This means that power can be structural. It does not depend on the decisions of individual policy-makers because only certain policy options are available. Although the state is not a capitalist state, it does favour some interests over others, and it is the nature of policy networks that ensure that this is the case.

Conclusion

To return to the propositions in Chapter 1, it is apparent from this book that the nature of state/group relations varies across policy sectors and that state interests are important in the development of these relationships. The types of policy networks that exist affect the degree of state autonomy and policy networks enstructure certain interests within the policy process. Policy communities do develop where the state needs highly resourced groups to assist in policy implementation, and issue networks develop in areas of lesser importance or where there is a high level of political controversy. Although policy communities do seem more likely in Britain than the United States, the book did identify some policy communities in the US.

Perhaps the most important point to emerge from this book is the complexity of the policy process. Notions of the state, pressure groups, state autonomy and policy networks are highly problematic. Consequently, it is difficult to make general claims about any of these concepts. The relationships between the state and groups have to be examined in a context that is historical, ideological and institutional. It also has to be remembered that the relationships between state actors and groups are relationships of dependence and therefore simplistic society- and state-centred approaches say little about empirical reality. Groups and state actors are continually trading resources. The state has advantages but ultimately it exists in an intricate relationship with civil society and so state actors cannot ignore group pressures.

BIBLIOGRAPHY

Aglietta, M. (1979) *A Theory of Capitalist Regulation: the US Experience*, London: New Left Books.

Ahearn, R.J. and Reifman, A. (1985) 'U.S. Trade Policy: Congress Sends a Message' in Baldwin, R.E. and Richardson, J.D. (eds) *Current US Trade Policy: Analysis, Agenda and Administration*, Cambridge, MA: NBER Conference Report.

Alderman, G. (1984) *Pressure Groups and Government in Great Britain*, London: Longman.

Alford, R. (1975) *Health Care Policy*, Chicago, IL: University of Chicago Press.

Allen, J. (1988a) 'Towards a Post-industrial Economy' in Allen, J. and Massey, D. (eds) *The Economy in Question*, London: Sage.

Allen, J. (1988b) 'Fragmented Firms, Disorganised Labour' in Allen, J. and Massey, D. (eds) *The Economy in Question*, London: Sage.

Allen, J. and Massey, D. (eds) (1988) *The Economy in Question*, London: Sage.

Allison, G. (1971) *Essence of Decisions*, Boston, MA: Little Brown.

Almond, G.A. (1988) 'The Return to the State', *American Political Science Review*, 82, pp. 853–74.

Althusser, L. (1971) *Lenin and Philosphy*, London: New Left Books.

Anker, L., Seybold, P. and Schwarz, M. (1987) 'The Ties that Bind Business and Government' in Schwarz, M. (ed.) *The Structure of Power in the United States*, New York: Holmes and Meier.

Atkinson, M.M. and Coleman, W.D. (1989) 'Strong States and Weak States: Sectoral Policy Networks in Advanced Capitalist Economies', *British Journal of Political Science*, 19, pp. 46–67.

Bachrach, P. and Baratz, M. (1962) 'The Two Faces of Power', *American Political Science Review*, 56, pp. 947–52.

Baldwin, R.E. (1984) 'The Changing Nature of US Trade Policy since World War II' in Baldwin, R.E. and Kruger, A.O. (eds) *The Structure and Evolution of Recent US Trade Policy*, Chicago, IL: University of Chicago Press.

Baldwin, R.E. (1985) *The Political Economy of US Import Policy*, Cambridge, MA: MIT Press.

Ball, A. and Millard, F. (1986) *Pressure Politics in Industrial Societies*, London: Macmillan.

Barbrook, A. and Bolt, C. (1980) *Power and Protest in American Life*, Oxford: Martin Robertson.

Barnett, J. (1982) *Inside the Treasury*, London: André Deutsch.

Barry, N.P. (1987) *The New Right*, London: Croom Helm.

Bauer, R.A., De Sola Pool, I. and Dexter, L.A. (1972) *American Business and Public Policy*, second edition, Chicago, IL: Aldine.

BBC (1986a) *Analysis*, Radio 4, 13 January.

BBC (1986b) *Today*, Radio 4, 25 November.

BBC (1987) *Analysis*, Radio 4, 11 March.

Beer, S. (1982) *Modern British Politics*, London: Faber.

Bell, D. (1974) *The Coming of Post-Industrial Society*, London: Heinemann.

Bell, D. (1989) 'Communication Technology: For Better or For Worse?' in Salvaggio, J.L. (ed.) *The Information Society*, Hillsdale, NJ: Lawrence Erlbaum Associates.

Benson, J.K. (1982) 'A Framework for Policy Analysis' in Rogers, D., Whitten, D. and Associates, *Interorganizational Coordination*, Ames, IA: Iowa State University Press.

Bentley, A. (1967) *The Process of Government*, Chicago, IL: University of Chicago Press.

Berger, P. and Luckman, T. (1967) *The Social Construction of Reality*, Harmondsworth: Penguin.

Berry, J.M. (1989) 'Subgovernments, Issue Networks and Political Conflicts' in Harris, R.A. and Milkis, S.M. (eds) *Remaking American Politics*, Boulder, CO: Westview Press.

Birkenshaw, P., Harden, I and Lewis, N. (1990) *Government by Moonlight*, London: Unwin Hyman.

Black, D. (1988) 'Medicine and Politics', *British Medical Journal*, 296, pp. 53–6.

Block, F. (1980) 'Beyond Relative Autonomy: State Managers As Historical Subjects', *The Socialist Register*, 1980.

Bloom, D.B. and Smith, R.B. (eds) (1986) *The Future of Consumerism*, Lexington, MA: Lexington Books.

Bloom, P.N. and Greyser, S.A. (1981) 'The Maturing of Consumerism', *Harvard Business Review*, 59, pp. 130–9.

Boddy, M. and Lambert, C. (1990) 'Corporatist Interest Intermediation: Government–Building Society Relations in the UK' in Crouch, C. and Dore, R. (eds) *Corporatism and Accountability*, Oxford: Clarendon.

Body, R. (1982) *Agriculture: the Triumph and the Shame*, London: Maurice Temple Smith.

Body, R. (1984) *Farming in the Clouds*, London: Maurice Temple Smith.

Bonefeld, W. (1987) 'Reformulation of State Theory', *Capital & Class*, 33, pp. 96–127.

Bonnett, K. (1985) 'Corporatism and Thatcherism: is There Life After Death?' in Cawson, A. (ed.) *Organised Interests and the State*, London: Sage.

Brand, D.R. (1984) 'Corporatism, the NRA and the Oil Industry', *Political Studies Quarterly*, 98, pp. 100–17.

Braverman, J. (1980) *Crisis in Health Care*, Washington D.C.: World Bank.

Brittan, S. (1964) *The Treasury Under the Tories 1951–1961*, Harmondsworth: Penguin.

Brittan, S. (1975) 'The Economic Consequences of Democracy', *British Journal of Political Science*, 5, pp. 129–59.

Brown, L.D. (1987) 'Introduction to a Decade of Transition' in Brown, L.D. (ed.) *Health Policy in Transition*, Durham, NC: Duke University Press.

Browne, W.P. (1986) 'Policy and Interests: Instability and Change in a Classic Issue Subsystem' in Cigler, A. and Loomis, B. (eds) *Interest Group Politics*, Washington D.C.: Congressional Quarterly.

Browne, W.P. (1988) *Private Interests, Public Policy and American Agriculture*, Lawrence, KS: University Press of Kansas.

Browne, W.P. (1989) 'Access and Influence in Agriculture and Rural Affairs: Congressional Staff and Lobbyists Perceptions of Organised Interests', *Rural Sociology*, 54, pp. 365–81.

Browne, W.P. (1991) 'Issue Niches and the Limits of Interest Group Influence' in Cigler,

A. and Loomis, B. (eds) *Interest Group Politics*, 3rd edn, Washington D.C.: Congressional Quarterly.

Bulpitt, J. (1986) 'The Discipline of the New Democracy: Mrs Thatcher's Statecraft', *Political Studies*, 34, pp. 19–39.

Burnett, J. (1989) *Plenty and Want*, London: Routledge.

Butler, D. and Stokes, D. (1974) *Political Change in Britain*, London: Macmillan.

CAB 27/619 *Committee on Trade and Agriculture*, London: Public Records Office.

CAB 71/6 *War Cabinet – Lord President's Committee*, London: Public Records Office.

CAB 124/24 *Cabinet Consideration, 1–50 1952*, London: Public Records Office.

CAB 124/572 *Cabinet – Post-War Agricultural Policy*, London: Public Records Office.

CAB 127/170 *Agricultural Policy*, London: Public Records Office.

CAB 128/19 *Cabinet Minutes 1951*, London: Public Records Office.

Callinicos, A. (1989) *Against Postmodernism*, Oxford: Basil Blackwell.

Cammack, P. (1989) 'Bringing the State Back In?', *British Journal of Political Science*, 19, pp. 261–90.

Cammack, P. (1990) 'Statism, New Institutionalism, and Marxism', *The Socialist Register*, 1990.

Campion, F.D. (1984) *The AMA and US Health Policy Since 1940*, Chicago, IL: University of Chicago Press.

Campbell, J.C., Baskin, M.A., Baumgartner, F.R. and Halpern, N.P. (1989) 'Afterword on Policy Communities: A Framework for Comparative Research', *Governance*, 2, pp. 86–94.

Carsberg, B. (1987) *The Regulation of the Telecommunications Industry*, London: The David Hume Institute.

Cawson, A. (1982) *Corporatism and Welfare*, London: Heinemann.

Cawson, A. (1985) (ed.) *Organised Interests and the State*, London: Sage.

Cawson, A. (1986) *Corporatism and Political Theory*, Oxford: Blackwell.

Cawson, A., Morgan, K., Webber, D., Holmes, P. and Stevens, A. (1990) *Hostile Brothers: Competition and Closure in the European Electronics Industry*, Oxford: Clarendon.

Cawson, A. and Saunders, P. (1983) 'Corporatism, Competitive Politics and Class Struggle' in King, R. (ed.) *Capital and Politics*, London: Routledge and Kegan Paul.

Cerny, P. (1990) *The Changing Architecture of the State*, London: Sage.

Cigler, A.J. and Loomis, B.A. (1983) 'Introduction: The Changing Nature of Interest Group Politics' in Cigler, A.J. and Loomis, B.A. (eds) *Interest Group Politics*, Washington, D.C.: Congressional Quarterly.

Clarke, D. (1984) *Post-Industrial America*, New York: Methuen.

Clawson, D. and Clawson, M.A. (1987) 'Reagan or Business? Foundations of the New Conservatism' in Schwarz, M. (ed.) *The Structure of Power in the United States*, New York: Holmes and Meier.

Cmd 2581 (1926) *Agricultural Policy*, London: HMSO.

Cmd 6879 (1946) *Second Review of the World Food Shortage July 1946*, London: HMSO.

Cmd 7072 (1947) *Post-War Contribution of British Agriculture to the Saving of Foreign Exchange*, London: HMSO.

Cmnd 1311 (1961) *Annual Review and Determination of Prices*, London: HMSO.

Cmnd 2764 (1965) *The National Plan*, London: HMSO.

Cmnd 4578 (1971) *Public Expenditure Plans 1969–70 to 1974–75*, London: HMSO.

Cmnd 7458 (1979) *Farming and the Nation*, London: HMSO.

Cm 555 (1989) *Working for Patients*, London: HMSO.

Coates, D. (1980) *Labour in Power?*, London: Longman.

Coates, D. (1983) 'The Character and Origin of Britain's Decline' in Coates, D. and Hillard, J. (eds) *The Economic Decline of Modern Britain*, Hemel Hempstead: Harvester Wheatsheaf.

Coates, D. (1989) *The Crisis of Labour*, London: Philip Allan.

Cobb, R.W. and Elder, C.D. (1983) *Participation in American Politics*, Baltimore, MD: Johns Hopkins University.

Cochrane, W.W. and Ryan, M.E. (1976) *American Farm Policy, 1948–73*, Minneapolis, MN: University of Minnesota Press.

Cohen, J.L. (1982) *Class and Civil Society: The Limits of Critical Theory*, Amherst, MA: University of Massachusetts Press.

Cohen, S.D. (1977) *The Making of United States International Economic Policy*, New York: Praeger Publishers.

Cohen, S.D. (1988) *The Making of United States International Economic Policy*, third edition, New York: Praeger Publishers.

Coleman, V. (1988) 'Labour Power and Social Equality: Union Politics in a Changing Economy', *Political Science Quarterly*, 103, pp. 687–705.

Coleman, W.D. (1990) 'State Traditions and Comprehensive Business Associations: A Comparative Structural Analysis', *Political Studies*, 38, pp. 231–52.

Com (85) 333 *Perspectives for the Common Agricultural Policy*, Commission of the EEC.

Conservative Party (1987) *The Next Move Forward*, London: Conservative Central Office.

Consumers in the European Community Group (1984) *Enough is Enough*, London: CECG.

Cox, A. (1988a) 'The Old and New Testament of Corporatism: Is it a State Form or a Method of Policy-Making', *Political Studies*, 36, pp. 294–308.

Cox, A. (1988b) 'Neo-Corporatism Versus the Corporate State' in Cox, A. and O'Sullivan, N. (eds) *The Corporate State*, Aldershot: Edward Elgar.

Cox, A. (1988c) 'The Failure of Corporatist State Forms and Policies in Postwar Britain' in Cox, A. and O'Sullivan, N. (eds) *The Corporate State*, Aldershot: Edward Elgar.

Cox, G., Lowe, P. and Winter, M. (1985) 'Changing Directions in Agricultural Policy: Corporatist Arrangements in Production and Conservation', *Sociologia Ruralis*, 25, 130–50.

Cox, G., Lowe, P. and Winter, M. (1986) 'Agriculture and Conservation in Britain: A Policy Community Under Seige' in Cox, G., Lowe, P. and Winter, M. (eds) *Agriculture: People and Policies*, London: Allen and Unwin.

Crewe, I. and Payne, C. (1971) 'Analysing the Census Data' in Butler, D. and Pinto-Duschinsky, M., *The British General Election of 1970*, London: Macmillan.

Crosland, A. (1974) *Socialism Now and Other Essays*, London: Jonathan Cape.

Crossman, R. (1972) *Inside View*, London: Jonathan Cape.

Crouch, C. (1977) *Class Conflict and the Industrial Relations Crisis*, London: Heinemann.

Crouch, C. (1979) 'The State, Capital and Liberal Democracy' in Crouch, C. (ed.) *State and Economy in Contemporary Capitalism*, London: Croom Helm.

Crouch, C. and Dore, R. (1990) 'Whatever Happened to Corporatism?' in Crouch, C. and Dore, R. (eds) *Corporatism and Accountability*, Oxford: Clarendon.

Cunningham, C. (1992) 'Sea Defences: A Professionalised Network?' in Marsh, D. and Rhodes, R.A.W. (eds) *Policy Networks in British Government*, Oxford: Oxford University Press.

Dahl, R.A. (1957) 'The Concept of Power', *Behavioural Science*, 2, pp. 201–15.

Dahl, R.A. (1961) *Who Governs?*, New Haven, CT: Yale University Press.

Day, P. and Klein, R. (1992) 'Consitutional and Distributional Conflict in British Medical Politics: The Case of General Practice, 1911–1991', *Political Studies*, 50, pp. 462–78.

Denton, G. (1976) 'Financial Assistance to British Industry' in Corden, W.M. and Fels, G. (eds) *Public Assistance to Industry*, London: Macmillan.

Destler, I.M. (1986) *American Trade Politics: System Under Stress*, Washington D.C.: Institute for International Economics.

Destler, I.M. (1992) *American Trade Politics*, second edition, Washington D.C.: Institute for International Economics.

Destler, I.M. and Odell, J.S. (1987) *Anti-Protection: Changing Forces in United States Trade Politics*, Washington D.C.: Institute for International Economics.

Devine, F. (1992) *The Affluent Worker Revisited*, Edinburgh: Edinburgh University Press.

De Witt, K. (1981) 'Reagan's Consumer Chief Notes Policy Shift', *New York Times*, 12 April.

Domhoff, W. (1967) *Who Rules America?*, New Jersey: Prentice-Hall.

Domhoff, W. (1978) *The Powers that Be*, New York: Vintage Books.

Dowding, K. (1991) *Political Power and Rational Choice*, Aldershot: Edward Elgar.

Downs, A. (1972) 'Up and Down with Ecology – The "Issue Attention Cycle"', *Public Interest*, 28, pp. 38–50.

Dunleavy, P. (1981) 'Professions and Policy Change: Notes Towards a Model of Ideological Corporatism', *Public Administration Bulletin*, 36, pp. 3–16.

Dunleavy, P. and Husbands, C. (1985) *Democracy at the Crossroads*, London: George Allen and Unwin.

Dunleavy, P. and O'Leary, B. (1987) *Theories of the State*, London: Macmillan.

Dyson, K. (1982) *The State Tradition in Western Europe*, Oxford: Martin Robertson.

Eads, G.C. and Fix, M. (1984) 'Introduction' in Eads, G.C and Fix, M. (eds) *The Reagan Regulatory Strategy: An Assessment*, Washington D.C.: The Urban Institute Press.

Easton, D. (1967) *The Political System*, New York: Alfred A. Knopf.

Eatwell, J. (1982) *Whatever Happenend to Britain?*, London: Duckworth/BBC.

Eckstein, H. (1960) *Pressure Group Politics*, London: George Allen and Unwin.

Edgell, S. and Duke, U. (1991) *A Measure of Thatcherism*, London: HarperCollins.

Edmonds, M. (1983) 'Market Ideology and Corporate Power: The United States' in Dyson, K. and Wilks, S. (eds) *Industrial Crisis*, Oxford: Blackwell.

Elfring, T. (1988) *Service Sector Employment in Advanced Economies*, Aldershot: Avebury.

Evans, J.R. (1980) *Consumerism in the United States*, New York: Praeger Publishers.

Falcone, D. and Hartwig, L.C. (1984) 'Congressional Process and Health Policy: Reform and Retrenchment' in Litman, T.J. and Robins, L.S. (eds) *Health Politics and Policy*, New York: John Wiley.

Featherstone, M. (1990) 'Perspectives on Consumer Culture', *Sociology*, 24, pp. 5–22.

Feldstein, P.J. (1988) *The Politics of Health Legislation*, Ann Arbor, MI: University of Michigan Press.

Finegold, K. (1981) 'From Agrarianism to Adjustment: the Political Origins of the New Deal', *Politics and Society*, 11, pp. 1–27.

Finegold, E. and Greenberg, G.D. (1984) 'Health Policy and the Federal Executive' in Litman, T.J. and Robins, L.S. (eds) *Health Politics and Policy*, New York: John Wiley.

Finer, S.E. (1956) 'The Political Power of Private Capital Part II', *Sociological Review*, IV, pp. 5–30.

Finer, S.E. (1966) *Anonymous Empire*, London: Pall Mall Press.

Flickinger, R.S. (1987) 'Consumer Policy: Qualified Divergence' in Waltman, J.C. and

Studler, D.T. (eds) *Political Economy*, Jackson and London: University Press of Mississippi.

Flynn, N. (1989) 'The New Right and Social Policy', *Policy and Politics*, 17, pp. 97–109.

Forbes, J.D. (1987) *The Consumer Interest*, London: Croom Helm.

Foster, J. and Woolfson, C. (1989) 'Corporate Reconstruction and Business Unionism: The Lessons of Caterpillar and Ford', *New Left Review*, 174, pp. 51–66.

Foucault, M. (1980) *Power/Knowledge*, Hemel Hempstead: Harvester Wheatsheaf.

Fox, D.M. (1986a) *Health Policies, Health Politics*, Princeton, NJ: Princeton University Press.

Fox, D.M. (1986b) 'The Consequence of Consensus: American Health Policy in the Twentieth Century', *Milbank Quarterly*, 64, pp. 76–99.

Freeman, J.L. (1965) *The Political Process: Executive Bureau–Legislative Committee Relations*, New York: Random House

Fritchler, A.L. (1983) *Smoking and Politics: Policymaking and the Federal Bureaucracy*, Englewood-Cliffs, NJ: Prentice-Hall.

Frolund Thomsen, J.P. (1991) 'A Strategic-Relational Account of Economic State Interventions' in Bertamsen, R.B., Frolund Thomsen, J.P. and Torfing, J., *State, Economy and Society*, London: Unwin Hyman.

Galbraith, J.K. (1953) *American Capitalism*, Harmondsworth: Penguin Books.

Galston, W.A. (1985) *The 1985 Farm Bill and Beyond*, Lanham, MD: Hamilton Press.

Gamble, A. (1982) *Britain in Decline*, Basingstoke: Macmillan.

Gamble, A. (1989) 'Individualism Rules, OK!', *The Sunday Correspondent*.

Gamble, A. (1990) *Britain in Decline*, 3rd edn, Basingstoke: Macmillan.

Gamble, A. and Walkland, S.A. (1984) *The British Party System and Economic Policy 1945–83*, Oxford: Clarendon.

Gardener, C. and Sheppard, J. (1989) *Consuming Passions: The Rise of Retail Culture*, London: Unwin Hyman.

Gardner, B. (1987) 'The Common Agricultural Policy: the Obstacles to Change', *The Political Quarterly*, 58, pp. 167–79.

Gaventa, J. (1980) *Power and Powerlessness*, Oxford: Clarendon Press.

Gershuny, J. (1978) *After Industrial Society*, London: Macmillan.

Gias, T.L., Peterson, M.A. and Walker, J.L. (1984) 'Interest Groups, Iron Triangles and Representative Institutions in American National Government', *British Journal of Political Science*, 14, pp. 161–85.

Gibb, F. (1988) 'Law Makes It Easier to Get Compensation for Poor Goods', *The Times*, 22 February.

Giddens, A. (1986) *The Constitution of Society*, Cambridge: Polity Press.

Gist, P. (1990) 'The Role of Oftel', *Telecommunications Policy*, 14, pp. 26–51.

Godber, G. (1988) 'Forty years of the NHS', *British Medical Journal*, 297, pp. 37–43.

Goldfield, M. (1986) 'Labor in American Politics – Its Current Weakness', *Journal of Politics*, 48, pp. 2–29.

Goldsmith, M. and Willetts, D. (1988) *Managed Health Care: a New System for a Better Health Service*, London: Centre for Policy Studies.

Goldstein, J. (1988) 'Ideas, Institutions, and American Trade Policy' in Ikenberry, G.J., Lake, D.A. and Mastanduno, M. (eds) *The State and American Foreign Economic Policy*, Ithaca and London: Cornell University Press.

Gorz, A. (1982) *Farewell to the Working Class*, Verso: London.

Gorz, A. (1989) 'A Land of Cockayne', *New Statesman and Society*, 2, pp. 27–31.

Gough, I. (1979) *The Political Economy of the Welfare State*, London: Macmillan.

Gramsci, A. (1971) *Selections from Prison Notebooks*, London: Lawrence and Wishart.

Grant, W.P. (1982) *The Political Economy of Industrial Policy*, London: Butterworths.

Grant, W.P. (1983) 'The National Farmers' Union: A Classic Case of Incorporation' in Marsh, D. (ed.) *Pressure Politics*, London: Junction Books.

Grant, W.P. (1985) 'Insider and Outsider Pressure Groups', *Social Science Review*, 1, pp. 31–4.

Grant, W.P. (1987) *Business and Politics in Britain*, Basingstoke: Macmillan.

Grant, W.P. (1988) *Government and Industry*, Aldershot: Edward Elgar.

Grant, W.P. (1989a) *Pressure Groups, Politics and Democracy in Britain*, London: Philip Allan.

Grant, W.P. (1989b) 'The Erosion of Intermediary Institutions', *Political Quarterly*, 60, pp. 10–21.

Grant, W.P. and Marsh, D. (1977) *The Confederation of British Industry*, London: Hodder and Stoughton.

Grant, W.P., Paterson, W. and Whitson, C. (1988) *Government and the Chemical Industry*, Oxford: Clarendon.

Grant, W.P. and Wilks, S. (1983) 'British Industrial Policy: Structural Change, Policy Inertia', *Journal of Public Policy*, 3, pp. 13–28.

Green, D. (1987) *The New Right*, Hemel Hempstead: Harvester Wheatsheaf.

Grey-Turner, E. and Sutherland, F.M. (1982) *History of the British Medical Association vol II*, London: British Medical Association.

Griffiths, R. (1988) 'Does the Public Service Serve? The Consumer Dimension', *Public Administration*, 66, pp. 195–204.

Griggs, E. (1991) 'The Politics of Health Care Reform in Britain', *Political Quarterly*, 62 (4), pp. 419–31.

Guth, J.L (1978) 'Consumer Organisation and Federal Dairy Policy', *Policy Journal*, 6, pp. 499–503.

Hall, J. and Ikenberry J. (1990) *The State*, Milton Keynes: Open University Press.

Hall, P. (1986) *Governing the Economy*, Oxford: Polity Press.

Hall, P. and Jacques, M. (1989) (eds) *New Times: The Changing Face of Politics in the 1990s*, London: Lawrence and Wishart.

Ham, C. (1981) *Policy Making in the National Health Service*, London: Macmillan.

Ham, C. (1985) *Health Policy in Britain*, London: Macmillan.

Hambleton, R. (1988) 'Consumerism, Decentralisation and Local Democracy', *Public Administration*, 66, pp. 125–47.

Hamelink, C.J. (1986) 'Is There Life After the Information Revolution?' in Traber, M. (ed.) *The Myth of the Information Revolution*, London: Sage.

Hamilton, D.E. (1991) *From New Day to New Deal*, Chapel Hill, NC: University of North Carolina Press.

Hansen, W.L. (1990) 'The International Trade Commission and the Politics of Protectionism', *American Political Science Review*, 84, pp. 21–45.

Hardin, C.M. (1978) 'Agricultural Price Policy: The Political Role of Bureaucracy' in Hadwiger, D.F. and Browne, W.P. (1978) *The New Politics of Food*, Lexington, MA: Lexington Books.

Harl, N.E. (1990) *The Farm Debt Crisis of the 1980s*, Ames, IO: Iowa State University Press.

Harris, L. (1988) 'The UK Economy at the Crossroads' in Allen, J. and Massey, D. (eds) *The Economy in Question*, London: Sage.

Harris, N. (1972) *Competition and the Corporate Society*, London: Methuen.

Harrison, S., Hunter, D.J. and Pollitt, C. (1990) *The Dynamics of British Health Policy*, London: Unwin Hyman.

Harvey, B.W. and Parry, D.L. (1987) *Consumer Protection and Fair Trading*, London: Butterworths.

Hathaway, D.E. (1963) *Government and Agriculture*, New York: Macmillan.

Havighurst, C.C. (1987) 'The Changing Locus of Decision Making' in Brown, L. (ed.) *Health Policy in Transition*, Durham, NC: Duke University Press.

Havighurst, C.C., Helms, R.B., Bladen, C. and Pauly, M.V. (1988) *American Health Care*, London: Institute of Economic Affairs.

Hayek, F.A. (1979) *Law, Legislation and Liberty Vol III*, London: Routledge and Kegan Paul.

Hayes, M. (1983) 'Interest Groups: Pluralism or Mass Society?' in Cigler, A.J. and Loomis, B.A. (eds) *Interest Group Politics*, Washington D.C.: Congressional Quarterly.

HC 254 (1957/58) *The Sixth Report of the Select Committee on Estimates*, Treasury Control of Expenditure, London: HMSO.

HC 77 (1961/62) *Second Report from the Estimates Committee*, Agriculture and Food Grants, etc., London: HMSO.

HC 137 (1968/69) *Report from the Select Committee on Agriculture*, Report, Minutes of Evidence and Index, London: HMSO.

HC 138 (1968/69) *Special Report of the Select Committee on Agriculture*, London: HMSO.

Headey, B. (1974) *British Cabinet Ministers*, London: George Allen and Unwin.

Heclo, H. (1978) 'Issue Networks and the Executive Establishment' in King, A. (ed.) *The New American Political System*, Washington D.C.: American Enterprise Institute.

Heclo, H. and Wildavsky, A. (1974) *The Private Government of Public Money*, London: Macmillan.

Hewitt, C.J. (1974) 'Elites and the Distribution of Power in British Society' in Giddens, A. and Stanworth, P., *Elites and Power in British Society*, Cambridge: Cambridge University Press.

Hindess, B. (1989) *Political Choice and Social Structure*, Aldershot: Edward Elgar.

Hirst, P. (1989) 'After Henry' in Hall, S. and Jacques, M. (eds) *New Times: the Changing Face of Politics in the 1990s*, London: Lawrence and Wishart.

HL 82-II (1982/83) *House of Lords Select Committee on the European Communities, The 1983–84 Farm Price Proposals Minutes of Evidence*, London: HMSO.

HL 153 (1983/84) *House of Lords Select Committee on the European Communities, The 1984–85 Farm Price Proposals*, London: HMSO.

HL 112 (1984/85) *House of Lords Select Committee on the European Communities, The 1985–86 Farm Price Proposals*, London: HMSO.

HL 237 (1984/85) *House of Lords Select Committee on the European Communities, The Reform of the Common Agricultural Policy*, London: HMSO.

HL 247 (1984/85) *House of Lords Select Committee on the European Communities, Agriculture and the Community*, London: HMSO.

HL 83 (1985/86) *House of Lords Select Committee on the European Communities, Cereals*, London: HMSO.

HL 107 (1985/86) *House of Lords Select Committee on the European Communities, The 1986–87 Farm Price Proposals*, London: HMSO.

HL 192, (1985/86) *House of Lords Select Committee on the European Communities, Consumer Protection Policy*, London: HMSO.

HL 83 (1987/88) *House of Lords Select Committee on the European Communities, Farm Price Review*, London: HMSO.

HL 34 (1989/90) *House of Lords Committee on the European Communities: Farm Price Proposals 1990–1991*, London: HMSO.

Hobsbawm, E. (1979) *The Forward March of Labour Halted?*, London: Verso.

Hogwood, B.W. (1986) 'If Consultation is Everything then Maybe it is Nothing', *Strathclyde Papers in Government and Politics*, No. 44.

Hogwood, B.W. (1987) *From Crisis to Complacency*, Oxford: Oxford University Press.

Hogwood, B.W. and Gunn, L. (1984) *Policy Analysis for the Real World*, Oxford: Oxford University Press.

Honigsbaum, F. (1989) *Health, Happiness and Security: The Creation of the National Health Service*, London: Routledge.

Honigsbaum, F. (1990) 'The Evolution of the NHS', *British Medical Journal*, 301, pp. 694–9.

Hood, J. and Harvey, K. (1958) *The British State*, London: Lawrence and Wishart.

Hooks, G. (1990) 'From an Autonomous to Captured State Agency: The Decline of the New Deal in Agriculture', *American Sociological Review*, 55, pp. 29–43.

House of Commons, *Parliamentary Debates*, Fifth Series, vol. 396, 26 January 1944.

House of Commons, *Parliamentary Debates*, Fifth Series, vol. 498, 4 April 1952.

House of Commons, *Parliamentary Debates*, Fifth Series, vol. 872, 9 April 1974.

House of Commons, *Parliamentary Debates*, Fifth Series, vol. 930, 27 April 1977.

House of Commons, *Parliamentary Debates*, Fifth Series, vol. 947, 7 April 1978.

House of Commons, *Parliamentary Debates*, Sixth Series, vol. 115, 27 April 1987.

Hufbauer, G.C., Berliner, D.T. and Elliot, K.A. (1986) *Trade Protection in the United States*, Washington D.C.: Institute for International Economics.

Hughes, C. and Wintour, P. (1990) *Labour Rebuilt: The New Model Party*, London: Fourth Estate.

Ikenberry, G.J. (1988a) 'An Institutional Approach to American Foreign Economic Policy' in Ikenberry, G.J., Lake, D.A. and Mastanduno, M. (eds) *The State and American Foreign Economic Policy*, Ithaca and London: Cornell University Press.

Ikenberry, G.J. (1988b) 'Conclusion: an Institutional Approach to American Foreign Economic Policy' in Ikenberry, G.J., Lake, D.A. and Mastanduno, M. (eds) *The State and American Foreign Economic Policy*, Ithaca and London: Cornell University Press.

Ikenberry, G.J., Lake, D.A. and Mastanduno, M. (1988) 'Introduction: Approaches to Explaining American Foreign Economic Policy' in Ikenberry, G.J., Lake, D.A. and Mastanduno, M. (eds) *The State and American Foreign Economic Policy*, Ithaca and London: Cornell University Press.

Infanger, C.L., Bailey, W.C. and Dyer, D.R. (1983) 'Agricultural Policy in Austerity: the Making of the 1981 Farm Bill', *American Journal of Agricultural Economics*, 65, pp. 1–9.

Ingham, G. (1984) *Capitalism Divided? The City and Industry in Britain*, London: Macmillan.

Inglehart, R. (1977) *The Silent Revolution*, Princeton, NJ: Princeton University Press.

Inglehart, R. (1990) 'Values, Ideology and Cognitive Mobilisation in New Social Movements' in Dalton, R.J. and Kuechler, M. (eds) *Challenging the Political Order*, Oxford: Polity Press.

Issel, W. (1985) *Social Change in the United States*, London: Macmillan.

Jenkins, P. (1988) *The Thatcher Revolution: the Post Socialist Era*, London: Jonathan Cape.

Jessop, B. (1980) 'The Transformation of the State in Post-war Britain' in Scase, R. (ed.) *The State in Western Europe*, London: Croom Helm.

Jessop, B. (1982) *The Capitalist State*, Oxford: Martin Robertson.

Jessop, B. (1983a) 'The Democratic State and the National Interest' in Coates, D. and Johnston, G. (eds) *Socialist Arguments*, Oxford: Martin Robertson.

Jessop, B. (1983b) 'The Capitalist State and the Rule of Capital: Problems in the Analysis of Business Associations', *West European Politics*, 6, pp. 139–62.

Jessop, B. (1988) 'Regulation Theory, Post-Fordism and the State', *Capital & Class*, 34, pp. 147–68.

Jessop, B. (1989) 'Thatcherism: The British Road to Post-Fordism', *Essex Papers in Politics and Government*, No. 68, Department of Government, University of Essex.

Jessop, B. (1990) *State Theory: Putting Capitalist States in their Place*, Cambridge: Polity Press.

Jessop, B., Bonnett, K., Bromley, S. and Ling, T. (1988) *Thatcherism: A Tale of Two Nations*, Cambridge: Polity Press.

Johnson, T.J. (1972) *Professions and Power*, London: Macmillan.

Jones, P.R. (1981) *Doctors and the BMA: A Case Study in Collective Action*, Farnborough: Gower.

Jordan, A.G. (1981) 'Iron Triangles, Woolly Corporatism and Elastic Nets: Images of the Policy Process', *The Journal of the Policy Process*, 1, pp. 95–123.

Jordan, A.G. (1984) 'Pluralistic Corporatism and Corporate Pluralism', *Scandanavian Political Studies*, 7, pp. 137–53.

Jordan, A.G. (1990a) 'Policy Community Realism versus "New" Institutionalist Ambiguity', *Political Studies*, 38, pp. 470–84.

Jordan, A.G. (1990b) 'Sub-governments, Policy Communities and Networks: Refilling the Old Bottles', *Journal of Theoretical Politics*, 2, pp. 319–38.

Jordan, A.G. (1990c) 'The Pluralism of Pluralism: An Anti-theory?', *Political Studies*, 38, pp. 286–301.

Jordan, A.G. and Richardson, J.J. (1982) 'The British Policy Style or the Logic of Negotiation?' in Richardson, J.J. (ed.) *Policy Styles in Western Europe*, London: George Allen and Unwin.

Jordan, A.G. and Richardson, J.J. (1987) *Government and Pressure Groups in Britain*, Oxford: Clarendon.

Katzenstein, P.J. (1978) 'Domestic Structures and Strategies of Foreign Economic Policy' in Katzenstein, P.J. (ed.) *Between Power and Plenty*, Madison, WI: University of Wisconsin Press.

Keane, J. (1988) *Democracy and Civil Society*, London: Verso.

Kelso, W.A. (1978) *American Democratic Theory: Pluralism and its Critics*, Connecticut: Greenwood Press.

Kenny, M., Laboa, L.M., Curry, J. and Goe, W.R. (1989) 'Midwestern Agriculture in US Fordism', *Sociologia Ruralis*, 29, pp. 131–48.

Keohane, R.A. (1984) *After Hegemony: Cooperation and Discord in the World Political Economy*, Princeton, NJ: Princeton University Press.

King, R. (1990) 'Policy and Process in the Modern State' in Simmie, J. and King, R. (eds) *The State in Action*, London: Pinter.

Klandersman, P.B. (1990) 'Linking the "Old" and "New" Movement Networks in the

Netherlands' in Dalton, R.J. and Keuchler, M. (eds) *Challenging the Political Order*, Cambridge: Polity Press.

Klein, R. (1979) 'Ideology, Class and the National Health Service', *Journal of Health Politics, Policy and Law*, 4, pp. 464–90.

Klein, R. (1984) 'The Politics of Ideology vs the Reality of Politics: The Case of Britain's National Health Service in the 1980s', *Milbank Quarterly*, 62, pp. 82–109

Klein, R. (1989) *The Politics of the NHS*, London: Longman.

Klein, R. (1990) 'The State and the Profession: The Politics of the Double Bed', *British Medical Journal*, 301, pp. 700–2.

Knoke, D. (1990) *Political Networks: The Structural Perspective*, Cambridge: Cambridge University Press.

Krasner, S.D. (1978) 'United States Commercial and Monetary Policy: Unravelling the Paradox of External Strength and Internal Weakness' in Katzenstein, P.J. (ed.) *Between Power and Plenty*, Madison, WI: University of Wisconsin Press.

Kreiger, J. (1986) *Reagan, Thatcher and the Politics of Decline*, Cambridge: Polity Press.

Kuechler, M. and Dalton, R.J. (1990) 'New Social Movements in Perspective' in Dalton, R.J. and Kuechler, M. (eds) *Challenging the Political Order*, Cambridge: Polity Press.

Kuhn, T. (1970) *The Structure of Scientific Revolution*, Chicago, IL: University of Chicago Press.

Kumar, K. (1978) *Prophecy or Progress*, London: Allen Lane.

Labour Party (1989) *Meet the Challenge Make the Change*, London: Labour Party.

Laffin, M. (1986) *Professionalism and Policy: The Role of the Professions in the Centre–Local Government Relations*, Aldershot: Gower.

Lake, D.A. (1988) 'The State and American Trade Strategy in the Pre-Hegemonic Era' in Ikenberry, G.J., Lake, D.A. and Mastanduno, M. (eds) *The State and American Foreign Economic Policy*, Ithaca and London: Cornell University Press.

Lane, C. (1988) 'Industrial Change in Europe: The Pursuit of Flexible Specialisation in Britain and West Germany', *Work, Employment and Society*, 2, pp. 141–68.

Larkin, G.V. (1988) 'Medical Dominance in Britain: Image and Historical Reality', *Milbank Quarterly*, 66, pp. 117–32.

Lash, S. and Urry, J. (1987) *The End of Organised Capitalism*, Cambridge: Polity Press.

Latham, E. (1953) *The Group Basis of Politics*, Ithaca, NY: Cornell University Press.

Laumann, E.O. and Knoke, D. (1987) *The Organisational State*, Madison, WI: The University of Wisconsin Press.

Leruez, J. (1975) *Economic Planning and Politics in Britain*, Oxford: Martin Robertson.

Lean, G. (1984) 'Thatcher Orders U–Turn for Farming', *Observer*, 14 October.

Levine, M.K. (1985) *Inside International Trade Policy Formulation*, New York: Praeger Special Studies.

Levitan, S.A. and Cooper, M.R. (1984) *Business Lobbies: The Public Good and the Bottom Line*, Baltimore and London: Johns Hopkins University Press.

Leys, C. (1985) 'Thatcherism and British Manufacturing', *New Left Review*, 151, pp. 5–21.

Lindblom, C.E. (1977) *Politics and Markets*, New York: Basic Books.

Lipietz, A. (1987) *Mirages and Miracles: The Crisis of Global Fordism*, London: Verso.

Lowe, P., Cox, G., MacEwan, M., O'Riordan, T. and Winter, M. (1986) *Countryside Conflicts*, Aldershot: Gower.

Lowi, T.J. (1969) *The End of Liberalism*, New York: Norton.

Lucco, J. (1992) 'Representing the Public Interest: Consumer Groups and the

Presidency' in Petracca, M.P. (ed.) *The Politics of Interests*, Boulder, CO: Westview Press.

Luhmann, N. (1982) *The Differentiation of Society*, New York: Columbia University Press.

Lukes, S. (1974) *Power: A Radical View*, London: Macmillan.

Mabie, J.E. (1978) 'Subsystems, Stability and Agricultural Policy Outputs' in Hadwiger, D.F. and Browne, W.P., *The New Politics of Food*, Lexington, MA: Lexington Books.

McConnell, G. (1953) *The Decline of Agrarian Democracy*, New York: Atheneum.

McConnell, G. (1966) *Private Power and American Democracy*, New York: Alfred A. Knopf.

McCool, D. (1990) 'Subgovernments as Determinants of Political Viability', *Political Science Quarterly*, 105, pp. 269–93.

McEachern, D. (1990) *The Expanding State*, Hemel Hempstead: Harvester Wheatsheaf.

McFadyen Campbell, C. (1962) *The Farm Bureau*, Urbana, IL: University of Illinois Press.

MacFarland, A.S. (1984) *Common Cause*, Chatham, NJ: Chatham House.

McInnes, J. (1987) *Thatcherism at Work*, Milton Keynes: Open University Press.

McKay, D. (1983) 'Industrial Policy and Non-Policy in the United States', *Journal of Public Policy*, 3, pp. 29–48.

McKay, D. (1989) *Domestic Policy and Ideology*, Cambridge: Cambridge University Press.

McKie, D. (1992) (ed.) *The Election*, London: Guardian Books.

McLennan, G. (1989) *Marxism, Pluralism and Beyond*, Oxford: Polity Press.

McQuaid, K. (1981) 'The Roundtable: Getting Results in Washington', *Harvard Business Review*, 61, pp. 114–23.

McQuaid, K. (1982) *Big Business and Presidential Power*, New York: William Morrow.

MAF 53/83 *Agricultural Conference 1930*, London: Public Records Office.

MAF 53/108 *Notes by the Minister of Agriculture on the Agricultural Bill*, London: Public Records Office.

MAF 53/134 *Statements on Talks with the NFU – Agricultural Policy 1936–40*, London: Public Records Office.

MAF 53/171 *Post-War Agricultural Policy*, London: Public Records Office.

MAF 53/182 *World Wheat Supplies*, London: Public Records Office.

Mann, M. (1984) 'The Autonomous Power of the State: its Origins, Mechanisms and Results', *Archives Européennes de Sociologie*, 25, pp. 185–213.

March, J. and Olsen, J.P. (1984) 'The New Institutionalism', *American Political Science Review*, 78, pp. 734–49.

Marmor, T. (1970) *The Politics of Medicare*, London: Routledge & Kegan Paul.

Marmor, T., Mashaw, J.L. and Harvey, P.L. (1990) *America's Misunderstood Welfare State*, New York: Basic Books.

Marmor, T. and Thomas, D. (1972) 'Doctors, Politics and Pay Disputes', *British Journal of Political Science*, 2, pp. 421–42.

Marquand, D. (1988) *The Unprincipled Society*, London: Fontana.

Marsh, D. (1984) 'The Politics of Private Investment', mimeo, Department of Government, University of Essex.

Marsh, D. (1991) 'Privatisation under Mrs Thatcher', *Public Administration*, 69, pp. 459–80.

Marsh, D. (1992a) *The New Politics of British Trade Unionism*, London: Macmillan.

Marsh, D. (1992b) 'Youth Employment Policy 1979–1990: Towards the Exclusion of Trade Unions' in Marsh, D. and Rhodes, R.A.W (eds) *Policy Networks in British Government*, Oxford: Oxford University Press.

Marsh, D. and Chambers, J. (1981) *Abortion Politics*, London: Junction Books.

Marsh, D. and Grant, W. (1977) 'Tripartism: Reality or Myth?', *Government and Opposition*, 12, pp. 194–211.

Marsh, D. and King, G. (1986) 'The Trade Unions under Thatcher', *Essex Papers in Politics and Government*, No. 27, Department of Government, University of Essex.

Marsh, D. and Locksley, G. (1983) 'Capital: The Neglected Face of Power?' in Marsh, D. (ed.) *Pressure Politics*, London: Junction Books.

Marsh, D. and Rhodes, R. (1989) 'Implementing "Thatcherism": A Policy Perspective', *Essex Papers in Politics and Government*, No. 62, Department of Government, University of Essex.

Marsh, D. and Rhodes, R.A.W (1992a) *Policy Networks in British Government*, Oxford: Oxford University Press.

Marsh, D. and Rhodes, R.A.W. (1992b) *Implementing Thatcherite Policies: Audit of an Era*, Milton Keynes: Open University Press.

Marsh, D. and Rhodes, R.A.W (1992c) 'Policy Communities and Issue Networks: Beyond Typology' in Marsh, D. and Rhodes, R.A.W (eds) *Policy Networks in British Government*, Oxford: Oxford University Press.

Marsh, D. and Rhodes, R.A.W (1992d) 'The Implementation Gap: Explaining Policy Change and Continuity' in Marsh, D. and Rhodes, R.A.W. (eds) *Implementing Thatcherite Policies: Audit of an Era*, Milton Keynes: Open University Press.

Marshall, G., Rose, D., Newby, H. and Vogler, C. (1988) *Social Class in Modern Britain*, London: Unwin Hyman.

Marshall, T.H. (1973) *Citizenship and Social Class*, London: Cambridge University Press.

Martin, R.M. (1983) 'Pluralism and the New Corporatism', *Political Studies*, 31, pp. 86–101.

Massey, D. (1988) 'What is Happening to UK Manufacturing' in Allen, J. and Massey, D. (eds) *The Economy in Question*, London: Sage.

Maynard, A. (1988) *Wither the National Health Service?*, University of York: Centre for Health Economics.

Maynard, G. (1988) *The Economy Under Mrs Thatcher*, London: Methuen.

Mazey, S. and Richardson, J.J. (1990) 'British Pressure Groups in the EC: Changing Lobbying Styles?', *Brunel Working Papers in Government*, Uxbridge: Brunel University.

Mechanic, D. (1981) 'Some Dilemmas in Health Care Policy', *Milbank Quarterly*, 59, pp. 1–15.

Meegan, R. (1988) 'A Crisis of Mass Production?' in Allen, J. and Massey, D. (eds) *The Economy in Question*, London: Sage.

Meier, K.J. (1978) 'Building Bureaucratic Coalitions: Client Representations in USDA Bureaus' in Hadwiger, D.F. and Browne, W.P. (1978) *The New Politics of Food*, Lexington, MA: Lexington Books.

Meier, K.J. and Browne, W.P. (1983) 'Interest Groups and Farm Structure' in Brewster, D.E., Rasmussen, W.D. and Youngberg, G. (eds) *Farms in Transition*, Ames, IA: Iowa State University.

Middlemas, K. (1979) *Politics in Industrial Society*, London: André Deutsch.

Middlemas, K. (1983) *Industry, Unions and Government*, London: Macmillan.

Middlemas, K. (1986) *Power, Competition and the State, Vol. 1: Britain in Search of Balance 1940–1961*, London: Macmillan.

Miliband, R. (1969) *The State in Capitalist Society*, London: Quartet Books.

Miliband, R. (1977) *Marxism and Politics*, Oxford: Oxford University Press.

Miliband, R. (1982) *Capitalist Democracy in Britain*, Oxford: Oxford University Press.

Mills, M. (1992) 'Networks and Policy on Diet and Heart Disease' in Marsh, D. and Rhodes, R.A.W (eds) *Policy Networks in British Government*, Oxford: Oxford University Press.

Millward, N. and Stevens, M. (1986) *British Workplace Industrial Relations 1980–1984*, Aldershot: Gower.

Milward, H.B. and Francisco, R.A. (1983) 'Subsystem Politics and Corporatism in the United States', *Policy and Politics*, 11, pp. 273–93.

Mintz, B. and Schwarz, M. (1987) 'Corporate Interlocks, Financial Hegemony and Intercorporate Coordination' in Schwarz, M. (ed.) *The Structure of Power in the United States*, New York: Holmes and Meier.

Mohan, J. (1990) 'Health Care Policy and the State in "Austerity Capitalism" ' in Simmie, J. and King, R. (eds) *The State in Action*, London: Pinter.

Moran, M. (1984) *The Politics of Banking*, London: Macmillan.

Moran, M. (1987) 'An Outpost of Corporatism: The Franchise State on Wall Street', *Government and Opposition*, 22, pp. 206–23.

Mort, F. (1989) 'The Politics of Consumption' in Hall, P. and Jacques, M. (eds) *New Times: The Changing Face of Politics in the 1990s*, London: Lawrence and Wishart.

Moyser, H.W. and Josling, T.E. (1990) *Agricultural Policy Reform*, Ames, IA: Iowa State University Press.

Murray, R. (1988) 'Life after Henry (Ford)', *Marxism Today*, October, pp. 8–13.

Nadel, M.V. (1971) *The Politics of Consumer Protection*, New York: Bobbs Merrill.

National Consumer Council (1979) *The Consumer and the State: Getting Value for Real Money*, London: National Consumer Council.

National Consumer Council (1990) *Annual Report*, London: National Consumer Council.

NFU (1984) *The Way Forward*, London: National Farmers' Union.

Newman, O. (1981) *The Challenge of Corporatism*, London: Macmillan.

Nordlinger, E. (1981) *On the Autonomy of the Democratic State*, Cambridge, MA: Harvard University Press.

Nordlinger, E. (1988) 'The Return to the State: Critiques', *American Political Science Review*, 82, pp. 875–85.

OECD (1983) *Consumer Policy in the Last Ten Years*, Paris: OECD.

Offe, C. (1981) 'The Attribution of Public Status to Interest Groups' in Berger, S. (ed.) *Organising Interests in Western Europe*, Cambridge: Cambridge University Press.

Offe, C. (1984) *Contradictions of the Welfare State*, London: Hutchinson.

Offe, C. and Wiesenthal, H. (1980) 'Two Logics of Collective Action', *Political Power and Social Theory*, 1, pp. 67–115.

Oliver, T.R. (1991) 'Health Care Market Reform in Congress: The Uncertain Path from Proposal to Policy', *Political Science Quarterly*, 106 (3), pp. 453–77.

Olson, M. (1965) *The Logic of Collective Action*, Cambridge, MA: Harvard University Press.

Olson, M. (1982) *The Ride and Decline of Nations*, New Haven, CT: Yale University Press.

O'Sullivan, N. (1988) 'The Political Theory of Neo-Corporatism' in Cox, A. and O'Sullivan, N. (ed.) *The Corporate State*, Aldershot: Edward Elgar.

Pahl, R. and Winkler, J. (1974) 'The Coming Corporatism', *New Society*, 10 October.

Palmer, J. and Woolf, J. (1990) 'EC Farm Subsidy Crisis Fuels Trade War Fears', *The Guardian*, 18 October.

Panitch, L. (1976) *Social Democracy and Industrial Militancy*, Cambridge: Cambridge University Press.

Panitch, L. (1977) 'The Development of Corporatism in Liberal Democracies', *Comparative Political Studies*, 10.

Parry, N. and Parry, J. (1976) *The Rise of the Medical Profession*, London: Croom Helm.

Pasour, E.C. (1990) *Agriculture and the State*, New York: Holmes and Meier.

Pastor, R.A. (1980) *Congress and the Politics of US Foreign Economic Policy 1929–76*, Berkeley, CA: University of California Press.

Pastor, R.A. (1983) 'The Cry-and-Sigh Syndrome: Congress and Trade Policy' in Schick, A. (ed.) *Making Economic Policy*, Washington D.C.: American Enterprise Institute.

Pater, J.E. (1981) *The Making of the National Health Service*, London: King Edwards Hospital Fund for London.

Paton, C.R. (1990) *US Health Politics*, Aldershot: Avebury.

Pearson, C. (1990) 'Free Trade, Fair Trade? The Reagan Record' in Pearson, C. and Riedel, J. (eds) *The Direction of Trade Policy*, Oxford: Basil Blackwell.

Pennock, J.R. (1962) ' "Responsible Government," Separated Powers, and Special Interests: Agricultural Subsidies in Britain and America', *American Political Science Review*, 56, pp. 621–33.

Peon, M.M. (1979) *Harry S. Truman Versus the Medical Lobby: The Genesis of Medicare*, Columbia, MO: University of Missouri Press.

Pertschuk, M. (1982) *Revolt Against Regulation*, Berkeley, CA: University of California Press.

Pertschuk, M. (1983) 'The Case for Consumerism', *New York Times*, 30 May.

Peters, B.G. (1986) *American Public Policy*, London: Macmillan.

Peters, B.G. and Hogwood, B.W. (1980) 'Policy Successions: The Dynamics of Policy Change', *Studies in Public Policy*, no. 69, University of Strathclyde.

Peterson, E. (1982) 'Is Consumerism Still a Marketing Tool?' in Bloom, P.N. (ed.) *Consumerism and Beyond*, Massachusetts: Marketing Science Institute.

Peterson, J. (1992a) 'The European Technology Community: Polity Networks in Supranational Settings' in Marsh, D. and Rhodes, R.A.W. (eds) *Policy Networks in British Government*, Oxford: Oxford University Press.

Peterson, J. (1992b) 'The European Community' in Marsh, D. and Rhodes, R.A.W (eds) *Implementing Thatcherism: Audit of an Era*, Milton Keynes: Open University Press.

Petit, M. (1985) *Determinants of Agricultural Policies in the United States and European Community*, Washington D.C.: International Food Policy Research Institute.

Petracca, M.P. (1992) *The Politics of Interests*, Boulder, CO: Westview Press.

Pierson, C. (1986) *Marxist Theory and Democratic Politics*, Cambridge: Polity Press.

Pika, J.A. (1983) 'Interest Groups and the Executive: Presidential Intervention' in Cigler, A.J. and Loomis, B.A. (eds) *Interest Group Politics*, Washington D.C.: Congressional Quarterly.

Plamping, D. (1991) 'The New NHS', *British Medical Journal*, 302, 30 March, pp. 737–8.

Pollard, S. (1979) 'The Rise of Service Industries and White Collar Employment' in Gustafsson (ed.) *Post-Industrial Society*, London: Croom Helm.

Pollard, S. (1981) *The Wasting of the British Economy*, London: Croom Helm.

Pollert, A. (1988) 'The "Flexible Firm": Fixation or Fact?', *Work Employment and Society*, 2, pp. 281–316.

Polsby, N. (1960) 'How to Study Community Power: the Pluralist Alternative', *Journal of Politics*, 22, pp. 474–84.

Polsby, N. (1980) *Community Power and Political Theory*, New Haven, CT: Yale University Press.

Porter, L. (1978) 'Congress and Agricultural Policy, 1977' in Hadwiger, D.F. and Browne, W.P. (1978) *The New Politics of Food*, Lexington, MA: Lexington Books.

Potter, J. (1988) 'Consumerism and the Public Sector: How Well Does the Coat Fit?', *Public Administration*, 66, pp. 149–64.

Poulantzas, N. (1969) 'The Problem of the Capitalist State', *New Left Review*, 58.

Poulantzas, N. (1973) *Political Power and Social Class*, London: New Left Books.

Poulantzas, N. (1978) *State, Power, Socialism*, London: New Left Books.

Powell, J. E. (1976) *Medicine and Politics: 1975 and After*, Tunbridge Wells: Pitman Medical Publishing.

Purdy, D. (1976) 'British Capitalism since the War', *Marxism Today*, September and October.

Read, M. (1992) 'Policy Networks and Issue Networks: The Politics of Smoking' in Marsh, D. and Rhodes, R.A.W. (eds) *Policy Networks in British Government*, Oxford: Oxford University Press.

Reagan, M. D. (1987) *Regulation: The Politics of Policy*, Boston, MA: Little Brown.

Rhodes, R.A.W. (1981) *Control and Power in Centre–Local Government Relations*, Farnborough: Gower/SSRC.

Rhodes, R.A.W. (1985) 'Power Dependence, Policy Communities and Inter-Governmental Networks', *Essex Papers in Politics and Government*, No. 30, University of Essex.

Rhodes, R.A.W. (1986) *The National World of Local Government*, London: Allen and Unwin.

Rhodes, R.A.W. (1988) *Beyond Westminster and Whitehall*, London: Unwin Hyman.

Rhodes, R.A.W. (1990) 'Policy Networks: A British Perspective', *Journal of Theoretical Politics*, 2, pp. 293–317.

Rhodes, R.A.W and Marsh, D. (1992a) 'Policy Networks in British Politics: A Critique of Existing Approaches' in Marsh, D. and Rhodes, R.A.W (eds) *Policy Networks in British Government*, Oxford: Oxford University Press.

Rhodes, R.A.W. and Marsh, D. (1992b) 'Thatcherism: An Implementation Perspective' in Marsh, D. and Rhodes, R.A.W. (eds) *Implementing Thatcherite Policies: Audit of an Era*, Milton Keynes: Open University Press.

Rhodes, R.A.W. and Marsh, D. (1992c) 'New Directions in the Study of Policy Networks', *European Journal of Political Research*, 21, pp. 181–205.

Richardson, J.J. and Jordan, A.G. (1979) *Governing Under Pressure*, Oxford: Martin Robertson.

Richardson, J.J. and Jordan, A.G. (1985) *Governing Under Pressure*, second edition, Oxford: Martin Robertson.

Richardson, J.J., Maloney, W.A. and Rudig, W. (1992) 'The Dynamics of Policy Change: Lobbying and Water Privatization', *Public Administration*, 70, pp. 157–75.

Riddell, P. (1983) *The Thatcher Government*, Oxford: Martin Robertson.

Riley, M. (1988) *Power, Politics and Voting Behaviour*, Hemel Hempstead: Harvester Wheatsheaf.

Ripley, R. and Franklin, G. (1980) *Congress, the Bureaucracy and Public Policy*, Illinois: Dorsey Press.

Riska, E. (1985) *Power, Politics and Health*, Helsinki: Socetas Scientarum Fennica.

Rochon, T.R. (1990) 'The West European Peace Movement and the Theory of New Social Movements', in Dalton, R.J. and Kuechler, M. (eds) *Challenging the Political Order*, Oxford: Polity Press.

Rodgers, W. (1985) 'Blurred Vision from the Commanding Heights', *The Guardian*, 12 April.

Rootes, C.A. (1991) 'The New Politics and the New Social Movements in Britain', *Paper Presented to Political Studies Association Annual Conference*, University of Lancaster.

Rose, R. (1990) 'Inheritance Before Choice in Public Policy', *Journal of Theoretical Politics*, 2, pp. 263–91.

Rothman Hasin, B. (1987) *Consumers, Commissions and Congress: Law, Theory and the Federal Trade Commission*, 1968–85, New Brunswick and Oxford: Transaction Books.

Rugman, A.M. and Anderson, D.M. (1987) *Administered Protection in America*, London: Croom Helm.

Rustin, M. (1989) 'The Trouble with New Times' in Hall, P. and Jacques, M. (eds) *New Times: The Changing Face of Politics in the 1990s*, London: Lawrence and Wishart.

Salisbury, R.H. (1979) 'Why No Corporatism in the United States?' in Schmitter, P.C and Lembruch, G. (eds) *Trends Towards Corporatist Intermediation*, London: Sage.

Salisbury, R.H. (1983) 'Interest Groups: Towards a New Understanding' in Cigler, A.J. and Loomis, A. (eds) *Interest Group Politics*, Washington D.C.: Congressional Quarterly.

Salisbury, R.H. (1990) 'The Paradox of Interest Groups in Washington, DC: More Groups and Less Clout' in King, A. (ed.) *The New American Political System*, second edition, Washington D.C.: American Enterprise Institute.

Salisbury, R.H., Heinz, J.P., Nelson, R.L. and Laumann, E.O. (1992) 'Triangles, Networks and Hollow Cores: The Complex Geometry of Washington Interest Representation' in Petracca, M.P. (eds) *The Politics of Interests*, Boulder, CO: Westview Press.

Saunders, P. (1975) 'They Make the Rules', *Policy and Politics*, 4, pp. 31–58.

Saunders, P. (1990) *A Nation of Home Owners*, London: Unwin Hyman.

Saunders, P. and Harris, C. (1990) 'Privatisation and the Consumer', *Sociology*, 24, pp. 57–75.

Saward, M. (1992) 'The Civil Nuclear Network in Britain' in Marsh, D. and Rhodes, R.A.W., *Policy Networks in British Government*, Oxford: Oxford University Press.

Schaetzel, J.R. (1986) 'Trade Relations' in Muskie, E., Rush, K. and Thompson, K. (eds) *The President, the Congress and Foreign Policy*, Lanham, MD: University Press of America.

Schmitter, P.C. (1974) 'Still the Century of Corporatism?', *Review of Politics*, 36, pp. 85–131.

Schmitter, P.C. (1979) 'Still the Century of Corporatism?' in Schmitter, P.C and Lembruch, G. (eds) *Trends Towards Corporatist Intermediation*, London: Sage.

Schnitther, J.A. (1987) 'Agricultural Reform Efforts in the United States' in Johnson, D.G. (ed.) *Agricultural Reform Efforts in the Unites States and Japan*, New York: New York University Press.

Schott, J.J. (1989) *More Free Trade Areas*, Washington DC: Institute for International Economics.

Schwartz, M. (1987) (ed.) *The Structure of Power in the United States*, New York: Holmes and Meier.

Self, P. and Storing, H.J. (1962) *The State and the Farmer*, London: George Allen.

Shanks, M. (1977) *Planning and Politics*, London: PEP/Allen and Unwin.

Shipper, F. and Jennings, M.M. (1984) *Business Strategy for the Political Arena*, Westpoint/ London: Quoram Books.

Short, J. (1985) *American Business and Foreign Policy: Cases in Coffee and Cocoa Trade*

Regulation, *1961–1974*, New York and London: Garland Publishing.

Silber, N.I. (1983) *Test and Protest: The Influence of Consumers Union*, London: Holmes and Meier.

Sked, A. and Cooke, C. (1979) *Post-War Britain*, Hemel Hempstead: Harvester Wheatsheaf.

Skocpol, T. (1980) 'Political Response to Capitalist Crisis: Neo-Marxist Theories and the Case of the New Deal', *Politics and Society*, 10, pp. 155–201.

Skocpol, T. (1985) 'Bringing the State Back In: Strategies of Analysis in Current Research' in Evans, P.B., Rieschemeyer, D. and Skocpol, T. (eds) *Bringing the State Back In*, Cambridge: Cambridge University Press.

Skocpol, T. and Finegold, K. (1982) 'State Capacity and Economic Intervention in the Early New Deal', *Political Science Quarterly*, 97, pp. 255–78.

Smith, B. (1976) *Policy Making in British Government*, Oxford: Martin Robertson.

Smith, D.B. and Bloom, P.N. (1986) 'Is Consumerism Dead or Alive? Some Empirical Evidence' in Bloom, D.B. and Smith, R.B. (eds) *The Future of Consumerism*, Lexington, MA: Lexington Books.

Smith, G. (1982) *The Consumer Interest*, London: John Martin Publishing.

Smith, M. (1986) *The Consumer Case for Socialism*, London: Fabian Society.

Smith, M.J. (1988) 'Consumers and Agricultural Policy: A Case of Long-term Exclusion', *Essex Papers in Politics and Government*, No. 48, Department of Government, University of Essex.

Smith, M.J. (1989a) 'The Annual Review: The Emergence of a Corporatist Institution?', *Political Studies*, 33, pp. 81–96.

Smith, M.J. (1989b) 'Changing Agendas and Policy Communities: Agricultural Issues in the 1930s and 1980s', *Public Administration*, 67, pp. 149–65.

Smith, M.J. (1989c) 'Land Nationalisation and the Agricultural Policy Community', *Public Policy and Administration*, 4, pp. 9–21.

Smith, M.J. (1989d) 'Specifying State Autonomy: The Development of Agricultural Policy in Britain', *Paper Presented at the ECPR Conference*, Paris, 10–15 April.

Smith, M.J. (1990a) *The Politics of Agricultural Support in Britain: The Development of the Agricultural Policy Community*, Aldershot: Dartmouth.

Smith, M.J. (1990b) 'The Impact of Social and Political Change on Policy Networks in Britain and the United States', *Paper Presented to ECPR Workshop: Institutions, Structures and the Intermediation of Interests*, Bochum, 2–7 April.

Smith, M.J. (1990c) 'From Policy Community to Issue Network: Salmonella in Eggs and the New Politics of Food', *Brunel Working Papers in Government*, No. 9, Uxbridge: Brunel University.

Smith, M.J. (1990d) 'Pluralism, Reformed Pluralism and Neopluralism: The Role of Pressure Groups in Policy Making', *Political Studies*, 38, pp. 302–22.

Smith, M.J. (1991) 'From Policy Community to Issue Network: Salmonella in Eggs and the New Politics of Food', *Public Administration*, 69, pp. 235–55.

Smith, M.J. (1993) 'Consumer Policy and the New Right' in Ashford, N. and Jordan, G. (eds) *Public Policy and the New Right* London: Pinter.

Social Services Select Committee (1984) *Griffiths NHS Management Inquiry Report*, HC 209 (1983/84), London: HMSO.

Social Services Select Committee (1988) *The Future of the National Health Service*, London: HMSO.

Social Services Select Committee (1989) *Resourcing the National Health Service: The*

Government's Plans for the Future of the National Health Service, London: HMSC

Solesbury, W. (1976) 'The Environmental Agenda', *Public Administration*, 54, pp. 379–97

Steinfeld, C. and Salvaggio, J. (1989) 'Towards a Definition of the Information Society' i Salvaggio, J. (ed.) *The Information Society*, New Jersey: Lawrence Erlbaum Associates

Stoeckle, J.D. (1988) 'Reflections on Modern Doctoring', *Milbank Memorial Fund*, 66 pp. 76–91.

Stones, R. (1988) 'The Myth of Betrayal: Structure and Agency in the Labou Government's Policy of Non-Devaluation 1964–1967', Ph.D thesis, University c Essex.

Street, J. (1988) 'Taking Control? Some Aspects of the Relationship Betwee Information, Technology, Government Policy and Democracy' in Plant, R., Gregory, F and Brier, A., *Information Technology: the Public Issues*, Manchester: Manchester University Press.

Strong, P. and Robinson, J. (1990) *The NHS Under New Management*, Milton Keynes Open University Press.

Talbot, R.B. and Hadwiger, D.F. (1968) *The Policy Process and American Agriculture*, Sa Franscisco, CA: Chandler.

Taylor, G. (1989) 'Policy Communities and the Coal Industry: A case for Redundancy' *Paper Presented at Conference on Policy Networks and Communities*, University of Essex July.

Taylor, M. (1987) *The Possibility of Cooperation*, Cambridge: Cambridge University Press.

Taylor, R. (1980) *Fifth Estate*, London: Pan Books.

Therborn, G. (1980) *The Power of Ideology and the Ideology of Power*, London, Verso.

Therborn, G. (1989) 'The Two-Thirds, One-Third Society' in Hall, P. and Jacques, M (eds) *New Times: The Changing Face of Politics in the 1990s*, London: Lawrence and Wishart.

Thompson, F.J. (1981) *Health Policy and Bureaucracy*, Cambridge, MA: MIT Press.

Thompson, R.L. (1988) 'Agriculture: Growing Government Control' in Boaz, D. (ed.) *Assessing the Reagan Years*, Washington D.C.: Cato Institute.

Thorelli, H.B. and Thorelli, S.V. (1974) *Consumer Information Handbook: Europe and North America*, New York: Praeger Publishers.

Thurber, J.A. (1991) 'Dynamics of Policy Subsystems in American Politics' in Cigler, A.J. and Loomis, A. (eds) *Interest Group Politics*, third edition, Washington D.C.: Congressional Quarterly.

Tivey, L. (1974) 'The Politics of the Consumer' in Kimber, R. and Richardson, J.J. (eds) *Pressure Groups in Britain*, London: Dent.

Touraine, A. (1976) *The Voice and the Eye*, Cambridge: Cambridge University Press.

Traber, M. (ed.) *The Myth of the Information Revolution*, London: Sage.

Truman, D. (1951) *The Governmental Process*, New York: Alfred A. Knopf.

Tucker, J. (1988) 'Free Trade, Protectionism and Investment: The Changing Shape of the Global Automobile Industry', *Essex Papers in Politics and Government*, No. 55, Department of Government, University of Essex.

Turner, B.S. (1987) *Medical Power and Social Knowledge*, London: Sage.

Tweeten, L.G. (1977) 'Agricultural Policy: A Review of Legislation, Programs, and Policy' in *Food and Agricultural Policy*, Washington D.C.: American Enterprise Institute.

Useem, M. (1987) 'The Inner Circle and the Political Voice of Business' in Schwarz, M. (ed.) *The Structure of Power in America*, New York: Holmes and Meier.

Vogel, D. (1978) 'Why Businessmen Distrust their State', *British Journal of Political Science*, 8, pp. 45–78.

ogel, D. (1980) 'The Public Interest Movement and the American Reform Tradition', *Political Science Quarterly*, 95, pp. 607–27.

ogel, D. (1983) 'The Power of Business in America: A Reappraisal', *British Journal of Political Science*, 13, pp. 19–41.

ogel, D. (1987) 'Political Science and the Study of Corporate Power: A Dissent for the New Conventional View', *British Journal of Political Science*, 17, pp. 385–408.

ogel, D. (1988) 'Government–Industry Relations in the United States: an Overview', in Wilks, S. and Wright, M. (eds) *Comparative Government–Industry Relations*, Oxford: Clarendon.

ogel, D. (1989) *Fluctuating Fortunes*, New York: Basic Books.

ogel, D. and Nadel, M. (1976) 'The Consumer Coalition: Dimensions of Political Conflict' in Katz, R.N. (ed.) *Protecting the Consumer Interest*, Cambridge, MA: Ballinger.

ogler, C. (1985) *The Nation State: the Neglected Dimension of Class*, Aldershot: Gower.

alker, D. (1990) 'Enter the Regulators', *Parliamentary Affairs*, 43, pp. 149–58.

alkland, S.A. (1984) 'Economic Planning and Dysfunctional Politics in Britain, 1945' in Gamble, A. and Walkland, S. *The British Party System and Economic Policy*, Oxford: Clarendon.

arland, R.H., Hermann, R.O. and Moore, D.E. (1986) 'Consumer Activism, Community Activism and the Consumer Movement', in Bloom, D.B. and Smith, R.B. (eds) *The Future of Consumerism*, Lexington, MA: Lexington Books.

eidenbaum, M.L. (1977) *Business, Government and the Public*, Englewood-Cliffs, NJ: Prentice-Hall.

eidenbaum, M.L. (1990) *Business, Government and the Public*, 4th edn, Englewood-Cliffs, NJ: Prentice-Hall.

eir, M., Orloff, A.S. and Skocpol, T. (1989) 'Understanding American Social Politics' in Castles, F.G. (ed.) *The Comparative History of Public Policy*, Cambridge: Polity Press.

eir, M. and Skocpol, T. (1985) 'State Structures and the Possibility of "Keynesian" Responses to the Great Depression in Sweden, Britain and the United States' in Evans, P.B., Rieschemeyer, D. and Skocpol, T. (eds) *Bringing the State Back In*, Cambridge: Cambridge University Press.

hitehead, P. (1985) *The Writing on the Wall*, London: Michael Joseph.

ilkinson, A. (1987) 'International Agricultural Trade Conflicts and Consequences', *Paper presented to the Agrarian Society of Northern Ireland*, 26 February.

ilks, S. (1984) 'Conservative Industrial Policy 1979–1983' in Jackson, P. (ed.) *Implementing Thatcherism*, London: RIPA.

ilks, S. and Wright, M. (1988a) 'Conclusion: Comparing Government–Industry Relations: States, Sectors, and Networks', in Wilks, S. and Wright, M. (eds) *Comparative Government–Industry Relations*, Oxford: Clarendon.

ilks, S. and Wright, M. (1988b) (eds) *Comparative Government–Industry Relations*, Oxford: Clarendon.

illiamson, P.J. (1989) *Corporatism in Perspective*, London: Sage.

ilson, G. (1977) *Special Interests and Policy Making*, London: John Wiley.

ilson, G. (1981) *Interest Groups in the United States*, Oxford: Clarendon.

ilson, G. (1982) 'Why is there no Corporatism in the United States?' in Lembruch, G. and Schmitter, P. (eds) *Patterns of Corporatist Policy Making*, London: Sage.

ilson, G. (1985) *Business and Politics*, London: Macmillan.

ilson, G. (1990) *Interest Groups*, Oxford: Blackwell.

ilson, H. (1974) *The Labour Government 1964–70*, Harmondsworth: Penguin Books.

Wilson, H.H. (1951) 'Techniques of Pressure – Anti-nationalisation Propaganda i Britain', *Public Opinion Quarterly*, 15, pp. 225–42.

Wilson, J. (1980) 'The Politics of Regulation' in Wilson, J. (ed.) *The Politics of Regulation* New York: Basic Books.

Winkler, J. (1976) 'Corporatism', *Archives Européennes de Sociologie*, 17, pp. 100–36.

Wistow, G. (1992a) 'The Health Service Policy Community: Professionals Pre-Eminer or Under Challenge?' in Marsh, D. and Rhodes, R.A.W. (eds) *Policy Networks in Britis Government*, Oxford: Oxford University Press.

Wistow, G. (1992b) 'The National Health Service' in Marsh, D. and Rhodes, R.A.W (eds) *Implementing Thatcherite Policies: Audit of an Era*, Milton Keynes: Open Universit Press

Wright, J.R. (1989) 'PAC Contributions, Lobbying and Representation', *Journal of Politic* 51, pp. 713–29.

Wright, M. (1988) 'Policy Community, Policy Network and Comparative Industria Policies', *Political Studies*, 36, pp. 593–612.

Young, H. (1992) *One of Us*, second edition, London: Macmillan.

Zysman, J. (1983) *Government, Markets and Growth*, Ithaca, NY: Cornell University Press

INDEX

Adam Smith Institute, 181
Agricultural Adjustment Act
[1933], 120–1
[1938], 119–29
agricultural expenditure, 120, 129, 131
agricultural policy, 55, 61, 65, 73, 89,
    93, 101–35, 151, 152, 155, 225,
    229
    community, 90, 101–35, 152, 22,
      226, 227, 230
    network, 118–35, 222, 223
    reform, 110–17, 129–32
agricultural subsidies 102, 104, 108,
    114–16, 120–1, 124, 130
Althusser, L., 7
American Farm Bureau Federation
    (AFBF), 118, 121–30
American Hospitals Association (AHA),
    185, 186, 191
American Medical Association (AMA),
    185–91
annual review, 102, 108–9

balance of payments, 108–9
Baldrige, M., 147, 151–2
Bell, D., 78
Bevan, A., 169–72
Bottemley, V., 183
Bretton Woods, 139, 141
British Medical Association (BMA), 66,
    166–8, 170–5, 179–80, 183
British Telecom, 214
Bureau of the Budget, 121–2
Bureau of Consumer Protection, 203
Bush, G., 130, 195, 202
business, 16, 18–25, 136–62, 199,
    210–11

council, 137
groups, 8, 221
policy networks, 136–62
Business Roundtable, 20–1

Cabinet, 17, 26
committee, 17, 26
capital, *see* business
capitalism, 39
Carter, J., 193, 202–3, 206–7
Cawson, A., 29, 32
central economic planning staff
    (CEPS), 153
Centre for Policy Studies, 180
chemical industry, 159
Chemical Industry Association, 159
City, 4, 22, 42–3, 157, 158
civil servants, 9, 38–9, 61, 166, 168,
    172
civil service, 157, 169
civil society, 2, 52–3, 55, 67, 84, 220–1,
    227
Clarke, K., 96, 179, 181
Class, 29, 37
forces, 40, 42, 55
fractions, 39, 42, 44
coal policy, 138
coffee policy, 149–50
Cold War, 140
collective action, 198, 216
collectivism, 157
Common Agricultural Policy (CAP),
    110–17, 131, 133
Confederation of British Industry
    (CBI), 19–21, 23, 24, 33, 34, 43